THE LAST DAYS OF
T. E. LAWRENCE

What I have done, what I am doing, what I am going to
do, puzzle me and bewilder me. Have you ever been
a leaf and fallen from your tree in autumn and
been really puzzled? That's the feeling.

Thomas Edward Shaw
6 May 1935

From *Leaves in the Wind*

A proposed addition to *The Mint*
But like his life, it was never fulfilled.

THE LAST DAYS OF
T. E. LAWRENCE
A Leaf in the Wind

PAUL MARRIOTT AND YVONNE ARGENT

THE
Alpha
PRESS

2 4 6 8 10 9 7 5 3 1
First published 1996 in Great Britain by
THE ALPHA PRESS
18 Chichester Place
Brighton BN2 1FF

and in the United States of America by
THE ALPHA PRESS
c/o International Specialized Book Services, Inc.
5804 N.E. Hassalo St.
Portland, Oregon 97213-3644

British Library Cataloguing in Publication Data

A CIP catalogue record for this book is available from the British Library.

ISBN 1–898595 16 X

Printed and bound by Biddles Ltd, King's Lynn and Guildford

Contents

Preface and Acknowledgements

T. E. Lawrence (1888–1935) was a complex and controversial man. As archaeologist, scholar, soldier and writer, he moved in the highest corridors of power, yet later he chose to hide from his fame as Lawrence of Arabia by enlisting as a serviceman in the RAF.

As evidenced in letters and people's remembrances, Lawrence possessed a strange "magic" which transformed people he met. He enabled others to realize their own potential abilities. Indeed, this influence is timeless. Sixty years after his death his achievements continue to inspire. John E. Mack's book *A Prince of Our Disorder* describes Lawrence's persuasive enchantment as a "spark" that lightens the darker sides of our psyches as we come to know of Lawrence's life and to empathize with the situations he faced.

Attempting to unravel Lawrence's last few weeks of life has brought both authors face to face with the nature of Lawrence's psychological make-up. While it is a truism that the act of one individual writing about another brings in its wake psychological changes, subtle or profound, in the case of Lawrence we are not the first to experience sleepless nights pondering the tangled Lawrence enigma.

The book purposely draws heavily on Lawrence's own written words, mainly from published and unpublished letters, where his private, gentle and tortuous feelings become unlocked. His last days are described in comprehensive, chronological order. The story begins with Lawrence's final three months in the RAF at Bridlington, supervising the redesign of rescue motorboats. During this period it was discovered that he received masochistic floggings in Edinburgh. Many chapters cover the specifics of his motorbike crash (13 May 1935), crash witnesses, and his five-day battle against death in hospital. The inquest reports are quoted, as well as full details of his funeral.

Once, when feeling despondent, Lawrence compared his depression to a leaf falling from a tree. "Leaves in the Wind" was Lawrence's last and unpublished writing project. It seemed natural to adopt the title for this book.

We would like to express our gratitude to many individuals, libraries, museums and societies for their help in the research for this book.

Many thanks are due to Nick Birnie, Lord David Cholmondesley, John Deheer, Friedericke Hilscher-Ehlert, Bob Hunt, Cliff Irwin, Lord Kennett, Ronald Knight, Mrs S. Lower, Andrew Morland, Arthur Russell, Andrew Simpson, and many others who wish to remain anonymous.

We extend special gratitude to the late R. W. Barchard, son of Mrs Hilda Barchard, for his extensive knowledge of Bridlington; to Tony Cripps for his detailed artwork on Lawrence's damaged Brough motorbike; to Frank Fletcher, the only survivor of the Lawrence crash, for patience and lively correspondence; to Roland Hammersley for many useful chats and crash information; to Stephen Hodson for hours of patient consultation in compiling computer maps and graphics; and to Squadron Leader J. R. Sims, retd., for permission to publish material from his father's (R. G. Sims) recollections and photographs.

We very much appreciate the help given by the following: the Ashmolean Museum, Oxford; Sgt. Green of the Bicester Traffic Centre, Oxon., for assistance in accident speed assimilation; Colin Harris of the Department of Western Manuscripts, Bodleian Library, Oxford, for invaluable help in photograph selection; to David Fletcher, archivist at the Bovington Tank Museum, Dorset; the British Library, London; the British Movietone News; Mike Leatherdale of the Brough Superior Club; RAF Cranwell Library, Lincolnshire, for Rupert de la Bere's long essay on Lawrence, reproduced by kind permission of the AOC and Commandant, Royal Air Force, Cranwell. Also thanks to the Hulton-Deutsch Picture Library, London.

We also acknowledge the help given by the Houghton Library, Cambridge, USA; Karen Hay, area librarian of Lincolnshire County Library; Mick Woods of the Meteorological Office Archives, Bracknell, for extracting daily weather records; R. A. Funnell, Deputy Keeper of Research and Information at the RAF Museum, Hendon, London; and Rodney Legg of Wincanton Press, Somerset, for help with many of the plates and maps.

We would especially like to show appreciation to the Trustees of the Seven Pillars of Wisdom Trust for copyright permission to publish an abundance of Lawrence material and to The Henry Williamson Literary Estate.

Finally, if any acknowledgements have been omitted, apologies are now rendered.

The authors and publishers wish to acknowledge permission to quote from copyright material as follows:

Ashmolean Museum, Oxford: Plates 17, 73. The late R. W. Barchard: Plates 1–3. Mrs T. W. Beaumont: Plate 5. Bodleian Library, Oxford: Plates 12, 14–16, 32, 39, 64–8, 70–1, 75. Bovington Tank Museum, Dorset: Plate 38. The British Library: Plates 11, 13, 23, 42. British Movietone News: Plates 74–5. John Deheer: Plates 6, 25. Roland Hammersley: Plate 72, Map 9. Hulton-Deutsch Collection: Plates 46, 51, 62. Lord Kennett: Plate 27. Joyce E. Knowles: Plate 36. The late Pat Knowles: Plates 53, 57–8. Mrs S. Lower: Plate 26. Paul Marriott: Plates 8, 10, 31, 35, 44B, 45B, 69, Maps 1–5, 8, Diagrams 2–4. Meteorological Office Archives: Plate 63, Table 3. Andrew Morland: back jacket picture, Plate 50. Controller, Ordnance Survey: Map 7. Royal Air Force Museum, Hendon: Plate 24. The Trustees of the Seven Pillars of Wisdom Trust: 40. Squadron-Leader J. R. Sims, retd.: Plate 19, front jacket picture. Total Home Entertainments: Plates 44A, 45A, 47–8, 52, 54–5, 60–1. Wincanton Press, Somerset: Plates 29, 41, Map 6.

Ashmolean Museum, Oxford: Plate 17; Cat. No. X422 – Plate 73. Bodleian Library, Oxford: MS. Eng. c. 2014, (dep c. 282) – Plate 39; MS. Photogr. c. 19, fol. 20 – Plate 12; MS. Res. c. 54, fol. 75r, 77r – Plate 19 (front jacket picture); MS. Res. e. 114, items 3, 5–6, 8–11, 13–14 – Plates 32, 64–8, 70–1, 76; Per, M356, c. 8 – Plates 14–16.

PAUL MARRIOTT
YVONNE ARGENT

THE LAST DAYS OF
T. E. LAWRENCE

1

Early Days at Bridlington, 15–21 November 1934

As far back as August 1934, while in Southampton, Lawrence had anticipated that he would be posted to the RAF Marine Detachment at Bridlington, on the east coast of Yorkshire, England. He spent the last four months (November 1934–February 1935) of his RAF days based in a large garage supervising the overhaul of ten RAF boats on behalf of the Air Ministry.[1]

He probably arrived at Bridlington by train on Thursday 15 November (see Appendix 5 for 1934–5 daily calendar), having already left his Southampton rooms at 13 Birmingham Street by at least 13 November.[2] He moved into the Ozone Hotel, a private Victorian hotel situated at the junction of Windsor Crescent and West Street opposite the South Pier and the RAF Marine Detachment shed (see Map 1).

During the summer of 1934 unmarried members of the Marine Craft unit were billeted on the top floor while seasonal seaside holiday-makers used the rest of the hotel. Guests included Herman Darewski's band who played at the Spa Royal Hall in the 1930s.[3] By November the whole building had been rented by the RAF. Mrs Hilda Barchard was the proprietor of the hotel, which was also the family home where she lived with her husband, son Reginald (22 years old) and daughter Katherine (16 years old). They had purchased the Ozone in 1928 and maintained a very high standard, which prompted the then (1934) civil adjutant, retired Flt. Lt. Sims, to write thanking Mrs Barchard for *"the excellence of the arrangements . . . The Wing Commander has noted with great pleasure several points in the Hotel that you have included for the comfort of the airmen, that are additional to your agreement, and he has observed the very high standard of board and lodgings that you provide for them. . . .*

This care and attention on your part have contributed, in no small degree, to the general efficiency of the Bridlington Detachment."[4] This letter was written on behalf of W/C Rice, Camp commandant of No. 1 Armament Training Camp, Catfoss, the main RAF station in the area in charge of the Marine Section at Bridlington.

Plate 1 shows the three-floored Ozone Hotel shaped in plan as a triangle, with an octagonal tower in one corner facing the sea. In November 1934 the top two floors were occupied by the RAF; each floor contained a long corridor with three different sized bedrooms on each side, making a total of six per landing, or twelve rooms in all, with two airmen sharing a room. The middle floor bedrooms had bay windows. The main entrance to the hotel was beneath the tower.

The RAF birthday party in Plate 2 was celebrated around this time, in a long room used by the family for meals situated on the ground floor looking into Windsor Crescent, beside the second entrance to the hotel. Immediately above lay a large lounge where there was a large alcove with French windows leading to a balcony.

Lawrence's accommodation was on the middle floor of the turret tower, a single bedroom smaller than the rest. It contained a bed, wardrobe, dressing table and open coal fire. The sea views from the east side of his bedroom were spectacular; he could see the cargo boats on the North Sea shipping lanes. To the rear of the Ozone was a small building to accommodate the Barchard's car; it later housed Lawrence's Brough Superior motorcycle GW 2275. This was adjoined to a narrow alleyway from West Street and a main entrance/exit lane through the back house to the west-north-west.

Mr Barchard, an official at the Hull Corporation Water and Gas Department, was a gifted pianist and Lawrence often joined the family to hear him play his beloved Beckstein grand. Mrs Hilda Barchard (see Plate 3 taken in *c.*1940) was a successful ballroom dancing teacher and once ran a studio in Margaret Street, Hull.

In the late 1930s the Barchards sold the Ozone to the Royal Yorkshire Yacht Club. The club almost completely refaced the building, although today it still has the original overall shape including part of the tower where Lawrence stayed.[5]

The evening of 15 November was wild and stormy. Lawrence must have heard the waves rolling up the seashore below his small comfortable upstairs room. The miserable weather matched the morbid thoughts of his uncertain civilian life ahead, *"It is a lamentable and paralysing future, about which I think all day and cannot bear it."*[6] Even before his Bridlington move the same mood prevailed. In a letter to Jonathan Cape (August 1934) Lawrence wrote, *"My civil date gallops towards me . . . I am promising myself a huge rest and sampletime, . . . My heart tells me that I'm finished."*

The following evening (16 November) Lawrence wrote his usual large number of letters. They covered a wide variety of subjects, some light and semi-serious, others of a more tormenting nature portraying his secret role and distressed state (which we shall discuss further in chapter 4). On this dark side Lawrence wrote three letters using the pseudonym *"R"*. The whole affair concerned a certain Scotsman called John Bruce who Lawrence met in the Tanks Corps at Bovington in 1922. There, and elsewhere, he had whipped and flogged Lawrence. Lawrence invented an uncle or "the old man", who, displeased with his nephew (Lawrence) for committing certain offences, would demand instructions for him to be whipped, later writing to the executioner for comments. All three letters were written to an observer of the floggings. Throughout Lawrence manipulated the whole charade.

Letter 1

Dear Sir,   *26 October 1934*

I am very much obliged to you for the long and careful report you have sent me on your visit to Scotland with Ted [Lawrence]; and for your kindness in agreeing to go there with the lad and look after him while he got his deserts. I am enclosing a fee of three pounds which I hope you will accept as some compensation for your trouble and inconvenience.

From what you tell me, and from the reports of those who have examined Ted since, it is clear that he had a sound thrashing, which was after all what he wanted. I hope he will take the lesson to heart, and not make it necessary for us to repeat it. Please take any chance his friendship for you gives, to impress upon him how wrong it is for him, at his age and standing, to force us to use these schoolboy measures against him. He should be ashamed to hold his head up amongst his fellows, knowing that he had suffered so humiliating and undignified a punishment. Try and drive some sense into his head. [Details of the whippings follow.] . . .

After being loosed [sic], did Ted stand quite steadily, or did he show any signs of trembling on his way from the club-room to the cafe or the train. Also you say that when they [Lawrence and Bruce] met you at the station, Ted was not looking too happy. Did his face remain pale to the end of the punishment, and after it? Did he say anything about his being glad the business was over?

Hills [Bruce] *reports that after the birching Ted cried out quite loudly, and begged for mercy. Can you confirm this, and do you recollect in what terms this plea was made? . . .*

. . . Does he take his whippings as something he has earned? Is he sorry after it? Does he feel justly treated? Has this year [1934] of harsh treatment made an improvement in his bearing?

I am sorry to bother you with all these difficult questions, but you have seen so much of Ted's private history this last twelve months, that your opinion is worth a great deal. One last question, too, if you say Yes to the main principle – are we at the end of our troubles with the lad? If not, must we give Hills his free hand, or will limited measures suffice? Can Hills be trusted again, or must I look elsewhere? And in that case, do you think your friend would be available or suitable?

> *With further thanks for your kindness*
> *Believe me*
> *Yours very sincerely*
> *R*

Letter 2

Dear Sir,   16 November 1934

I must apologize for having taken so long to answer the additional report you were good enough to send me. Your information was exactly what I needed and I am most grateful.

You have aroused my curiosity by your remark that from your service with Ted you know something that might replace corporal punishment in making him behave himself. You must understand that this is a matter of the first importance to me and to Ted. By his wishes which I must respect, according to my promise, we are prevented from meeting; but if you can get your information on paper, you will put me further into your debt.

I note what you say about Hills, and it only confirms my own impression. You will recollect how he came to go to him this time, Ted's punishment at X had proved not enough, due to the inadequacy of a belt for use upon a grown lad, and not through any fault of yours or your friend's. Unfortunately you could not arrange another dose at the time, and while we were thinking about it Ted allowed himself to give offence upon quite another subject. It was with this second offence that Hills dealt with last month. Ted still owes us (as he very well knows) proper payment for his very mean action in trying to steal money in transit from me to you.

4

I do not know, of course, what your hinted remedy is worth, as a corrective. If it proved effective I might save you and me from a repetition of his punishment. I gather that your friend is not yet available, and it is not fair to the lad himself to keep such a punishment hanging over him for month after month. Yet it is equally impossible for me, having solemnly promised it to him. I always do what I promise, and I have brought Ted to know it.

So will you please try to take me into your confidence on this alternative; and please also inquire into the arrangements of the friend who helped you last time, so that we may fall back on him, if necessary.
    Yours sincerely
    R[7]

Letter 2 was written directly after Letter 1 with no Lawrence correspondence in between to his companion, who, with John Bruce, had perceived the floggings.

Letter 1 is a reply to the companion's previous report on a flogging. In it Lawrence asked many direct questions about the Scottish whipping – *"Can you confirm this, . . . Does he take his whippings as something he has earned? . . . Has this year of harsh treatment made an improvement . . . "* and so on. Lawrence asked for a further report to these questions (which he probably received a reply a few days later) because in Letter 2 he apologises *"for having taken so long to answer the additional report . . . "*

Hence in Letter 1 the *"visit to Scotland with Ted . . . "* for flogging is the same as *"Ted's punishment at X . . . "* in Letter 2.

It becomes apparent that Lawrence and the companion journeyed separately by train to the Scottish rendezvous. We have in Letter 1 *"when they met you at the station, Ted was not looking too happy "* and *"on your visit to Scotland with Ted."*

The flogging took place in October 1934, *"Hills dealt with last month"* in Letter 2 and probably a week or so before its date of 26 October (possibly the weekend of 20–21 October). This would agree with Bruce's suggestion of *"another [beating] in 1934 at Maitland Buildings, Elm Row, Edinburgh."*[8] In the *Edinburgh Valuation Roll* for 1934, 41–44A Elm Row was owned by Elm Row Palace and rented by the Studio Theatre Company Limited. They occupied 41, the first floor of 42 continuing above a confectioners at 43 into 44 and 44A. The latter was a billiard hall called the Bellevue Billiard Rooms. In 1934 there were no other social or club establishments in Elm Row so the Maitland Buildings that Bruce referred to can only have been the Studio Theatre. The whole business operated on a membership basis for private functions and was, therefore, probably the venue for Lawrence's flogging.[9] A resident recalled a club with a billiard room above Pringle's Picture Palace in 1934 which was also the same site as the Studio Theatre Company. Today it is occupied by the studios of Scottish Television.[10] A fact even more intriguing concerns the 1934 Edinburgh and Leith street directory which registered the occupants of 41 as J. Bruce, H. Butler and Henry Jamieson. Undoubtedly this refers to John Bruce and possibly his two attendants at Lawrence's 1934 flogging.

On more normal matters, Lawrence continued his avid love of reading and criticizing books. C. Day Lewis had sent him a copy of his book *A Hope For Poetry*. In his first reply, Lawrence remarked about the omission of the poets Donne, Vaughan and Crashan and continued to describe his dislike of the metaphysical poets of the day. *"They were afraid of plain statement . . . So they splash something about shirt-sleeves or oysters quickly into every sentimental sentence."* Ending *"Thank you for an exciting and quite unsatisfying book: but if you want to make us really happy, you will expose yourself to the risk of writing some more poems: and for the ear, not the eye. These cheap typewriters do poets much harm."*[11]

The theme continued in remarks to the author Frederic Manning who Lawrence knew was trying to rekindle another book masterpiece, *"I beg of you don't . . . There are many books, and you have written two of the best of them* [Her Privates We *and* Scenes and Portraits]. *To covet a third is greedy. Don't be a book-hog."*[12] When writing to Charlotte Shaw, Bernard Shaw's wife, Lawrence expressed his disappointment at not receiving a book detrimental to himself. *"Somebody called Bray, they say, has lately published a book* [Shifting Sands *by Major N. N. E. Bray, Unicorn Press, 1934*] *which proves that I was a dud, in the war."*[13]

Again the gloom of the uncertain future emerged *"Candidly, the prospect of unalloyed leisure terrifies me, . . . "*[14] Nevertheless, at Bridlington, amongst his RAF pals, he felt at ease, *"My sort seems to be the plain sort, for with them I can chat away and reach common ground."*[15]

It is amusing to recall Lawrence's descriptions of the meaning of *Ozone Hotel*. *"The name of the Hotel is real. So, I think, is the ozone, or is it the fishmarket that smells?"*[16] – *"No: the address is not a spoof."*[17] – *"Ozone (Ugh!) Hotel, . . . Doesn't the name of the Hotel give you shivers? I'm sure it was meant for the summer visitor: . . . "*[18]

Lawrence's Brough Superior 996 cc motorcycle, which he called *George VII* (with each new bike the number would change – for example his third was called *George III*), and also nicknamed *Boanerges* ('son of thunder'), was housed in his thatched garage at his home in far off Clouds Hill, near Bovington Army Camp in Dorset. To improve mobility in and around Bridlington he purchased a push-bike between 17 and 25 November, as on the 16th he had *"a halfmind to buy a good light push-bike . . . "*[19] and on the 26th *"Here I go about, less splendidly, on a push-bike."*[20]

His daily work times were *"8 till 6, with a dinner hour and two 'smokes', . . . "*[21] with weekends free for leisure.

Lawrence had a lifelong interest in boats. He possessed his own canoe in the Isle of Wight and nearly drowned in the river Cherwell in 1906 whilst canoeing in treacherous winter floods. He pioneered a trip through the Saxon underground Trill Mill stream at Oxford; canoed while in Carchemish; and in August 1929 was working on RAF boats at Cattewater, Plymouth.

The catalyst for this marine interest was an *Iris III* flying boat that he had witnessed crashing into the sea in Plymouth Sound on 4 February 1931. Although the RAF rescue launch was one of the first on the scene, Lawrence perceived that a faster boat might have saved more of the aircraft's crew. During the next few months Lawrence was to head a team, including a Corporal Bradbury, to carry out trials on the new *'Fast Seaplane Tender 200'* known as *RAF 200* at Plymouth.[22]

Lawrence also used his own boat, the *Biscuit* (Plate 4), during the summer of 1931 to experiment in the towing of targets (used for bombing practice from aircraft) by line. He continued his investigations, introducing numerous modifications over the next few months into the *RAF 200*, which resulted in a large and detailed report in March 1932. He completed it on 83 foolscap stencils, dealing with every possible aspect of the speedboat. He called the report *Provisional Issue of Notes* and it remained the bible for training staff and crews for many years.[23]

In mid-April 1932 the RAF were interested in the bombing of marine craft and not the towing of targets. Lawrence, together with Flt. Lt. Beauforte-Greenwood, was engaged to look into the problem. They contracted Hadfield Ltd of Sheffield to armour plate a new boat based on the *RAF 200* class boat. During the first trials at Hythe in June 1932, Lawrence, characteristically, took the experience to extreme lengths by being present when one of the 8½ lb practice bombs hit his prototype boat. This foolhardy keenness backfired with headlines in the Press. The Air Ministry recalled him to more mundane duties.

The Air Ministry were displeased with any Lawrence/newspaper publicity. However, they agreed a new contract on 2 May 1933, which read:

"a. Generally to watch the Air Ministry's interests at contractors' yards during construction of marine craft, various types of bombing target, moorings, engines, and equipment.

b. Assist in preparation of trial reports and notes on running and maintenance of various types of craft.

c. Assist in production of craft and equipment generally and in particular the high speed vessel for crashwork, life saving and also salvage of boat planes."[24]

Lawrence took on this more apt and purposeful role. He travelled the country visiting various manufacturing and engineering works amassing information and commissioning appropriate equipment for the new boat bombing programme. By late March 1934 the British Power Boat Company, a company involved in the project, had completed five of these new armoured boats.

This short precis of Lawrence's involvement with boats brings us to his last four RAF months at Bridlington where the armoured speedboats were being bomb tested at sea for final completion before operational use.

The RAF Marine Craft detachment at Bridlington was based in a garage cum workshop shed by the South Pier. There were ten RAF boats, all in different condition, placed in different garages throughout the town. The five seaplane tenders seem to have been housed in the Marine Craft shed and the other five armoured boats in the other rented garages, such as the Tooth and Twelvemen in York Place (now a supermarket)[25] and the Alexandra Garage underneath the Alexandra Hotel in nearby Sewerby Terrace (now a car park).[26]

Up to now the Bridlington detachment had operated only during the summer but with an overall expansion plan the Air Ministry required a year-round effort as more boats were commissioned.

When ready for sea trials, an armoured boat was towed on a large trolley from its garage through the streets of Bridlington to the harbour. Civilian contractors then launched it ready for mooring.[27] The boat cruised out into the North Sea opposite Skipsea to the bombing range. They were the target for 8½ lb practice bombs dropped from 10,000–16,000 ft by RAF aircraft based at inland RAF stations. Each boat's armoured plating covered the engines, fuel tanks, cockpit and exterior. They were reconditioned at the Scott Payne boatyard in Hythe, armour plated by Hadfields in Sheffield and any remaining repairs carried out at Bridlington (see Plate 5).

The conditions aboard each armoured boat were cramped, hot and uncomfortable. The 40-ft craft was unsinkable, even if bombed, because of its inner hull lining, which was made from an extremely light substance called onazote.[28] Should a bomb hole appear, conical plugs were immediately hammered in to seal the leak. In the event of taking in large amounts of sea water, the compartmentalized structured hull could easily isolate the offending section.

Many of the early sea tests were horrific experiences for the three-man crew of coxswain, deckhand and wireless operator. Lawrence often took part, recalling the boats as *"damned uncomfortable! Hellish hot, smelly and noisy. They wear ear-defenders, crash helmets and gas-masks and little else!"*[29] Forward steering was complicated by peering through tiny slits in the cockpit and a series of mirrors offered restricted stern observation. The three-manned crew sometimes had to endure up to twelve hours in these appalling conditions.[30]

Partly because of Lawrence's constant pressure on the authorities the crews received an extra sixpence per day or 'discomfort money' to compensate for the deafening noises, excessive heat and repugnant fumes of the engines.

Lawrence's second main objective was the continuing improvement of the now fast seaplane tenders which were altogether more luxurious and streamline. The interior was comfortable for the crew and gave adequate space for emergency stretchers. It was his dream that they would be launched in a few seconds without any preliminary fire lighting or boiler heating, and achieve a speed of 30 knots or more. Although having a three-foot draught at anchor, at speed the tenders could achieve two feet, uniquely sliding through the waves owing to their streamline designed hull and the excessive power of the engines. As Lawrence explained, *"they have (power for power) three times the speed of their predecessors, less weight, less cost, more room, more safety, more seaworthiness. As their speed increases they rise out of the water and run over its face. They cannot roll, nor pitch, having no pendulum, nor period, but a subtly modelled planing bottom and sharp edges."*[31]

During these first days Lawrence was searching for woodwork and metalwork instruments to complete a tool kit. They were to be kept in a large wooden box with *Shaw* painted on its front.[32] On Tuesday evening, 20 November, he wrote to his friend Arthur

Hall, once an RAF carpenter, *"I need a set of twist bits: or if not a set, as near a set as I can get. I've been to the only tool shop and they say 37/6* [£1/17/6 = £1.875 – see Appendix 6]. *This is beyond me. The only other place at Bridlington is Woolworth's . . . .Tell me – are there any shops in Brum* [Birmingham] *which sell second-hand carpenter's tools . . . and if so, could you give me a look-see upon twist bits? I want decent ones, to do the R.A.F. job here: . . . I need a draw-knife, bradawls, two gimlets, a morticing chisel, mallet, bench-vice, soldering iron, tenon saw. Just that."*[33]

He also wrote to J. G. Wilson of Bumpus bookshop about the proposed move of its premises from 350 to 477 Oxford Street, London. He was entertained by the news that his copy of the William Morris Kelmscott *Chaucer*, lent for a Bumpus book exhibition, was remarked upon and examined by H.M. Queen Mary.[34]

On most Wednesday evenings his friend Ian Deheer invited Lawrence for a meal to his cottage, the *Cuddy*, in nearby Flamborough village. It was in the garden that Deheer photographed Lawrence in RAF uniform (Plate 6). Deheer was a shipbuilder, lighter (barge used for loading and unloading ships anchored off shore), tug and salvage contractor who had business premises next door to the Marine shed. Together at the *Cuddy* they discussed a multitude of topics but if Mrs Deheer entered the room Lawrence became very quiet. Even so he joined in the family fun, and was known to bounce the elder daughter on his knee.[35] The cosy 1920s bungalow, built of brick and wood, still retains its fashionable style.

About this time Reginald Barchard possessed a small portable Remington typewriter. Lawrence asked if he could borrow it and many an evening he could be heard typing away in his small upstairs room.[36]

He was so content in Yorkshire that he once remarked to Henry Williamson, *"Virtually I'm webbed-footed now, and quack before meals."*[37]

2

Surroundings,
22 November–19 December 1934

On Thursday 22 November, Flt. Lt. Reginald G. Sims, Equipment Officer and Civil Adjutant at RAF Catfoss (see Plate 7), rang up Bridlington and asked for A. C. Shaw to invite him over to Catfoss (see Map 2). Lawrence was out on the boats so Sims left a message saying that if he could not manage transport, knowing full well he had none, he could arrange it, having a baby Ford car of his own.

Sims recalls, *"The next day* [Friday 23 November] *I heard nothing, so I rode over and went to a large dark garage where the boats were out for overhaul under his charge as representing the Air Ministry. I saw two men standing in the lee of a boat, and went up, meaning to ask them where Shaw was. As I got near them I noticed a small man in a rough fisherman's jersey, reading a blue print nearby, and although I could not see his face, which he kept completely hidden with the print, I knew, without hesitation, who it was. I stood respectfully in front of the blue print. This was slowly lowered, and a pair of the bluest, most flashing eyes I had ever seen blazed forth, while a vast forehead, equal in size to the terrific chin beneath, simply radiated scorn and hate at me. Although this reception should have struck terror I afterwards realized that it did nothing of the sort. I was full of admiration and joy at the sheer beauty of his face. It was that of a very small boy, angelically fair, from whom another boy has just pinched an apple. I murmured that I was Flight-Lieutenant Sims of Catfoss. Instantly the glare disappeared, and a slight smile replaced it (incidentally, from looking like a very young boy, he assumed the appearance of a man of about thirty or so) and he said with an engaging air: 'Oh, I am so sorry, sir, but for a moment I took you for a reporter.' He then said how sorry he had been to have kept the book* [a collection of photographs of insects taken by Sims in Iraq with descriptions, all bound in book form, was lent to Lawrence who took months to return it – with no comments enclosed] *for so long, but that it was one that had to be taken in homoeopathic doses, and that he did not want to return it until he had finished it. He went on to say that the cost of publication would be very high, although he would like to have it published.*

After a few minutes I asked him if he would come back to Hornsea with me for lunch. He engagingly excused himself on the pleas that (i) he was not dressed for the part; (ii) he felt dirty and shopsoiled, having clambered over the boats for most of the morning; and (iii) he had to be back at Bridlington within two hours. I suggested use of our bath-room and indicated the baby Ford. He listened with gravity. 'Then all that remains is for me to say thank you,' he said.

I asked him if he would not drive, but he did not drive cars, he said. Fast motor cycles he liked, but a car was of too stable an equilibrium for him to enjoy driving. He gave me the impression that he was slightly nervous of cars, and I do not think I took my eye off the road then, or at any other time afterwards when he was my passenger.

On arriving at Hornsea he looked at our cottage, and stood for a moment in a favourite position, holding his left fist tightly with his right, with the index finger of his right hand bent and pressed against his chin. He then said: 'Ah, yes. Cobble built, repaired with brick facings, about sixteenth or early seventeenth century. Nice cottage' [see Plate 8]. He had an attractive way of saying Yes, slightly biting the first part, and making the end a little bit sibilant. His voice and choice of words were both quite perfect.

He set my wife, child, and dog, all at ease immediately. After lunch we ensconced him in a large chair and listened open-eared to his tales of books, people, music, and R.A.F. experiences, and very much against the grain at 3.15 I reminded him of the time, whereon he pulled himself out of his chair in one movement like a steel spring unbending, and said everything had conspired to make him forget that there was such a thing as work. He shook hands very cordially, and thanked us.

I duly delivered him at his garage, and he again shook hands."[1]

After work that evening Lawrence walked through a cold drizzly south-west wind the short distance from the Marine shed to his room. A few days earlier he had been offered the important post of Secretary to the Bank of England by its Governor Sir Montague Norman via a message from the Honourable Francis Rodd.[2] Friends had become worried about his moodiness and plans for lazy retirement, and were genuinely trying to support a man of exceptional skills for a stable future. The compliment had pleased him, but after wrestling with the decision he resolved that evening, in a letter to Francis Rodd, *"You will please say No, for me, but not a plain No. Make it a coloured No, . . . "*[3] Even then he wished to hide the apparent long delay in coming to a decision, *"Please explain how by accident it only came to me tonight, when I got back after work, too late to catch the evening mail from this petty seaboard town."*[4]

He also playfully reprimanded Rodd, as a banker, for causing possible future inflation. This could affect the 25/- a week interest he had anticipated for his retirement following the advice of Robin Buxton, banker and personal friend.

Lawrence was also concerned with the future of the RAF. The proposed increase of fighter over bomber squadrons worried him as he believed it would lead to a pile of obsolete planes, *"I fear we are going to waste money, for no object. The international horizon is quite clear for the near future, and we might with gain to ourselves have breathed peacefully and built up our efficiency."*[5]

That same evening (Friday 23 November) he pondered over his thoughts of the previous Friday (16 November) concerning the book *The Shifting Sands*: *"Good Lord, No! One dosn't answer this sort of thing. Bray is quite an honest muddle-headed sort of chap, who believed everything he wrote. His publishers are just splashing what little he wrote about me in the hopes that people will take it up and talk about it and so buy the book. It is pure advertisement and unfortunately it advertises me as well as the book, bother them. . . . Only, I don't want notice, and the only way to gain quiet is to be quiet."*[6]

Over the weekend (24–25 November) Lawrence was due to take one of the Bridlington boats to Felixstowe. Before setting out he wrote a letter to Bruce Rogers asking him to *"promenade the Oxford Press of N.Y. to send me one of the new and cheap* Odysseys, *thither."*[7]

A more pressing concern was the request from the President (Walter Williams) of the University of Missouri, Columbia, to supply him with an autograph for the University Library's copy of the *Odyssey* amongst a list of the *"'best and most important' books of 1932–1934."*[8] Lawrence took exception to this noting that the majority of them were useless and of a very low standard. It troubled him so much that after completing the 200 miles or so North Sea trip south to Felixstowe (about seven hours duration) he wrote immediately to the President. *"I glanced through the list of selected books which accompanied your letter. That completed my astonishment, for I found (besides the inevitable names of Shaw,*

Houseman and Tomlinson) only two names, Archibald MacLeish and Halper, that stood in any way for the considerable body of people trying to write ahead of this time, today." He goes on to mention seventeen authors not included and adds *"but it is not flattering to find one's work included in a collection from which nearly everything one cares for is shut out."* He hopes that the Library readers will *"treat them as decorations or as scalps, and not as encitements towards thinking; but it does seem to throw a lavid reflection upon the state of mind of your selectors. I should change them."*⁹

Sunday at Felixstowe seems to have been a lazy rest day as he was free to read the *Observer* newspaper.¹⁰

Before leaving Felixstowe on the Monday morning (26 November) he found time to write a reply to a curious letter, in French, from a certain "Mademoiselle Schneegans" who was interested in tracing the origins of her name. Apparently the envelope had been incorrectly addressed taking six months to reach Felixstowe. He usually made it a rule never to answer letters from strangers but since it came from Cahors in France, a town that inspired his early architectural studies during his cycling tours of 1906–8, he made an exception. Also the etymological appeal of her surname obviously intrigued his diverse sense of history. *"I think it improbable that any family name of the Rhineland can go back even into the early Middle Ages, much less to the epoch of St. Columba, who was a Celt, and a religious, as were his companions. I do not think they are likely to have had acknowledged descendants, and I do not remember that their mission was accomplished by any movement of families from Celtic Ireland to Middle-Europe.*

*Would you not be content to establish a claim to descend from one of these famous later 'Wild geese' as Europe called them, . . . "*¹¹

After the long sea trip back north to Bridlington Lawrence returned to his hotel room to indulge in light-hearted scribble with Lady Astor, *"I'm very romantic, they say: I often think of it over my evening fish and chips. As for Miss Cohen* [Harriet Cohen 1895–1967, international concert pianist], *she is apparently romantic too. I heard long ago she wanted to marry me: but Harriet is not one of my pet names, and there is no piano at my cottage, and I like her gramophone records. Yet I cannot imagine playing one's wife to oneself on the gramophone. Can you? . . . Mrs —— (wife of RAF officer) wrote to me ever so often at first. Am I a beast? But she wants something which I want to keep, and she ought to understand. There are Untouchables, thank Heaven, still."*

On more serious matters he was sorrowful about the death of

Mrs Knowles (Henrietta Knowles died on 20 November 1934 aged 52 years, who was found ill by Joyce Dorey, Pat Knowles' future wife), his immediate neighbour, *"I would like to reach my Dorset cottage, for my neighbour and tenant* [Lawrence had recently taken over her lease at £12 per year, mainly to ease her financial problems], *Mrs Knowles who was a great friend, dropped dead suddenly last week – or rather she was found dead on the floor, having apparently fainted and hurt herself falling. That strands me, rather. I have very much I should see to."*

On an intimate note, Lady Astor had sent Lawrence a latch-key to her Plymouth house where a room was at his disposal and although he intended to live on his 25/- a week at Clouds Hill, he was obviously tempted, *"That room idea . . . do you know I almost dally with it? . . . Yet to live on you would be either charity or a confession of failure to keep myself. I think I won't. I hope I won't. It would be a hole in my armour."*

Regarding family matters he felt trepidation concerning the return of his domineering mother, next winter, from China with Dr Robert Lawrence (his brother) and was very keen and concerned to search for *"some do-good medical job in England . . . "* for him.[12]

On Wednesday evening, 28 November, amongst an almost infinite backlog of mail, he found a June letter from an American historian, Professor Earle, seeking answers to Middle East affairs since the Great War. Explaining to Liddell Hart he wrote *"I found this today, digging deep into the pile of slowly-rotting letters that await a reply: . . . "*[13]

Lawrence liked the coastal town in the quiet season, *"Bridlington in winter is a silent place, where cats and landladies' husbands walk gently down the middles* [sic] *of the streets. I prefer it to the hustle of summer."*[14]

Again despondent forebodings of the future emerged. To friends he wrote, *"my February-looming discharge from the Air Force makes me low-toned. It is like a hermit crab losing his twelve-year-old shell, and I hate the pleasure that my service has been, coming thus to an arbitrary end.*

. . . then my plan is to move to Clouds Hill, Moreton, Dorset (the cottage) and stay there till I feel I can stay there no more: there being a hope behind my heart that perhaps I shall like it and not wish to come away."[15] Also, *"and then my R.A.F. embodiment ends, and . . . and what?*

Probably I go to my cottage and sit still there till sitting still irks me, if ever it does: . . . "[16] Furthermore, *"After that I plan to go to Clouds*

15

Hill . . . *I'm afraid of what may follow, and of what may not follow. It feels like – not an end which would be welcome I think, but like something interminable. I've always wanted less from life than I've had . . .* "[17]

At the end of November several more RAF personnel arrived at Bridlington and after a few days Lawrence remarked, with a smile, to his officer-in-charge, ex-Lt. Cdr. W. E. E. Weblin (soon to retire), *"they are all doing exactly as I tell them already. I suppose one day some N.C.O. will tell me to mind my own business – but I doubt it!"*[18] His influence was genuinely appreciated by all RAF ranks and civilian contractors, especially at boat conferences and discussions where he would let everybody exhaust their opinions and then at the end would say, *"If I might be allowed to suggest, sir . . . "*. Weblin then explained that Lawrence *"would present what was obviously the best solution of the problem under discussion. This suggestion was invariably adopted."*[19]

His thoughts turned to his beloved *Boanerges* Brough motorbike. On Wednesday, 17 October, he had visited the Brough stand at the Olympia motor show in London, where he met its representative, a Mr Prestwich Jnr, who stated that a new Brough SS 100 motorbike would be available when the present machine was handed back to the Brough works in Nottingham for exchange. In a letter to George Brough, Lawrence remarks, *"For the present the poor thing* [George VII] *is standing on its two stands in the garage of my cottage in Dorset, while I flash about Bridlington less magnificently (but with what quiet) on a push-bike.*

. . . and wondered if it would be convenient to you if I cleaned the grease off, blew the oil out of the heads, and made for Nottingham, on my way back, just before the end of the year? . . .

I am looking forward very much to this new '100' from you, . . .

G.VII is still running superbly, . . . of course he's cold and miserable on his legs, just now. It's the first time I've laid a bike up for years."[20]

Perhaps these diverse subjects written in a small seaside room appear trivial to some but they show the many aspects of this complex man. Lawrence's continuing drive to achieve perfection still remained, for his manuscript about RAF barrack-room days, called *The Mint*, was still being lent to various people for their serious criticism. Indeed he asked A. S. Frere-Reeves, *"will you (if convenient) post me back (here) those RAF notes, if they are still to your hand? Another poor chap wants to see them. Ah well."*[21]

On Monday, 26 November, Flt. Lt. Sims asked Lawrence to a concert. *"For three days* [due to the weekend] *I kept silent and then rang him up. He started at once to talk of the progress he was making on his boats, and we got caught up in a welter of detail as to stores and gear that he wanted. I suggested his coming over again, but he regretted that he could not see his way for a day or two, and then I mentioned that there was a Celebrity Concert, conducted by Sir Henry Wood, in Hull, on the following Thursday [29 November]. He considered for a moment and seemed to think that was quite an important matter, but was uncertain how to get back to Bridlington. I made the obvious suggestion, or as an alternative, would he stay the night, and I would deliver him to the garage by nine o'clock the next morning? He then proceeded to do a little sum. 'This seems to rather overdriving your car and kindness. It is thirty miles return to Bridlington, and doing it twice over makes that sixty miles, just to get me into Hull. Does not that seem a lot of miles to eat up?' Again I answered in the only obvious manner, and he agreed. He never again mentioned the sixty-mile journey his visiting us entailed on our car. I just called for him, and took him back to the hotel as a matter of course. He had a very subtle way of paying a compliment by* **not** *saying or doing. Also for the few little services it was our pleasure to render during that winter he gave no thanks: it was perhaps his unique manner of an admission of friendship.*

The concert to which we took him was good. The Schubert, he considered, had 'just one piece of sugar too much.' We gathered he thought as little of singing as we did ourselves. One rather futuristic piece, that conveyed little to me beyond discordant notes, I said I was unable to appreciate, to which he replied that it was perfectly conventional music underneath. The overlay was modern in style only, but it was quite good basically. He also said, looking straight at me, 'The tympanum's [Norman stone section between a door's lintel and arch found in English churches] *very good.' Now, I am not at all sure that I know what a tympanum is, although one guesses it is a drum of sorts, so I simply answered that I knew too little to judge either the piece itself, or the individual instruments. He continued to look at me for a second or so, and then looked away. I remember this very distinctly, and rather feel it was a test remark. Answering as I did only proved ignorance, with which he was never impatient, but to profess a knowledge which was absent, was one of the things he detested."*[22]

Sir Henry Wood was giving the first of his usual three annual winter performances as guest conductor with the Hull Philharmonic Society. The programme that evening featured the pianist Irene Scharrer. The music covered a wide selection, including William Walton's *Façade*, Beethoven's 2nd Symphony, Ravell, short piano pieces (including Chopin), and a Schuman piano concerto – the one Lawrence thought had *"just one piece of sugar too much."*[23]

During the next weekend (1–2 December) Lawrence went to stay with the Sims for the first time. *"The first week-end he came arrayed peerlessly in a French print shirt with starched collar to match. Then he was being very polite and formal. He never afterwards wore a collar. The fisherman's jersey was his standard attire. I mentioned that I would start wearing one of a gay colour myself, but he was comically impressive.' No. You are in a very important position,' he said, 'It would never do.' This was accompanied by an engaging grin.*

He complained that the neck of his jersey stretched and did not come back, so that a draughty gap was caused. He suggested that necks and wrists should be sprayed with cellulose or other elastic fluid, so that the yarn would always remain elastic. We suggested that there were jerseys obtainable . . . [24]

Neither that night, nor any other night when he had seen us, did we get to sleep until the early hours of the following morning. Words cannot describe the terrific charm of T. E. He walked as on silent wheels, perfectly smoothly, without any perceptible jolt. In fact, he made no noise at all. I never heard him clear his throat, cough, sneeze, or even splash about in the bathroom. His voice was particularly quiet, but so clearly did he speak that one never lost a syllable. His face was roughened and red, or as he referred to it, sandblasted, but although we knew he was about forty-five or so, the vivid impression he gave us was of eternal youth, and very beautiful youth at that. He emanated a mental stimulus that affected everyone, especially if he spoke." [25]

For their return to Bridlington on Monday, 3 December, Sims and Lawrence took their usual walk from the cottage to the garage (a distance of 100 yards) where Sims kept his car. On entering the garage somebody called out for a Mr Shaw, which was ironically intended for the garage proprietor of the same name.[26]

The greats of the literary world continued writing to him and on Friday, 7 December, he replied to a typically unorthodox cursing letter from Ezra Pound. In it Lawrence condemned economics, the English monetary system and the organization of Society. He is sad at the loss of A. R. Orage (editor of *The New Age* 1907–22 and *New English Weekly* 1931–4) and reiterates his liking for the labourer: *"The English working men are another creation from us. Abstract ideas are another name for maggots of the brain. Heads are happy when they employ hands, not when they earn idleness for them."* [27]

During Saturday, 8 December, he made a visit to York. In one of the bookshops there he purchased Henry Williamson's *The Linhay on The Downs; "yesterday I had to go to York and lay out three day's pay on* The Linhay . . . "28

The weather on Sunday, 9 December, at Bridlington was cloudy and dull with afternoon and evening showers. Lawrence stayed in his room reading "The Linhay . . . *which I have been dipping into, with satisfaction, all this too rough Sunday. Too rough for a walk from lodgings. No clothes, poor* [coal] *fire for drying. . . . but this sea rushing and sliding in my ears won't stop . . . .and the waves roll all day like green swiss rolls over the yellow sand, till they hit the wall and run back like spinning rope. I want to walk out in the wind and the wet, like at Clouds Hill, and can't, for my landlady's sake"*29 (see Plate 9).

Having read and reviewed Williamson's book Lawrence proceeded to read some of Ernest Altounyan's verses. As he scoured the words they became indistinct, *"I haven't got on well with them. I don't know what it is, but my eyes are letting me down. In open daylight I can read, perfectly: and my far sight is as good as good. But by night, or in dull daylight, something goes wrong. I have to put pressure on some nerve within my head, and say 'focus yourself on that line:* **see** *it' before I can read it, and then not for long . . .* As the light goes now by four o'clock (and we work till 5, from 8) this is cutting into the enjoyment of your script. One cannot get the picture of it in spasms between blind times." Even so Lawrence persisted and offered his usual honest judgement, which was slightly unfavourable, *"Your verses twist and turn like eels with your thought ever slipping away from me, and with never a stop. It moves and moves, and moves, until I find myself longing for somewhere to sit down and rest."*30

During this dismal Sunday, confined to his books and reading, he reflected his own shortcomings to Henry Williamson, *"(By the way, did I ever lend you the typescript of my R.A.F. book? Surely I did, poor return though it is.) . . . If only I could write like I read."*31

In addition to Lawrence's letter to Wilson on 20 November about the Bumpus bookshop display, he recently heard from an airman friend, G.W.W. Dunn, that an extra item, one of his Oxford Editions of *The Seven Pillars of Wisdom,* lent for private use, was also exhibited in another window display along with an original letter from him to Bernard Shaw. Feeling embarrassed he penned to Charlotte Shaw on Tuesday, 11 December, *"I cannot understand how Wilson can do these things: I wonder how I'm to get out of it . . . I didn't know that any of my G. B. S. letters had gone astray.*

Nor do I like the Oxford printing being shown. I let him keep it in his little room, because I could see how he enjoyed showing it to his private

19

collectors: but that's a long way from public exhibition: and I'd never show a letter to anyone."[32]

Lawrence's old friend Lord Trenchard, founder of the RAF, had been in the news. During his role as Commissioner of London's Metropolitan Police many cases of bribery and corruption emerged. He swiftly succeeded in quelling the disorder, and introduced the Metropolitan Police Act which incorporated many important reforms. Lawrence wrote to congratulate him on the reorganization. He had received from Trenchard the memoirs of Sir Sefton Brankley, killed in the tragic R101 airship crash, for scholarly comment which *"brought back you and the war and the beginning of the R.A.F. very distinctly to my mind. Not a good book, but interesting to those who know something and are something about the time and subject."*[33] The usual regards were expressed to Trenchard's son, the Hon. Hugh Trenchard (killed in action in 1943), who Lawrence dubbed Hugh the Second or Hugh the Younger.[34]

Again his despondent thoughts of the future emanated, *"My time is almost out: two months to go . . . I shall feel like a lost dog outside.*

Plans? . . . I plan to settle in my cottage . . . and live on it and in it till I no longer want to live in it! That is as good plan as any, I think. Leisure is about the only experience I have never yet had and it will, I hope, suit me."[35]

On Friday 14 December a high-ranking officer came to inspect RAF Bridlington. Flt. Lt. Sims recalls, *" On that day, T. E. had arranged to let me call for him in the afternoon for the week-end. I arrived at the garage about three o'clock. It was dark, forbidding, and vast. At first it seemed nothing stirred or lived there, but when the eyes and ears lately confronted with sights and sounds of the busy world became more used to the gloomy silence, a faint light was visible at the far end, and a very low murmur became audible. On tip-toe I approached. Surely, one thought, the ceremony is taking place. A slight upright blue-clad figure stood high up in the bows of a boat, with one electric light turning his hair into gold. He was giving a masterly lecture on the major features of the boats. The officer was listening in rapt silence, supported by two other Air Ministry officers. Behind them stood the contractor and engineer, one or two workmen with bared heads stood hushed on each side, and a couple of odd airmen formed the rest of the congregation. With infinite solemnity the precession visited boat after boat. The Air Ministry officials and the contractor occasionally breathed a quick word to T. E., prompting him so that he should not omit to describe, to their delight, one or two little points, that they could never tire of hearing, and patently desiring him to show off their boats, of which they were proud, and also himself, whom they worshipped. It was a ceremony of pure delight. T. E., perfectly sure of himself, and of every detail in his boats, was the complete encyclopaedia, as well as the beautifully respectful airman."*[36]

On his first weekend visit he complained of a jersey with loose neck and wrists. *"On his next visit* [during this weekend], *we produced the actual article* [an elastic fitting jersey], *with which he was as pleased as a small boy, trying it on at once and approving its quality."*[37]

One highlight to follow on Monday, 17 December, was the reading of Siegfried Sassoon's new book of poems called *Vigils.* With his usual deep sensitivity and understanding of poetry in all its subtle tones Lawrence scrutinized every delicate phrase and offered *"They have deeply moved me. They are so . . . gentle, I think I want to say. . . . These poems are like wood-violets and could easily be passed over by a man in a hurry. . . . Every other one of the 22 looks forward. I can feel the solidarity of the war-anger and the peace-bitterness under the feet, as it were, of these poems: they are all the better for it, but so far from it: so far above and beyond.*

Sometimes, in a lyrical phrase or an adjective of accumulated beauty, I can link them to your earlier work: . . . You are not ashamed of 'suddenly burst out singing' but growing shy of it. Just a word or two hint at happiness, and then your blotting paper comes down. . . . They are human and very careful and faint and solitary. Each seemed to me to shut one more door of your gigantic house . . .

But these are exquisite poems, exquisite. First reading was like sitting under an autumn tree, and seeing its early leaves falling one by one . . . these things are streets ahead, in power and beauty and calmness, of anything of yours I've ever before seen."[38]

Sassoon was overjoyed with the praise and replied in a letter *"Every window of* [draws arrow to his home address at Heytersbury House, Wiltshire] *has been lit up by your letter, & Hester* [wife] *is sending up mental rockets regardless of expense."*[39]

Lawrence became worried about his closest friend, Charlotte Shaw, who had caught a bad chill, *"Annually you have them, now (before going around the world) and again, soon after you get back . . . But it sounds uncomfortable,"*[40] he wrote late at night (17th December). Recently she had sent him *Shifting Sands* by Major N. E. E. Bray but Lawrence had already devoured it the previous month passing it on to Reginald Sims.[41] However, he had serious thoughts of writing a short biography about Roger Casement, the Irish rebel leader, *"Casement. Yes, I still hanker after the thought of writing a short book on him. As I see it, his was a heroic nature. I should like to write upon him subtly, so that his enemies would think I was with them till they finished my book and rose from reading it to call him a hero. He had the appeal of a broken archangel. But unless the P.M. will release the 'diary' material, nobody can write of him."*[42]

3

Clouds Hill for Christmas, 20–31 December 1934

Before Christmas on Thursday 20 December he wrote to Flt. Lt. Jinman, who together with Flt. Lt. Beauforte-Greenwood, was in charge of the MAEE (Marine Aircraft Experimental Establishment) at RAF Felixstowe, Bridlington's main command headquarters. In 1932 Jinman, an engineering officer, had taken part in the preliminary trials of the *RAF 200* boats, now the major task of MAEE. One of the many subjects discussed in the letter concerned Lawrence's own motorboat, *Biscuit* (see Plate 4). It is interesting to record the influence this tiny craft had on Lawrence's involvement in boat evolution and ideas.

At the Schneider Trophy held in September 1929, Lawrence was working on the motor yacht *Karen*, which was used as a floating headquarters for the race; it was moored off Calshot near the Isle of Wight. The yacht had as a tender a Biscayne Baby two-seater speedboat with a 100 h.p. Scripps engine, built by the Purdy Boat Company of Port Washington, Long Island, which Lawrence used for ferrying duty during the contest. Major Colin Cooper, owner of the *Karen*, had received it from Sir Henry Seagrave, who had brought it over from the United States. Cooper was so impressed with Lawrence's knowledge and piloting of the boat that he kindly offered it to him and the Sidney Smiths, other friends of Lawrence, as a gift, which was very gratefully received.

Although it was operative, many repairs were required. It was also an unstable craft for manoeuvring, which displeased Cooper's wife and obviously formed another reason for its bequest. Lawrence jumped at the marvellous offer and named it *BB* or the *Biscuit*.[1]

After the Schneider Trophy it was taken to RAF Mountbatten,

Plymouth, where it was scraped, repainted and the engine stripped. Lawrence anchored it amongst the rocks of a small local creek, and fitted it with old rubber tyres to save scratching its paintwork. Because of tidal problems he transferred *Biscuit's* mooring site to where a mechanical crane could lift it in and out of the sea for future trips.[2] By early April 1930 *Biscuit's* overhaul was completed and he took it to sea for trials.[3] Unfortunately the boat, built for speeds up to 45 m.p.h., proved to be temperamental and in July it was moored in a shed with engine, water, oil and coupling problems.[4] Its spirit-driven engine was also a fire hazard, but Lawrence never lost enthusiasm and had a motorcar headlamp fitted near the bows for potential trips.[5]

Lawrence's main dilemma was the non-availability of the American spare parts in the UK, so he wrote to an old friend, F.N. Doubleday (USA publisher of the translation of his *Odyssey*), and acquired his surety to purchase directly from the Purdy Company, New York works. In early September 1930 he had written for a spare shaft and gear wheel. Also in that month the *Biscuit* burnt out its dynamo which had been sent to London for rewiring.[6]

These temporary misfortunes ended when the spare parts arrived during December, with Lawrence's London bank providing the necessary dollar payments.[7] With the new 100 h.p. engine installed he refloated the craft on two good weather days in late April 1931.[8]

The summer proved successful for sea runs, with local trips inland up the creeks off Plymouth Sound, taking Clare Sydney Smith and friends. On 25 June he visited Polpero in Cornwall[9] and promised an excursion on 15 July with Lady Astor in his beloved *Biscuit*.[10]

By late October the speedboat was berthed in its shed for a winter service. Due to long working hours on RAF boats his keenness for the *Biscuit* waned. Throughout 1932 very few nautical expeditions were made; apart from doping its hull, little maintenance work was achieved.[11]

Even on 17 November 1932, when a new battery was added, his lethargic attitude continued with the *Biscuit* permanently secure in its shed.[12] This inaction continued throughout the winter of 1932–3 but by the spring his interest was rekindled and in early March 1933 he had manoeuvred her along the coast and on 3 April it was *"going beautifully."*[13]

With his posting to RAF Felixstowe in May 1933 the *Biscuit* was left at Plymouth, almost ending a glorious marine attachment. During June the original owner, Colin Cooper, agreed to transport it to Hythe later that summer[14] and in November Lawrence steered his beloved *Biscuit* for the last time in a 15–minute run at Hythe.[15] Further to the Jinman letter of 20 December 1934, Lawrence requested that the boat's condition should be conveyed to the new owner, *"If they ask your help, to put her right, you'll have to say the dynamo dosn't charge (you remember its a 6-volt, pushed . . . to charge 12V and used 15 mins on and 15 mins off, so as not to burn out). I think it's alright, but it didn't charge last time at Hythe. I had only one 15 minute run. Carbs not synchronised. Water overheating (I didn't take down the water-pump. It may be worn, or the inlet choked) an oil-leak somewhere. Ignition too advanced. That sounds a lot, but actually isn't very much."*[16] On Thursday 3 January 1935 *"The parting with my motor boat (a jewel of a creature: 37 m.p.h.) was a wrench, . . . "*[17] During mid-January 1935 the *Biscuit* journeyed to Felixstowe to the new owner, Flt. Lt. Barlow.[18]

Lawrence's knowledge of speed boats was invaluable with regard to the Bridlington craft, as a further twelve boats were due to arrive from Hythe. One of them, No 159, he was very keen to install with his own invented chrome-tested cowls.[19] Writing to Flt. Lt. Jinman, *"The Brid-engines are being all modified to date:* [with] *the latest oil pump with filter-and-release valve, A/C petrol pumps, git seals on main gland and Hyland pump shafts, big greasers on water pumps (11/4' greasers, very effective), . . . "*[20]

Many more letters were written on Thursday, 20 December. He updated criticism on C. Day Lewis' book *Hope For Poetry*[21] begun on the 16 November. The previous week he wrote to A. S. Frere-Reeves criticising another book, *"I read the Branker book. I hope it is being carefully revised for press. It is **rottenly** compiled. Grave doubt, often, who was writing, him or his editor. And heaps of names spelt wrong. . . . The book was very interesting, where it affected the Air Ministry politics. I have lent it to Lord Carlow, who shares my interest in that."* Similarly, *"Thanks for the Tomlinson. It was really good, in parts. His reflections on England strike me as ill-informed. His reflections on Spain strike me as admirable. . . . He writes now at one remove; no line, all shading. Excellent, but allusive and sometimes ambiguous."*[22] Lawrence also requested to read Cpl. Dixon's book *Tinned Soldier.*[23]

With only two months to go to demob he wrote with gratitude to thank John Buchan and Stanley Baldwin for making it possible for him to rejoin the RAF in 1925. *"If you meet Mr Baldwin in the near future, will you please tell him that the return to the Air Force secured me by him (on your initiation) has given me the only really contented years of my life?"*[24]

And it was that unknown period ahead that prompted him again to reflect, *"I have determined to keep my mind wholly blank about futures, till the time comes."*[25]

Lawrence had also amassed a number of books for his ex-Tank Corps pal A. E. 'Jock' Chambers. Over the years he periodically posted him a batch of literature both for pleasure and educational instruction. *"I hope you got your books. They were piled ready for post at Christmas. . . . "*[26]

Christmas, the festive season, was a time for fun and Lawrence did not forget his younger companions. In a charming, child-like, impish letter to his godson James Newcombe (aged 14 years) he stated, *"Dear James, (alias Stewart a word I only cry out when about to be sick – alias Monster, plus or minus other things),*

Dear James, as I said Ahem

*Dear **James***

Third time lucky. We're off. Merry Christmas. . . . Avoid gluttony, above all. Remember your figure, and the figures your parents ought to have. If you observe them over-eating clear your throat gently, to attract attention, and say 'A bit high, this bird?' That will put them off. If they bring in plum puddings and things, remark in a blase accent . . . the normal speech, I mean, of Eton . . . 'Isn't it jolly, papa, to keep up these old customs? It's like Dickens, isn't it, I mean, what?' That will throw a chill over the whole meal-time – I mean orgy."[27]

Lawrence caught the train from Bridlington to London late on Thursday, 20 December and spent the night there. On the 21st he visited the Air Ministry.

On Friday the 21st he travelled north from London to Sir Philip Sassoon's home at Trent Hall, Barnet in Herefordshire to stay the night. Sims recalls, *"At Trent Hall the visit had just ended of the Duke of Kent, and Princess Marina, so that the next guest Sir Philip entertained was T. E. . . . 'It was a very small and undistinguished party. Only myself and a Royal Air Force officer, Squadron Leader Pope. We were the aftermath of Royalty, and were very quiet.*

When we left, Philip brought out his visitors' book for us to sign. I turned it over, and the most recent names were

> *George*
> *Mary*
> *Edward*
> *Marina*

> *Henry*
> *etc., etc.*
> *So Squadron Leader Pope signed himself*
> *Pope*
> *And I signed myself*
> *Shaw*

These two names seemed to me to be very insignificant, after those immediately preceeding them, so after 'Pope', I inserted a note. (NOT THE Pope), and after mine I added similarly; (NOT THE Shaw.)

I was thinking how else this page could be improved, when Philip snatched the volume away, angrily saying that we were merely messing up his visitors' book.'"[28] In actual fact the visitors' book is signed,

> *"S H Pope*
> *338171 A/C Shaw"*

and the page is dated 22 December 1934.[29]

Lawrence eventually trained down from London to Clouds Hill on Sunday the 23rd. While at his cottage (see Plate 10) he sent his usual laconic reply-paid telegram to Lady Astor saying *"Merry Xmas,"* to which she always replied *"Same to you."*[30] Another annual Christmas custom was for Charlotte Shaw to send him a box of chocolates.[31] He later recalled *"I spent three nights at Clouds Hill, liking the place, but not easy in mind, for Mrs Knowles died suddenly a few weeks ago, and her son, Pat, wants to take on her place and is puzzled how to do it. So we camped there, he in her house and I in mine, and ate a chicken for Christmas and wondered how we were going to work out."*[32] Also *"I spent Christmas at my cottage . . . it was necessary to talk leases and arrangements. Fortunately her eldest son, who I like, is hovering on the edges of marriage and wishes to settle there after it. So the peace of Clouds Hill continues."*[33]

One of Lawrence's passionate life-long ambitions was to produce fine, privately printed pages on hand-made paper. During the Christmas with Pat Knowles (see Plate 11) they made plans for such an enterprise. *"We discussed the erection of a building over the firetank; a good place, for the atmosphere would always be damp and good for printing. He intended to get a small hand press but at that time he was not certain what type; after* The Mint *he intended to print 'some good but obscure poet.'"*[34] The fire tank referred to was a four-walled wood, brick, concrete and glass construction partly filled with a tank of water for summer heath fire-fighting, erected at the southern end of the Knowles' garden. Pat Knowles later recalled that the printing press was to be ready by January 1936 when Lawrence thought the newspaper interest in him would have died. He planned only to make a few shillings a copy to earn bread and butter.[35]

Riding his Brough, Lawrence left Clouds Hill on Wednesday, 26 December and visited Augustus John at Fryern Court, Fordingbridge, with the intention of making arrangements for some fresh portrait sittings for his forthcoming RAF book, *The Mint*. He was anxious to complete the unfinished drawings, sketched in the old timbered studio at Fordingbridge, which John had begun the previous March. Although Lawrence always revered the artistic genius in John, who was often drunk, he was only too aware of his incapacity to finish a painting during this period. Even so, he still maintained that John could accomplish the portraits required. On arrival Lawrence was made welcome and a place was set for him to join a Christmas dinner party.

Lady Pansy Lamb remembered meeting him for the first time, *"There was a crowd of people, amongst them a little bright-eyed man in a white sweater, . . . No instructions, but we all had our places marked with our names and my younger sister found herself next to the stranger. – he picked up his name ticket and said, 'Ah – Shaw – I wondered what name they would put.' My sister, in the dark, thought he was joking, and asked, 'Have you many aliases?' He replied, 'Quite a few.' 'And many nationalities?' 'Always Irish,' he answered firmly."*[36]

Nicolette Devas recalled, *"Lawrence came to lunch one Christmas day at Fryern, . . .*

The curtains were pulled to hide the cold daylight and candles bloomed to give the tables a party look. There were too many of us for the refectory table, and some people sat at a round table . . .

Lawrence sat at the top of the table near Augustus, and I was further down on the opposite side, so I had a good view of him during the meal. . . . His head was impressive, intelligent, cupped in the neck of his polo-necked white sweater, seemed to be resting a pedestal. . . . Yet there was something very self-conscious about him, and he held off from all the family frivolity and Christmassy conversation as though he were too grand for such nonsense.

After lunch, as we were all trooping over to the studio, I overcame my shyness and spoke to him. In a few tentative words I told him that I had read the Seven Pillars *and thought it 'absolutely marvellous'. He glanced at me, took three quick steps forward and joined Augustus and started to talk to him. I was too silly to know that I had been snubbed. Inside the studio near the the door, there was a pile of drawings and I joined Lawrence as he looked through them and offered comments. 'This is one of the best, don't you think?' After one or two such remarks on my part, he dropped the drawings and moved away. I had never been snubbed quite like that.*"[37]

On Thursday 27 December he motorcycled to London[38] because, *"The sting is in the tail – and I, alas, am the stung. My Air Ministry chief wants a copy of Liddell Hart's book about me* ['T. E. Lawrence' In Arabia and After first published in March 1934]. *Will you* [G. Wren Howard, a director of Jonathan Cape the publishers] *please send it to Captain W. E. Beauforte-Greenwood, Room 366, Air Ministry, Kingsway, W.C.2 . . . **and may no other blitherer ever write a book about me till I'm dead, for heaven's sake.***"[39]

The book presented a two-edged problem. First, he couldn't have forseen, through insisting that Liddell Hart included inverted commas around 'T. E. Lawrence' in the book title, that the Press would probe for his real identity and family name. Second, the Air Ministry insisted that no adverse publicity would accompany him whilst still serving in the RAF. All through Friday 28 December he remained at Kingsway, *"They kept me there till afternoon at Air Ministry."*[40]

So on a very wet night Lawrence motorcycled from London to Bridlington, *"It was pouring with rain as I left London and rode up the Great North Road . . . the Brough purred smoothly, to Royston and Biggleswade and Stamford and Grantham and Bawtry and Goole and Bridlington. Even the rain ceased after a while, and I got in warm and dry."*[41]

It was possibly on Sunday 30 December that an accidental meeting with a nearby resident, Mr K. Lester, who lived opposite the *Ozone* at 2 West Street, occurred. In 1992 he vividly recalled the chance encounter, *"I was sixteen years old . . . we both had the same make of motor cycle which was the 'Brough Superior,' his bike was brand new, . . . whereas my bike was very old and cost me £2/10/ – [£2.50]. I was riding up the back of the* Ozone *at the same time as Lawrence was pushing his bike out of the* Ozone *back passage [see p. 2]. My bike conked out as I was passing him, he laughed and asked me what the trouble was. I said I didn't know so he came to have a look and tried to kick start my bike off but it refused to start.*

He went back to his own bike, opened his pannier and came back with a new spark plug – five shillings in those days . . . he fitted the plug, checked the engine, kicked the start and the engine fired first time. I thanked him very much and told him I would pay him for the plug later. He just laughed and said 'that's OK son just watch what you are doing' and sped off up the back way."[42]

On Monday, 31 December, back at Bridlington he cleaned his

Brough.[43] Lawrence also went to see Ian Deheer who remembered him saying, *"I have brought my bike up, would you like to see it?"* Eager to view the Brough, Deheer was amazed at its enormous size when Lawrence stood beside it. *"You will be breaking your blinking neck on it,"* and Lawrence replied, *"Well, better than that than dying in bed."*[44] During the evening he wrote to G. Wren Howard about three of the firm's new books: Nesbitt's *Desert and Forest* which he thought had *"a benediction of old-fashioned decency over it. A classic of the XIX th Century, written out of its time."* He asks how Cecil Gray's *Peter Warlock: A Memoir of Philip Heseltine* is faring. V.M. Yeates' *Winged Victory* is highly praised, *"How good that he did it in time. It is a very good book, and every R.A.F. mess has a copy. I advise everybody to get it, and hear nothing but praise of it."*[45]

Yeates had very recently died and it was significant that Lawrence had been instrumental in helping him produce the book, *"Thank heaven you got him delivered of that book, while he could."*[46] Henry Williamson wrote to Lawrence in late December 1934. Eventually, in late January 1935, he answered the letter, *"Thank you for . . . your article upon Yeates. I suppose it was too late: but one reads it with a sense of shame. He ought not to have been let die. The book would have helped him in time, for I'm sure it will go to some thousands in the end. . . . I cannot see* Winged Victory *dying short. How about his wife and children? They are more than half the tragedy. Is there any prospect of help for them? . . .*

The poor chap. I wish we had been able to do something. It was good of you to offer him the means to go south, for you haven't anything to spare. In such cases I fancy the south is only a last illusion, so perhaps he was right to say no."[47] It was somewhat ironic that Yeates always signed himself as the *"Wingless Victor"* in his letters.

Lawrence complimented Liddell Hart on securing the job as War Correspondent with *The Times* newspaper, *"Returned to find your note, upon which the warmest congratulations . . . . On the **Times** you will be permanent and safe and dignified and opulent. Most admirable. You are now on the Treetop of your profession . . . I am sure that you will be able to correlate the three Defences and Offences to the general benefit."*[48]

He also complained of too much time consumed and money spent in sending letters to friends. To remedy this he devised a new year resolution to reduce such activities to a minimum, *"Next year I am going to draw in my ink-horns: for this year I have tried – vainly! – not to spend more than 2/- a week* [16 letters at 1½d per letter] *on post. After February . . . I shall not spend more than three pence weekly upon post; after the first week, when I have to warn people that I am ceasing to write."* [49] This proposed reduction in correspondence was the forerunner of a card he had printed in February 1935 (see Diagram 1), simply stating *'To tell you that in future I shall write few letters,'* although on 16 June 1933 he had mentioned to Alan Dawnay, *"Upon withdrawal to Clouds Hill I will go through my address book and to each name send a printed card 'To announce cessation of correspondence.'"* [50] But the idea went even further back to 22 March 1928 in letters to Edward Garnett and Sydney Cockerell. He wrote to Garnett *"I think I will print cards, 'to announce cessation of non-business correspondence: 'and send them to every address I can remember, at the rate of 20 a week."* [51]

In his last letter of the year to Charlotte Shaw, eating her chocolates between paragraphs, he wishes GBS and Charlotte good fortune in their impending sea voyage, *"I hope you get securely and well on to your Reina del Pacifico, and I hope the cruise is a success."* but is genuinely worried about their well being, *"Your news of health makes me feel a little unquiet. . . . As for G. B. S . . . the strain of that collapse will hang behind his eyes for weeks. Beg him to be careful: or perhaps better not, for he is wilful enough to react against advice."* [52]

Lawrence's despondent moods of civilian life were increasing at an alarming rate. He ends the year on a low note, *"The R.A.F. leaves me out of its rolls in February next, and I'm facing a rather blank future in something like unhappiness. I've been serving for 12 years, and the assurance has stayed me, like his shell a hermit crab. Now life's to begin again, with all the 24 hours of the day given to me – and I particularly don't want so much."* [53] Also to Liddell Hart *"For myself, I am going to taste the flavour of true leisure. For 46 years have I worked and been worked. Remaineth 23 years (of expectancy). May they be like Flecker's.*
'a great Sunday that goes on and on.'
If I like this leisure when it comes, do me the favour of hoping that I may be able to afford its prolongation for ever and ever." [54]

4

The Old Man,
1–20 January 1935

On Thursday, 3 January 1935, more letters arrived. Finance becomes an important item, especially after the RAF. Lawrence had invested money for the interest as part of his future income, but was also due his RAF bonus, *"Actually, I'll be full of money in March, for they give me a gratuity of £12. I'll have an income of 25/- per week, clear: and hope to live comfortably on that, without work, for at least 1935."*[1] Similarly, *"I have a little money (enough to bring me in about 25/- a week) . . . ."*[2]

Lawrence was contemplating staying incognito in Coventry immediately after his military service. In a letter to his old Tank Corps friend Arthur Russell, *"Do you think, if I came to Coventry, that you could find me some quiet place in which to settle for a little time, to make up my mind? Nothing definite to be fixed yet: perhaps when March comes I won't need it: but I may want to get away from myself, somewhere where I will not be talked about or known. . . . I thought of getting a room, or a bed, anyway, with some working family; till I can pull myself together. . . . Don't let this worry you; and don't fix anything up: but as you go round, just keep an eye open for a backwater in which I could be quiet (and cheap) for a spell. I don't want to do anything: just to moon about and think!"*[3] Later he added *"I shall come, either for a look-see, or for a stay-put-for-a-while."*[4] Despite this, Lawrence had concrete thoughts on his Clouds Hill cottage, *"I want a rest of rests. Much cottage-fitting and fixing to do too."*[5] and *"Clouds Hill is charming, now, I think. I hope to live there, after the change has happened and been forgotten: . . . "*[6]

Once again his gloomy forebodings emerged, *"I hate leaving the R.A.F. and feel like a snail whose shell is being pulled off him!"*[7] He opened his thoughts to his friend H. S. Ede, *"If to that I find myself in possession of a quiet mind, then I shall be fortunate. I think I have to 'draw' this mind when I draw my discharge; and dare only hope to find it full and quiet. I do not often confess, it to people, but I am almost aware that madness lies very near me, always. The R.A.F's solidity and routine have been anchors holding me to life and the world. I wish they had not to be cut."* [8]

Lawrence most likely visited the Sims' *White Cottage* at Hornsea for the third time during the weekend of 5–6 January. As Sims recalls, *"With children, his manner was perfect. I came in to the room one day, and found T. E. and my small son* [aged 11 years] *discussing the comparative merits of certain persons included in a book entitled* Heroes of Modern Adventure. *He gave thumbnail sketches of each, as he came to them, and at last: 'Oh, John, what have we here?' he said. 'Not quite right. Bad shot. Very inaccurate.' He was reading 'Lawrence of Arabia'. 'Give me a pencil and let us make notes.' So John produced one of his very many pencils, and T. E. wrote in the margins.* [9]

It happened that a boy friend had lent us, that Christmas, three books of which one was identical with John's. To our horror, we found that T. E. had noted the loan book. We dared not tell John, but the next time T. E. came, I explained, and would he mind? He instantly took a pencil and made notes in John's own book which are slightly different, and a little fuller than those he had previously inserted in the other book. Later, although we felt that he did not want to meet anyone at all, he agreed instantly that this boy should come and dine with us, to round off the affair, and that night, it seemed that there were three, very young and lovable little boys, who, as a treat, had been allowed to sit up to dinner with us . . . .

*He enjoyed quite large meals, did not seem to care what was given to him to eat, but always finished everything. . . . He drank nothing but water, tea and coffee. Smoked only two cigarettes yearly – one on Christmas Day and one on Easter Day, not because he liked to smoke, but because whilst doing so, he could feel how lucky he was that it was not his habit as a general rule. He liked fruit, especially apples. These he would eat holding in his hands. After getting close to the core all round, he invariably ate that too, including the pips, but he once explained to us, he **never** ate the stalk.*

Before he rose in the mornings, I took him up a cup of tea and some fruit. He selected one or the other – never both. It was a delight to knock at his door and hear that very low quiet voice say 'Come in' and see him, fully awake, not at all tousled, and smiling a greeting. My small son would seize the opportunity of rushing in; we would hear low voices, until we thought it only kind to call him away.

33

At tea, he would always take a very large slice of cake for my dogs, giving it, if possible, without that polite animal thanking him. He was not an animal lover in the full sense . . . .

He was worried as to what slippers or shoes he would wear at Clouds Hill. If he wore socks, they would be more articles to wash – he contemplated doing his own – and yet without them, leather shoes were uncomfortable, but footgear would be necessary, as he would have to go in and out of the cottage. We said nothing, but remembered seeing advertisements of high sheepskin slippers with zip fasteners and rubber soles. We got a pair and he came downstairs the next morning without his socks, to 'show us how comfortable they were'." [10]

A new Commanding Officer arrived at Catfoss, Pilot Officer F. J. Manning, who attended a dinner for the artist Eric Kennington given by the Sims at their cottage probably during this weekend. At first Manning had some misgivings, as he wondered whether a C.O. should dine with one of his airmen, even though it was Lawrence. However, the evening went off very well without the slightest trace of embarrassment on anyone's part, particularly as Kennington got going on the illustrations he had done for *Seven Pillars* and described how one of the Arab sitters had attacked him with a knife while he was engrossed in the drawing. [11] On this occasion Manning remarked to A. C. Shaw that, for a young man, it was quite a distinction in that presumably his first, and certainly one of his first, Commanding Officers, was General Allenby. Now he (Manning) was *"at the other end of the line,"* and in due course he would have something to say to his grandchildren about it. *"This actually drew a little titter of a laugh from Shaw,"* Manning remarked, *"so he certainly didn't take objection to it."* [12]

After returning Lawrence to Bridlington, on Monday, 7 January, Sims had to visit Scarborough. Having heard that an Air Ministry officer was to be at Bridlington that day, and in case he wished to see him, Sims called at the boat garage on his return journey. Finding the garage empty Sims went to the *Ozone* hotel anticipating the officer might be there.

Sims recalled, *"The officer was not there, but T. E. was in I was told. I said I would not come in, as I had only left him that morning, and had no excuse for taking up more of his time.*

'But do come in' said the proprietress [Mrs Barchard], 'I am sure he would not like you to go without speaking to him.'

'You know his room, will you go straight up?' I was asked.

I went through the hall and, from certain signs, suspected that fish and chips figured on the evening's menu. As I went upstairs I felt that my first impression was correct. A crack of light gleamed under T. E.'s door but all was silent. I knocked. Again, silence, utter and profound, for quite five seconds. Then a still, small, beautifully clear, voice said, 'Come in' and I entered, what I always felt was, The Presence.

T. E. was sitting on an armchair, hands on knees, bold upright, looking straight ahead, calm immobile, like a small Buddha, and surrounded by an aura of impenetrable dignity. I have never seen such aloof calm . . . .

The odour of fish and chips, like incense, took the place of perfumed smoke from hanging censers. The remains of one fish tail and two small chips, together with a knife and fork, lay on a plate nearby, very neatly arranged.

For quite three seconds he brooded, motionless. I perforce remained still and silent. Then with one graceful movement he levitated himself out of the chair and came to greet me, giving at the same time the impression that he expected, and wanted me to come.

We spoke of unimportant things, and eventually he saw me into the car, dismissing with grave, smiling courtesy." [13]

Lawrence kept his motorcycle at Bridlington during the period 28 December 1934 to 21 January 1935. On the wettest day, Monday, 7 January (daily total of 8.2mm of rainfall at Bridlington) he rode his Brough on Air Ministry business. Ian Deheer remembered, *"he had been out on his motor cycle and had been caught in a bad storm and the cycle was covered with mud. He was beginning to clean it when I suggested that one of my men, who was a keen motor cyclist, would be only too pleased to clean it, so T. E. agreed.*

I have since heard from my man that when he had finished it T. E. came up and thanked him, and as the man was leaving he was called back; T. E., unscrewing the petrol filler cap, lifted out the gauze strainer and it was seen to contain seven or eight half-crowns. He handed one to the man who received it in amazement.

T. E. then explained, with the remark, 'It saves a lot of trouble getting half undressed to get at your money pocket to pay for petrol, etc., on the road.'" [14]

During the evening Lawrence wrote, in his role as literary critic, to Frere-Reeves (a director of *Heinemann*, book publishers) shouting the praises of Ford Madox Ford's (1873–1939) book *It Was a Nightingale*. There are numerous lines of acclamation, shown by a few short extracts: *"I began by tossing through its first pages, but soon stopped and went back and digested them one by one. The thing is beautifully fine-knit, and has not a spare word in it – except that swarm of nasty thats, of course!* [Lawrence had a hatred of link words] *. . . and it seems to me that at last he has risen to his full* *height. . . . It seems to me almost perfect as writing, quite perfect in taste, and lovely in matter."*[15]

The most private, secretive part of Lawrence's make-up is revealed with another letter, written on Friday, 11 January, to one of his flagellate assistants.

Letter 3

Dear Sir,   *11 January 1935*

Your letter showed me that I was perhaps being rather hard on Ted, by repeating that punishment at short interval. So upon reconsideration I informed him that it will be indefinitely postponed. I asked him to give you prompt notice that your help would not be immediately required. We will hold our hands and watch to see if the lad justifies this kindness.

I need not say that I am very much obliged to you for being ready to take the further responsibility. I shall call upon you with confidence if Ted again makes it necessary. Please let me correct one misapprehension in your letter, however. Unless he strips, the birch is quite ineffective. The twigs are so light that even the thinnest clothing prevents their hurting. I fully understand your reluctance to strip him; so I was making up my mind to ask you to use either your friend's jute whip (which you mentioned to me in a former letter) or a useful little dogwhip which I could send you by post.

If the emergency arises, I shall agree to Ted's coming to you in flannels.

Yours sincerely
R[16]

There is a two-month gap between letter 3 and letter 2 written on 16 November 1934. The present correspondence states, *"by repeating that punishment at short interval."* This shows that one or more floggings occurred since 16 November. Obviously Lawrence controlled the whole operation with all observer letters going to him at Bridlington where he would plan this elaborate play – actor, director and author (see chapter 1 for earlier letters).

There seem to be four main reasons for his pursuit of flogging. Firstly, raised in a strict disciplinary Victorian period, strong sexual taboos existed. Instead of the child's natural curiosity and self-discovery of the body, masturbation for example was parentally instructed as filthy, sinful and would lead to lingering illness, stupidity, sexual insatiability, loss of hair, madness and so on. It was a subject swept under the carpet, a hypocritical dirtiness not to be explored.

Secondly, the fraud of Lawrence's mother preaching the rules of religion by day, but herself a slave of carnal desire at night, had its repercussions. He sensed, and eventually found out, that the whole family had been born out of wedlock. This led to a sense of betrayal, and refusal of all things of the flesh.

Thirdly, there was the hatred of his own smallness: a large head with a small, slight body, a schoolboy figure and an immature shrill voice.

Fourthly, his obsessive need to write numerous letters to people, mainly friends and colleagues, was his main expression of close contact with people, and was indicative of the way he viewed personal relationships.

With the burden of these four traumatic problems, Lawrence trained his sensitivity to an extreme degree in order to survive. Each time he was aroused by his sexuality he repressed it, ran away from it. His worldly success remained on the surface but a never-sleeping beast remained beneath his thin skin. The fight was constantly between his enjoyable spiritual triumphs and the strong desires of his hated body. When the body dominated with its demands, he despaired – with physical pain, flogging. He felt physical pain from sexual attacks and countered it in the same way.

The driving force, apart from countering pain with pain, was the seeking of hope or remission. The sinner seeks redemption – the stronger the pain the greater the release. Boundless lightning fills his soul like a brain spilling over with sparkling wine – a brain ejaculation! Most masochists seek pain not for pain's sake but for a hopeful salvation. His mother's favourite saying, *"God hates the sin but loves the sinner,"*[17] must many times have been at the forefront of his mind.

During the weekend of 12–13 January he motorcycled to Birmingham to stay with his old pal Corporal Arthur Hall, nicknamed 'Brum', his wife and daughter (nearly three years old). During this short break they had their photographs taken, *"Dear Brum, Back again, and the photos here. Thank you very much for them. I call them pretty good: we are as regimental as two button sticks. I look like an S.P. [Service Policeman] who has just caught you in the Bricklayers' Arms. . . . I had no idea I was so tall and thin and hard looking.*

If you see the damsel who took them, please thank her from me for painting my face so smooth. She has done us both good: for you arn't (in real life) much more of a masterpiece than myself. Ask your wife for her candid opinion of us as beauty chorus"[18] (see Plate 12).

Although Lawrence was fulfilling his new year resolution of writing fewer letters, on 13 January a long correspondence occurred with his life-long friend Robert Graves. Apart from repeating his liking for *Winged Victory, Desert and Forest* and *It Was a Nightingale*, he purposely omitted to mention his dislike for Graves' *I Claudius* and tried to be kind by picking on a small character like Herod to praise, *"your sympathetic picture of Herod . . . . Herod is charming:"* The overall flavour of the letter possesses an awkward sugary taste – more to read in the unwritten. Again Lawrence spoke of his future at Clouds Hill, *"People offer me jobs, but I've never had much leisure yet, and want to try it."*[19] Ironically Graves wrote on the same day to Lawrence.

During January the brother of Lawrence's friend, R. A. M. Guy, arrived at Bridlington late one night, trying to find Lawrence to tell him of their mother's serious illness. He called in at the *Ozone* only to be told that Lawrence was in bed and since the hotel was not open to civilians, he would have to find other accommodation. Only a brief breakfast encounter took place as Lawrence was pressed with visiting hierarchy. He was always on his guard against curious strangers seeking his attention and this must have been uppermost in his mind when writing to Guy, *"He was not a bit like you . . . and I was worried all the time trying to find a likeness, and wondering if he was really your brother or not! Apologise to him, if you see him soon."*[20]

By Friday 18 January the Bridlington workload was extremely active, *"I work all day at the boat-shed, and have to visit York, Sheffield and London frequently, at irregular times"*[21] – *"Meanwhile I work away at the boats, and find myself everlastingly putting up suggestions for new devices or improvements."*[22] So it was a pleasant surprise to hear that Sydney Smith had been promoted, *"Excellent: this letter is addressed to the Air Commodore. I wish I could see the blue plumes nodding down the main roads of Singapore. . . . I am so glad you have reached Air Rank. It is almost the top of the tree . . . . and commodoring is usually only a brief act before the baton comes."*[23]

By now Lawrence had become a celebrity in Bridlington and to his annoyance the public were frequently asking his whereabouts. To offset this unwelcome predicament his RAF colleagues decided to select a willing scapegoat. They chose a red-headed Scotsman with a broad accent, 'Ginger' Colgan, to be Lawrence of Arabia to the enquiring public. Once a man asked Shaw where Lawrence was, and with impish delight he pointed to the foreign imposter. This amusing procedure became standard practice.[24]

Another incident was remembered by H. E. E. Weblin, *"He was in dirty overalls stripping an engine in the open hold of a vessel alongside the pier, when one of the sailors from H.M. Ships visiting the port, remarked to the other, 'You see that chap down there with fair hair? That's Lawrence of Arabia.' Shaw looked up with annoyance and instantly said, 'I thought you fellows belonged to the silent Navy!'"*[25]

With only six weeks to go to Lawrence's RAF discharge each letter portrayed some melancholy note, *"This going out makes me sad, for I shall miss the work and the companionship . . . "*[26] – *"The sands run out, continually. Another six weeks and the R.A.F. loses its smallest ornament."*[27] – *"The losing of the R.A.F. is going to hit me quite hard."*[28] – *"Leaving here is a preliminary training for the wrench next month when I lose the service too."*[29]

Lawrence spent his fourth weekend with the Sims at the *White Cottage*, Hornsea, on 19–20 January. Afterwards he had planned to journey to London. *"T. E. had spent the weekend at our cottage, and the next day went to the South. He intended seeing Korda, about his film."*[30]

5

RAF Finale,
21 January–17 February 1935

Early on Monday morning of 21 January, Lawrence left Hornsea and motorcycled south via the Great North road to London, covering about 210 miles in about four hours, to meet the Honourable Edward Eliot, his solicitor and a trustee of *Revolt in The Desert*, and to lunch with the film magnate Alexander Korda who was anticipating the production of a film about Lawrence. Lawrence had arranged the meeting to try and persuade Korda to drop the film. The trouble began back on 24 May 1934 when he wrote to Eliot "*A splurge in the* Daily Mail *talking of a film to be made around my squalid past.*"[1] Rumours continued and eventually Korda bought the film rights to *Revolt in The Desert*. Lawrence correctly assumed that filming preparations were nearing a climax. Plate 13 shows Leslie Howard, who was one of the many stars booked to play Lawrence in the proposed film. A meeting was arranged, "*I am confident of persuading him off it,*"[2] he announced to Charlotte Shaw.

The luncheon turned out to be a huge success, "*No, there will be no Korda movie of me. The rumours grew thick, so I bearded the lion-maker and persuaded him to leave me alone. It would have been more ballyhoo, and after March I want retirement.*"[3] He wrote to Charlotte Shaw, "*He was quite unexpectedly sensitive, for a king; seemed to understand at once when I put to him the inconveniences his proposed film of* Revolt *would set in my path . . . and ended the discussion by agreeing that it should not be attempted without my consent. He will not announce its abandonment, because while he has it on his list other producers will avoid thought of it. But it will not be done. You can imagine how this gladdens me. Eliot took it like a dear.*"[4]

And to Lord Carlow, "*There is **not** going to be a film of me.*

Korda proved most reasonable and decent, upon acquaintance."[5] Also to Robert Graves, *"I had not taken seriously the rumours that he meant to make a film of me, but they were persistent, so at last I asked for a meeting and explained that I was inflexibly opposed to the whole notion. He was most decent and understanding and has agreed to put it off till I die or welcome it. Is it age coming on, or what? But I loathe the notion of being celluloided. . . . So there won't be a film of me."*[6]

The final word is recorded in a conversation Lawrence had with Ralph Isham. *"He said he would however co-operate with any film based on his Arabian career if it were done in the spirit of Mickey Mouse. Example: a Turkish troop-train blown into the air in bits – re-forms in space – and perfectly united, lands gracefully and proceeds merrily on its way. Treated thus, his affairs would make a great picture. He said this without any irony or bitterness, but beaming and chuckling at the idea."*[7]

Flt. Lt. Sims also recalled, in his book *The Sayings and The Doings of T. E.* the same theme, when Lawrence remarked that he would have loved to have seen the film executed in the style of *Three Little Pigs* and *The Grasshopper and The Ant*: *"Me and my army jogging across a skyline on camels could have been very amusing."*[8]

Lawrence motorcycled to Augustus John's house at Fryern Court, Fordingbridge, on Wednesday, 23 January, where he stayed for two days and one night. The main idea was to secure a life-like sketch of himself to be used as the frontispiece for his forthcoming private Clouds Hill edition of *The Mint*. John sketched Lawrence in the new *Studio* (see Plates 14–16) in his garden. *"Thereafter I sat to John for two days, twice each day; and he painted with great ease and surety (a new John, this) a little head-and-shoulders of me in oil, R.A.F. uniform, with cap on head. I think it much the best thing of me he has ever done. It sparks with life, is gay-coloured and probably not unlike my real face when thinking. So lively and clean. He himself agreed that it had come off and was comforted, as lately he has found it hard to finish anything. In his pleasure he went on to do two charcoal drawings of me, three-quarter lengths, standing – and then gave me the better of them. . . . A fine swagger drawing: small head, thin body and big knees"*[9] (Plate 17).

Lawrence wrote to G. W. Dunn *"John is on the water wagon, and was well, strong and interesting. Worried somewhat at the difficulty he is finding in continuing a picture. Many good starts, but no second wind. However he set out on a small head and shoulders, and in four bouts (morning and afternoon, for two days) it became a little jewel of a portrait. He felt it full of sparkle, and to be lovely paint. He was quite cheered by the success, his first for weeks: and at the end of it he took up a block of drawing paper and did two black charcoal studies of me. Each was also an R.A.F. fashion plate, much better than that foul 'walking out' diagram in the Drill Book. The first he said was good about the knees, but poor in the head. The second he called a good drawing and wrote on it 'John to Shaw' and gave it to me* [see Plate 17]. *It goes down to my puttees, and we tied it at once on my back with a cord and it sat there, en pillion, till I reached Clouds Hill, my cottage. . . . Alas, why have I not a face like Ivor Novello and a figure like Weismuller, so that John may have a real birthday whenever I come?"*[10] Also to Bruce Rogers, *"and a sitting to Augustus John who finished a head of me in oils and did a drawing . . . "*[11] Similarly *"John (Augustus) painted a small head of me last month. It is very good. He also drew me (in R.A.F. togs) ¾ length in charcoal. Also good. And he gave me the drawing, which is also good: very good indeed, in fact. John is a great man."*[12] And finally, *"Augustus John was in a ripe and happy mood . . . . "*[13]

He left Fordingbridge on his Brough on Thursday, 24 January, for Clouds Hill, taking with him the best of the two charcoal sketches. At home he inspected all buildings and assessories, and had long chats with Pat Knowles about future plans, *"The ram is working strongly, and the cisterns and taps are all full of water, my side and Pat's. The big tank has cracked at its north end, and will have to be undercut and buttressed. I shall get this in hand as soon as the weather permits, so as to have my water ready against the summer fire menace. . . . Pat still camps his side of the road. He has an idea of marriage in the offing* [sic]*, and a definite girl in view."*[14] (See chapter 19 for an explanation of Clouds Hill and its contents/buildings.)

Lawrence stayed, *"one night in my cottage – all very well- . . . "*[15] and on Friday, 25 January, Pat Knowles rode the Brough from Clouds Hill to Wool railway station with Lawrence as pillion clutching his suitcase and John's sketch of him, *"I caught the train just after you went (it was a good idea, that pillion ride – though pretty awful pillioning with a suitcase and masterpiece in one's arms!) . . . "*[16]

Lawrence travelled by train from Wool to Waterloo station in London. He then took the underground to Tottenham Court Road to see Wilfred Merton (who had recently taken over Emery Walker's business) at nearby 45 Great Russell Street, London WC1, to get the John portrait collotyped into 100 copies for the forthcoming *Mint* publication, *"and dumped the m-p* [masterpiece] *in London on Emery Walker, to be photographed half size and collotyped, 100 copies. That is my frontispiece – 'airman 1934 type' – if ever I put together my notes on the R.A.F."*[17] Also *"I have put it with Merton, who took over the business from Emery Walker, and have asked him to copy it, for safety."*[18] After having sent a copy to John he received the acknowledgement, *"Thanks for the collotypes, they are excellent. Say you can sure hustle!"*[19]

During the Friday evening he boarded a number 77 bus to King's Cross station to catch a train and returned to the *Ozone Hotel*, Bridlington. Reading through his accumulated mail he discovered a package from Bruce Rogers containing his letter and a manuscript of a play by Helen Kittredge. Immediate permission to use some phrases from his translation of the *Odyssey*, privately published by Rogers in 1932 in a limited edition of 530, in the chapter on *Nausicha*, was urgently required. Early the next morning on Saturday, 26 January, Lawrence cabled *"Yes"* to Rogers and followed it later that day with a letter saying *"But I shall not expect it to be accepted. It is too thin for our complicated generations. Her doing it is a compliment to us: to you, me and Homer. Where she quotes, there is a limpid remoteness in the words and I feel them to be beautiful.*

No remarks . . . what could I say. But kangaroo and bombardment both project rather from the background . . . .

As I said, it is too simple."[20]

The Oxford University Press had sent a new edition of the *Odyssey* to Lawrence, *"A good looking book, great value at six shillings, which I suppose is its present cost. I saw it only for a little while, but thought it to be the same plates as the former Oxford Press edition, not re-set, but smaller-looking. Probably they have trimmed the margins."*[21]

In sympathetic tone he commiserates with Rogers' friend Alan Villiers, who had experienced a major mishap with his sailing frigate *The Conrad.*[22]

To his pal 'Jock' Chambers a more frivolous letter was composed, *"I had hoped the new nerves would have reformed your handwriting into legibility. God alone knows how you got into the Post Office with it* [Chambers was a sorter with the Paddington branch of the London Post Office] *. . . or did they mean you for the cryptographic department?"*[23] Chambers was hoping to take a spring holiday at Clouds Hill, *"The cottage will never be less than partly yours, whenever you want it, . . . It may be wholly yours, if I'm away: . . .*

Your coming will be a delightful change, if I'm there. You know the conditions, so I needn't explain them."[24]

Gale force winds blasted Bridlington on Saturday evening (26

43

January) as Lawrence scribbled to Charlotte Shaw in his lonely room; the storm was *"starring all the black windows with wild hail . . . But what a night! A harbour-night, for sure."*[25] Despite receiving no mail this year from the Shaws, Lawrence religiously continued to write to them. He believed they had already left for a sea voyage, *"May you and G. B. S. be prospering, wherever your ship is."*[26] On 28 January G. B. S. wrote to him explaining the situation. Charlotte had booked an eight-week South American tour to begin in January to improve her husband's health from the English winter. In early January *"She hurt her shin packing. It woke up the old South African wound and produced blood poisoning. Three doctors, 1, local g.p., 2, Harley St homeopath (Sir John Weir), 3 [William] Cooper the osteopath. Yet she lives!"*[27] She refused to move from their home at 4 Whitehall Court, London, SW1. In the meantime G. B. S *"had to cancel the South American trip, and engage for another tour round Africa to the Dutch East Indies."*[28]

On reading this Lawrence was deeply shaken, *"This is very bad news. I had been imagining you both off safely for South America, acquiring your winter dose of sunlight. I am so sorry. You say she is making ground, which is so far good; but that return of blood poison may be very severe on the heart. . . . Please, when she is better, say how very much I'd like to come and see her, . . . I won't write, because you'll have worry enough as it is: but do take care of yourself."*[29] Charlotte steadily improved and they both sailed from Tilbury on 21 March for Gibraltar.[30]

On Sunday, 27 January, Lawrence stated that he went to see Bernard Shaw's *Too True To Be Good* (which he read in December 1932 saying that it *"pleases me beyond measure . . . ,"*[31]). It was performed at the *Spa Pavilion*, Bridlington,[32] in which he was portrayed as Private Meek. A few days later, however, he admitted to G. B. S. that *"I funked going to see the play,"* adding" *Too True made an awful lot of talk. Bridlington in winter is a large village only, and I'm known as a character. . . . They would have cheered or jeered, probably: cheered, I'm afraid; so I funked it. Sorry."*[33]

Also he had just finished reading James Hanley's book *The Furys*. Lawrence wrote to Hanley, *"In the Furys you go forward. The good qualities of your writing; its force and conviction and heat and violence, come through the stronger the more you control them."* He favourably described many of the book's characters, ending, *"A special word about the writing. It began perhaps with labour: at least I noticed a staccato style, sentence after sentence being simple, and independent. Then it warmed to the job (or I did) and for the last 200 pages I galloped right through, never noticing how perfectly the manner fitted the job."*[34]

On Thursday, 31 January he wrote at least seven or eight letters. In one to G. Wren Howard he praised his recent books and the author Leo Walmsley, who had spent his early years in Robin Hood's Bay just south of Whitby further up the coast. It was his particular graphic, detailed and true descriptions of the north-east Yorkshire coastal scene that so delighted Lawrence. *"My sense of fitness makes me feel that all book people should take their hats off to Walmsley . . . whose* Three Fevers *has proved not a flash in the pan but the hefty beginning of a family . . . these coastal sketches, which are charming . . . "* and in impish mood adds *"but if he still sticks close to Robin Hood Bay wouldn't it be fitting if I ran up there late in February with one of those R.A.F. boats we are overhauling here (I could call the jaunt a trial, and it would take an hour each way, weather being good . . .) and blow my Klaxon towards his beach? He is not reverenced in his own county, I find. In Hull and York and elsewhere I have had mild rows with the local booksellers for their not selling him in basketsfull. . . . If it was summer time, I'd take the fleet of ten boats up and serenade him properly: . . . "*[35]

Clouds Hill, his future home, was uppermost in his mind. Lawrence sent a number of large stamped envelopes to Pat Knowles who could, at regular intervals, fill them with Clouds Hill letters and post them to Bridlington.[36] *"I am trying tonight to write some letters to Yorkshire fellows, and if I manage them, will enclose them for you to post* [from Clouds Hill]. *If I send them from Bridlington they may make efforts to see me . . . and that is inconvenient."*[37]

Tom Beaumont, who served with Lawrence in 1918 and is listed in *Seven Pillars of Wisdom* as a member of the Hejaz Armoured Car Company, wrote to offer his services as valet in Dorset. Lawrence replied on Saturday, 31 January, *"No, Clouds Hill wouldn't look right with a valet!"* Unfortunately he went on to mention his demob date, *"My time runs out a month hence, . . . Let us leave it till after March 1."*[38] Beaumont, possibly with financial reasons in mind, informed a National newspaper of this impending news with potentially disastrous results (see Chapter 6).

Lawrence's apprehension of his unknown future deepened, *"One month to go! Only a month. I can feel it happening now."*[39] – *"March 1 is my sad date, when I go:"*[40] – *"Only a month more: I cannot persuade myself that it is really all coming to an end."*[41] – *"After my discharge I have somehow to pick up a new life and occupy myself – but beforehand it looks and feels like an utterly blank wall. Old age coming, I suppose; at any rate I can admit to being quite a bit afraid for myself, which is a new feeling. Up till now I've never come to the end of anything. Ah well. We shall see after the Kalends of March."* [42] – *"My clock is running down: another month, and it's 'out' for me. I'm still all amazed at what to do next. I want a rest, and time to think about things, and I'd like a holiday, and to wander about England for a bit . . . "* [43]

Lawrence was becoming uncertain about his finances in the far future, *"I don't think I'll have enough cash even for bread and butter after the first year. However, we'll see."* [44] – *"I've got to look after myself: not immediately, for I have enough for at least six months, but as soon as is convenient. I have not an idea in my head: various jobs have been offered, but none of them attractive. Possibly I shall fall back on my cottage and see how much – or rather how little – I really need."* [45]

Also on 31 January Lawrence wrote to Edward Spurr,[46] a young engineer from Bradford, who was working in Southampton at the time. With no other available correspondence it would be fair to assume that they had known each other for only a few months. According to Spurr's memory *"he first met Lawrence in 1935 . . .* [and] *related how, together with Lawrence, he built 'nearly 70 miniature models'* [searching for a new type of speedboat].*"* Also, *"the two together evolved the dramatically new form of craft . . . . "* [47] Spurr continued this experimental work after Lawrence's death which on 24 May 1938 resulted in the launching of the strangely designed speedboat *Empire Day* with *"To L of A: a compte* ["To Lawrence of Arabia : on account"]*"* painted on its bows. It is just possible that the two did meet to experiment on such a programme but with Lawrence's hectic time schedule during this period the reality points to Spurr, in conversations with Lawrence, becoming fired with enthusiasm and Lawrence's fame, proposing the partnership to such an extent that he emblazoned Lawrence's name on the final prototype. In fact *Empire Day* was not very successful in its trials.[48] (See Jeremy Wilson's *Lawrence of Arabia*, pp. 1153–4 for similar views.)

Lawrence wrote to Pat Knowles at Clouds Hill asking him to *"enquire re-clinker from Dulleston* [R. Dulleston, fuel merchant at Bovington Camp]. *Fire-logs from Wareham. Digging out the end of the tank for putting in a reinforcement. The last should be done and dry by April, for us to fill against the fire raiders: I am nearly complete with the engine-and-hose-and-pump order."* [49]

A casual meeting with one of his old pals, J. T. Parsons, occurred on Friday, 1 February, *"I met him again the beginning of February 1935, two months before his discharge from the R.A.F.; he was working at Bridlington, supervising the refit of power boats by contractors. He was still the same man, considerate in detail, and would do anything for the 'troops', and even when talking to 'Big Noises', he would always find time for the men. One little incident I recall happening at that particular time was: half a dozen of us had just been posted from Felixstowe and not having drawn any pay for a fortnight, we were, like the average airman, rather pushed for cash; Shaw had an inkling of this and walking into the dining-room one day he placed £2 on the table saying, 'Perhaps this will help to relieve the tension, share it between you,' he then walked out again. That was typical of Shaw, always ready to help the lads."*[50]

Because of this generosity Lawrence wrote to Arthur Hall during the evening and explained his cash shortage. *"I'd hoped to send you some tool-money, but luck is still dead out. Wait a bit, before you get anything please. It might be another fortnight before Felixstowe send me my credits. It is not easy to arrange that sort of thing by post, when you don't know the pay bloke you are writing to."*[51]

Lawrence was involved in another incident which concerned a vociferous woman who, with two grown sons, had written for two years begging him to return home. Lawrence explained the story in the same letter to Arthur Hall, *"Meanwhile I've been having a dust-up with the Chief Constable of your town [Birmingham]. A Mrs [name omitted] kept on writing me letters, calling me Jim and begging me to go back to her and all would be forgiven. I answered the first one, saying I wasn't her Jim and didn't know her from Eve: but she went on writing about twice a week, from a place called [name omitted].*

So finally after about two years of it, I wrote to your Chief Copper and asked if as a favour he'd send an officer to ask her to abate her nuisance. I asked him to do it gently, because I thought the poor woman was mad.

He replied in a letter (not even marked confidential) addressed to the C. O. Bridlington R.A.F. saying that Mrs [name omitted again] had been interviewed, was 53, eccentric, a widow, two grown-up sons: that she had lived with me during the war, while I served in an Anti Aircraft Battery at Birmingham – and that she had no intention of ceasing to write to me.

I sent him back a snorter, saying that I had written to him personally, and he had no right to communicate with my supposed C.O. . . . but that fortunately there was no C.O. at Bridlington, and so his letter had come direct to myself!

*Since then, complete silence from my abandoned widow **and** from the Chief Copper."*[52]

Also during that evening he replied to a letter from K. W. Marshall, a director of the publishers Boriswood Ltd. They were to be prosecuted at Manchester Assizes for publishing an obscene book called *Boy* by James Hanley (see Plate 18). Lawrence had already read the book and praised it. Fully aware of possible indecent phrases, he still maintained it was a text of high literary value. He advised Marshall, that since its first issue in 1931 all reviews were good and nobody objected to its content, *"But in cold fact, you'll be in the hands of your counsel. . . . If you can find out who at Bury initiated the prosecution, and send me his name and address, I will try and get him sent from Paris, by post, a regular supply of really indecent literature: something that will show him the difference between pornography and works of art."*[53]

James Hanley (1901–85) was a self-taught writer, almost a recluse. After his boyhood in Liverpool he went to sea at age 13 and sailed around the world. Jumping ship at New Brunswick he joined the Black Watch Battalion of the Canadian Expeditionary Force where he saw action at Bapaum. He was gassed, hospitalized, discharged and eventually returned to Liverpool. During the next few years Hanley pursued diverse interests. Apart from studying French, Russian literature and the piano, he worked for a number of years at a railway station.[54]

Hanley drew on his merchant navy experiences when creating *Boy*, which he wrote in ten days. The book is dedicated to Nancy Cunard who provided him with a typewriter during the hard times when creating his book. By the early 1930s he had settled down with his wife Yimothy in Merionethshire.

Boy is the story about a lad who escapes from his tyrannical father by stowing away on a merchant ship bound for Alexandria. The major part and meat of the narrative centres around his ill-treatment and sexual manipulation by the crew. He loses his virginity in an Alexandrian brothel and catches syphilis. The situation gets out of hand and the frightened captain suffocates the boy and throws him overboard. Although unpleasant and foul in taste to some, the lively movement and fresh colloquial phrasing of the text holds together a manuscript of extreme brilliance.

Boy was first published by Boriswood Ltd in 1931 in a limited edition of 145 copies. After many editions, a cheap version appeared in 1934 with a highly provocative cover of an almost naked body. A Lancashire taxi driver borrowed the book from a library. By chance his wife, after only reading the publisher's blurb, took it to Bury police complaining of its licentiousness. The police in turn prosecuted the publishers (not the author James Hanley) for obscene libel.[55]

Lawrence first met Hanley in 1930. A year later he wrote to him *"I will not throw* Boy *away. I propose to read it more. It is good. I like it better than* Sheila *. . . for subjective reasons, because I like men, and ships and Alexandria."*[56]

Even in 1931 Lawrence was well aware that *Boy* could provoke censorship, *"I hope you* [C. J. Greenwood, a partner in Boriswood] *are not riding for a row with the Home Office . . . Hanley is too good to be labelled by them."*[57]

Later that year, *"*Boy *is being reprinted, with the asterisks cut or replaced by words. . . . I think it would have gone much better if you had made the cheap edition a new book, rather than a mutilation."*[58]

Although his hands were tied he later enlisted the help of E. M. Forster. Meanwhile Boriswood were advised to plead guilty – as a not guilty could have led to imprisonment. The police seized 99 copies of *Boy* and the jury at Manchester Assizes found the publishers guilty, fining them £400 and ordering *Boy* to be withdrawn from circulation.[59]

Another item Lawrence mentions in his letter to K. W. Marshall was Heinrich Hauser's *Bitter Water, "a real good book . . . ."* with *"the middle section, of life on the Baltic or N. German island, was most admirable reading."*[60]

A group, headed by Lawrence, visited York Minster on Sunday, 3 February, *"I was able to take a solemn party over York Minster, and detail its glass and distinguished Nottingham alabaster . . . "*[61]

On Monday, 4 February, Lawrence wrote to Lord Carlow explaining about the hectic workload at Bridlington,*"Boats are going well. All armour has been returned, modified from Hadfields, and we are keen on keeping our promised finishing date for March; for all boats. Into the water, that is; not necessarily finished test . . . . to-day, . . . we sketched out an oil-hydraulic fitting gadget for the armoured hatches."*[62]

In late January Robert Graves wrote a scathing letter to Lawrence concerning his friendship with Laura Riding, Graves' closest friend, *"I have felt very unhappy about the breach between you and Laura and would give a great deal to have it healed."* He raps Lawrence for acting in an averse manner to Laura at their last meeting. *"Instead, you wrote a long chatty letter to* me *and as a sort of afterthought made some light-hearted reference to Laura's obscure style. The protest I registered did not convey anything to you. You merely wrote to* me *again, and your whole tone conveyed the sense of Laura as a sort of intellectual freak and worse than that, of Laura as having no status of her own as being some sort of appendage of mine . . . . but the nearest*

I can get to a comparison is the junior partner in a third-rate New York publishing firm, & I mean this literally as a counter-insult."[63]

Lawrence is equally blunt when replying on 4 February, *"If you remember the history you will see that Laura and I never met. . . . Laura saw me too late, after I had changed my direction. She is, was, absolutely right to avoid communication with me. There is no woman in the machines, in any machines . . . but you can understand a mechanic serving his bits-and-pieces, whereas she could not. I do not know or care if you are better, or she: . . . Whereas she and I could never have changed places. The bar between us was not her artistry, but her self and mine: and quite likely her sex and mine."*[64]

However they were great life-long friends and Graves offered to increase Lawrence's proposed weekly income to 42/- for a year or more from his sales of *I Claudius*.[65] Lawrence thanked him but was *"guilty of a great fault in taste . . . when I told you I was able to help you when you were in difficulties. I was stupidly thinking aloud.* [Lawrence helped Graves and his first wife with debts that accumulated with their shop venture at Boars Hill, Oxford. In 1921 Lawrence gave four chapters of his *Seven Pillars of Wisdom* to Graves which he sold for serial publication in the USA.] *It is very good of you to offer to share the job with me. . . . You will be a reserve, only if ever I get meshed (like you at Boar's Hill) and unable to help myself."*

In the same letter Lawrence sent his own obituary to Graves, to be used in the event of his death, in answer to a request from *The Times* newspaper to Graves.[66]

On Wednesday, 6 February, Lawrence sent a collotyped print of the John portrait of himself to Lord Trenchard who replied the following day, *"I am very glad to have it."*[67]

On the 6th he also wrote, *"I must not try to sign on again in the R.A.F. as in 12 years time I should be too old to be efficient. The wrench this is; I shall feel like a lost dog when I leave – or when it leaves me, rather, for the R.A.F. goes on. The strange attraction is the feel of the clothes, the work, the companionship. A direct touch with men, obtained no other way in my life."*[68] This fragmented piece was intended to form part of a collection of descriptions of his RAF days called *Leaves in the Wind*. It was additional material to his *Mint* manuscript and it seems to have been his intention to add it as a sequel.

At Clouds Hill, after his death on 19 May 1935, pencilled notes were found in a manuscript which were also to be included in the sequel. It describes, as far back as December 1926, his crowded and filthy journey aboard the troopship *Derbyshire* on his posting to India. One very vivid account is of an ex-naval Warrant Officer manually unblocking a woman's toilet.[69] From another source he describes the *Iris III* Flying Boat that crashed into the sea near Plymouth on 4 February 1931. He witnessed the fatal plunge when the *Iris* sank and helped to rescue the few lucky survivors.[70]

Writing from the *Alexandra Garage*, Bridlington, where boats were taken for reconditioning under Air Ministry contract, to Flt. Lt. Jinman on Saturday, 9 February, he was extremely pleased at the success being achieved with the RAF motorboats, *"We launch our first boats on the 18th of this month, and the last on the 27th, weather permitting: but the target boats (which represent 15 engines) are not required for duty for weeks . . . .*

We have made a smooth overhaul and thorough recondition of all the hulls here, and corpl Bradbury has done very thorough work on the engines. So Bridlington ought to have a light season, so far as upkeep goes." And remarking on Jinman's future, *"I believe you have heard of the prospect of your moving to C/A* [Coastal Area] *. . . which would be the best thing imaginable for the R.A.F. fleet however inconvenient to yourself. . . . I see the boat question increasing every year in importance, and if large boats come along, and the Marine Branch gets organised, the need to have somebody who understands design at C/A will become paramount."*[71]

During the last few days, Lawrence, with his RAF colleagues, launched their own small boat, *"the quietest and sweetest tick-over of any Dinghy yet! It kicked back, when cold. So we put the ignition back a trifle. Then the front rocker ran dry, and there was no oil flowing down the front lead from head to camshaft front bearing. So we pulled down the rocker assembly, and found more bits of Harry M's string in the rocker-fulcrum pipe! Took 'em out, and all's perfect."*[72]

Further details of the last few remaining boats showed that his Bridlington job was ending smoothly, *"Send the last engine of 217 when you can. We aim to get the Garage empty by February 27, and haven't too much time. Recasting the controls of 190 and 191 will be a slow job.*

Felixstowe are pleased with 159 – but they ran down her battery, starting up! They'll learn, like we did.

Interesting about the Lion [proposed marine use of the Napier Lion engine]. *More trouble coming, I think."*[73]

Another mechanical letter is sent to Cpl. Bradbury on Friday, 15 February, requesting different tools and parts. The inevitable sadness also appears, *" I find these last days rather wearing, and will be glad to end them suddenly."*[74]

Lawrence paid his fifth weekend visit to the Sims' cottage at Hornsea on 16–17 February where they *"noticed a certain relaxing of his manners and body."*[75] Reginald Sims, a very good photographer, took four excellent photographs of Lawrence, of which two are reproduced in Plate 19 and the jacket.

On Monday, 18 February, Sims finally recalled, *"On leaving he took his seat beside me and waved through the window his farewell as we turned the corner.*

We were very silent during the ride back to Bridlington. When we reached his hotel he got out, and I tried to tell him, haltingly and stumblingly, how much we treasured the last four months, and what it had meant to us.

He did not attempt to help me out, but watched me silently.

'We shall see you again?' I asked.

He still looked at, and through me. Then, after another moment he replied, 'Nothing is more certain than that I shall see you again.'

Since T. E. himself said that, we often wonder."[76]

6

Explosion,
17–25 February 1935

A bombshell hit Lawrence's world on Sunday, 17 February. Although the Air Ministry had warned him as early as the 13th that the Press were curious about his movements, he couldn't have expected the explosive article and headlines in the *Sunday Express:*

"LAWRENCE OF ARABIA
LEAVING THE AIR FORCE ON MARCH 1
'REALLY SORRY'

Lawrence of Arabia, now aircraftsman T. E. Shaw, is to leave the Royal Air Force on March 1, when his discharge becomes effective.

In a letter to a Yorkshireman who served under him in Arabia, he wrote: 'My time runs out in a month hence, and I shall be very sorry. The work passes my time. The last twelve years would have been long without it. Yes. I shall be really sorry!'

The letter, dated January 31st last, from Bridlington, was received by Mr. T. W. Beaumont, now a foreman in a Dewsbury textile mill. Mr. Beaumont was a machine-gunner in the 'Suicide Club', a detachment of twenty-six men, sent to Arabia in 1917 for secret service work under Lawrence.

FEELING OF PEACE

Lawrence plans to retire to his cottage in Dorset. This is how he describes it in his last letter to Mr. Beaumont. 'It is a cottage in the middle of a great heath of bracken and heather. Two rooms, no bed, no kitchen, and no drains, but a spring in the garden and a feeling of utter peace. I may go there for a while after my discharge . . . '

T. E. Shaw has written four times to Mr. Beaumont since 1931. All the letters reveal uncertainty as to the future. 'I shall be rather lost in charge of myself after all these years,' he writes."[1]

The prospect of the Press hounding him on his discharge and at Clouds Hill cottage filled him with extreme anger and horror, but he controlled his rage and only mildly rebuked Tom Beaumont, *"Your contribution sent the pressmen scurrying about Bridlington, I believe: but vainly. They are proper tripe hounds, keep clear of them, for your own sake.*

If it's true that you got a good offer for my letters [A collector was prepared to pay £20 for one of them] *by all means take it! They are your property but the copyright (that is the right is publish) remains mine always. Sell them cheerfully but for the Lord's sake don't let the pressmen read or repeat them, it's pretty beastly to have them snooping around the place."*[2] However the damage has been done, an action that Lawrence would regret for the rest of his short life.

As the steam train drew into Bridlington station at 18.15 hours on Tuesday evening, 19 February, Lawrence, waiting on the platform, met his old RAF pal Corporal W. Bradbury who had travelled up from Hythe to officially replace him. Bradbury was in civies and had brought his personal mechanical spares book with details of numbers and prices.[3] Lawrence had known back in November 1934 that Bradbury was to carry on his work, *"I've found a fitter corporal, Bradbury (ex Birmingham) who promised nicely to take my place . . . a tough sensible knowledgeable chap."*[4]

In a short note to Pat Knowles on Wednesday, 20 February, he wrote, *"No more to here* [mail from Clouds Hill to Bridlington] *. I've finished, and shall push off by bike* [push-bike] *in a day or two for Clouds Hill, travelling by very slow stages, but arriving there in very scruff order some time in early March.*

I shall be glad to get away, now."[5]

During this week he went to see Cecil B. DeMille's film *Cleopatra* at one of the evening performances between 18.15 and 22.30 hours at *The Winter Gardens* (see Plate 20). The film starred Claudette Colbert[6] and Lawrence *"considered both photography and acting to be one hundred per cent."*[7]

The hectic schedule had paid dividends,*"Actually I've been frantically busy, working all the time to finish these R.A.F. boats – and successfully too. They are in the water two days ahead of schedule. It is comforting to plan a campaign of overhaul, and work it all out according to plan. And a minor benefit has been that in the rush I have not had time to listen to my last minutes in the Air Force, ticking out."*[8]

The official log page for the technical description of his last boat overhaul was completed on Saturday, 23 February and signed *"T. E. Shaw A/C (His last R.A.F. work)"*[9] (see Appendix 1).

On the same day a young pressman asked about his future plans; with impish displeasure Lawrence replied *"I shall make a list of all the press representatives in London, and shall then assassinate them one by one. Your turn will come in about five years time."*[10]

As Saturday was the last day of sea testing the speed boats a number of officers attended the occasion, including Weblin and Beauforte-Greenwood. Later that evening, Lawrence, with his fellow officers and brother airmen, called in at a local club for the RAF tradition of 'ginning up',[11] where he *"occasionally ate the red cherries on small sticks from his friends' glasses. One of the waitresses brought an entire dish of these dainties, and he ate every one with the zest of a schoolboy raiding a tuck-shop."*[12] Afterwards they attended the *Spa Theatre*, a few yards south of the *Ozone*, to see John Galworthy's play *Windows* (first performed on 25 April 1922 at the *Royal Court Theatre*, London). The theatre was a grand building with lush Victorian decor. The plush seating ranged from the 1/- upper circle to the 2/- stalls.[13]

The play was in three acts with only one stage set which consisted of a dining room looking out to a garden with "windows" in between. The main characters were the March family who rambled on and on in one of those awful pseudo-melodramatic farces. The philosophic window cleaner uttered such remarks as, *"You can clean yer windows and clean 'em, but that don't change the colour of the glass. . . . I see through it; I see my girl's temptations. I see what she is – likes a bit o'life, likes a flower, an'a dance. She's a natural morganatic."*[14] No wonder Lawrence laughed throughout, *"Shaw watched the play very attentively, and seemed to comprehend more amusing passages than the rest of us, frequently chuckling to himself, when the rest of the party were silent and 'po-faced'. He sat right in the middle of us all, again with the scarf and the sports jacket. The wives of Ian Deheer and Weblin were there, and he was extremely sociable with them: . . ."*[15] Another account of that evening remembers that *"During the play, he sat quietly mostly with his head on his hands and gave a little giggle, sometimes when there was otherwise complete silence in the auditorium. He afterwards said that the play was good. Very good. It must have been, because I hardly understood what it was about."*[16]

Afterwards in the foyer he *"looked quite immaculate in his cheap ready-made coat, slacks, and blue fisherman's jersey, was crowned by a friend with a very large, hard, bowler hat. T. E. rose to the occasion nobly, and paraded around the foyer with lordly dignity and a gloriously fierce air which matched the bowler hat perfectly."* [17] He even autographed some of the officers' wives' programmes. [18]

On Sunday, 24 February, he took out a dinghy around the harbour mouth for a last nautical reminder of his Bridlington days. [19] With the rest of the day free he generally put things in order and wrote letters. One of the final tasks was to post his unpublished typed manuscript of *The Mint* to John Buchan at Elsfield, just east of Oxford, *"Today I have posted you the typescript (about 60000 words) of my R.A.F. journal. You said I might, in your last letter; but I send it apologetically. Typescripts are messy to read. . . . The story has more shadow than sunlight in it. Its language is often grossly obscene, for it is the language of the troops. And besides I have a fear that in it I have given away my limitations more bluntly than I would wish.*

However, there it is. The fragment is unpublished, and not likely-to-be-published. I suspect it is better writing than my Seven Pillars, and if you could confirm that suspicion, I might be tempted into trying to write something again." [20]

On bookish matters he also refuses a request from Sir Ronald Storrs to write an introduction to a book on Bedouin life, *"No: I won't; Forewards are sceptic things, . . . but to strangers it is easy to say 'NO': he must understand that he has no claim on me: nor do I even know what he has written, or why, or who he is. No, most certainly No."* [21]

On Monday morning, 25 February, he put on his RAF uniform for the last time and presented himself at the C.O.'s (Flying officer F. J. Manning) office where the Flight Sergeant marched him in. Lawrence said, *"I have come to say goodbye, sir."* They talked about boats and Clouds Hill. Lawrence also mentioned the reason for not signing on for another term of service, and with that he returned to the *Ozone*. [22]

During his last evening on Monday, 25 February, Cpl. Bradbury joined him, *"I helped him pack his kit the evening before he went off, and during the packing I could not help but feel that he was very miserable at leaving it all."* [23]

Officially, his discharge papers contained a summary stating that *"He is an exceptional airman in every respect and his character and general conduct have at all times been 'very good'."* In another document from the Ministry of Labour, found amongst his discharge papers, it said *"This airman has a habit of pushing any job too far. He can do rather too many things. He prefers a small job to a big one. Job preferred: motor yacht hand. Seasonally only and in a small craft. . . . References: None – best reference probably manager British Power Boat Company or Wing Commander."*[24]

He wrote a final word to his Air Chief Marshall, *"Dear Sir Edward, Not many airmen, fortunately, write to their Chief of Staff upon discharge; but I was admitted by the first C.A.S. [Trenchard] so hesitantly that perhaps it is in order for me to thank his successor for the forbearance which has let me complete the twelve years.*

I've been at home in the ranks, and well and happy: consequently I leave with a sense of obligation, though always I have tried in return to do everything that the rules – or my chiefs – would allow.

So if you still keep that old file about me, will you please close it with this note which says how sadly I am going? The R.A.F. has been much more than my profession."[25]

7

The Long Ride Home,
26 February–5 March 1935

The day Lawrence dreaded had arrived. On Tuesday, 26 February, he presented himself at the Marine Shed and posed, sitting on his push-bike and leaning against the brick harbour wall opposite (still there in 1992), for a photograph (see Plate 21) taken by Ian Deheer. Lawrence was attired in his usual scarf, sports jacket and flannel trousers. A few friends turned up to see him off including his C.O. Pilot Officer F. J. Manning. Somehow he was able to scribble a quick note saying *"I'm riding out of Bridlington at this moment* [10.00 hours], *aiming South but with no destination in view."*[1] Similar impressions about his vague itinerary were expressed during the previous week, *"My cottage is waiting for me, . . . I shall not get there for a couple of weeks, . . . "*[2] – *"travelling by very slow stages, but arriving there, . . . in early March,"*[3] and *"I shall cycle down in slow stages from here to Dorset, to my cottage. The road passes near Elsfield* [near Oxford], *and I may, if dry and warmish, call at your house as I pass."*[4]

The route and timing of his push-bike southward towards Clouds Hill are sketchy but an attempt has been made (see Maps 3–4). The few available facts have to be stated:

First, to estimate his speed it was convenient to take the ride he was to make on the same push-bike from Romsey to London on 17–18 March 1935, covering 75 miles in about eight hours.[5] This gave an average of nine miles per hour.

Second, in very wet or windy conditions his progress would be reduced so the authors have monitored each day's weather situation on route. All weather reports were taken from the nearest three weather stations along the route for each day.

Third, Lawrence wrote to the publisher Peter Davies on Thursday, 28 February, saying *"On Tuesday* [26th February] *I took my discharge from the R.A.F. and started southward by road, meaning to call at Bourne and see Manning:* **but today** [28th] **I turned eastward,** *instead, hearing that he was dead."* [6] The letter was written on headed notepaper from the *Talbot Hotel,* Holbeach, where he obviously stayed the night of 28 February/1 March, arriving there in the late afternoon – darkness then fell around 17.30 hours.

Fourth, Lawrence visited RAF Cranwell to see Rupert de la Bere on the morning of 28 February, because of its convenient location well north of Bourne, even though Lawrence never mentioned it in his letter to Peter Davies.

So Lawrence left Bridlington at 10.00 hours on Tuesday, 26 February, on a sunny day with a moderate westerly breeze. He cycled south, probably along the coastal road to Beverley and Hull, covering 32 miles and arrived at Hull in the early afternoon. He caught the Hull ferry, which took an hour to cross the Humber. Travelling south for the rest of the daylight, Lawrence passed through the more familiar county of Lincolnshire through Caistor and Market Rasen. Just south of here was then sited the Youth Hostel at Lynwode, a possible night stop.

Rain, heavy at times, with a south-easterly gale, continued all through Wednesday the 27th making cycling very arduous. Lawrence would have covered only a small distance, say 15 or so miles. It seems highly probable that drenched through he travelled to his old favourite haunt, Lincoln, where he might have lodged overnight (27–28 February). It is quite possible that he stayed at a guest house on Steep Hill – one used often in his Cranwell days.

Conditions were ideal on Thursday morning (the 28th). The rain had passed over and only a mist and overcast sky greeted Lawrence as he pushed south the 17 or so miles to RAF Cranwell. He went to visit Rupert de la Bere, an old friend he had known for about 15 years, *"he paid me a long visit at the College only a few weeks before his death."* [7]

There are two versions of Lawrence's Cranwell visit by de la Bere.[8] They provide definite pointers to the timing of his visit and his following destination. *"I was having tea in my quarters at Cranwell . . . Lawrence came in."* [9] and *"It was during the morning break. . . . I saw him standing humbly out-side."* [10] Hence he arrived at the mid-morning break (10.00–11.00 hours). They walked around the College for *"about an hour and a half."* [11] Lastly *"he was just going off on his push-bike from Cranwell to Cambridge."* [12] and *"he was proceeding to Cambridge."* [13]

Combining the two accounts we obtain a graphic account of Lawrence's appearance, visit and conversations held.

"The last time I saw Lawrence was last term, a few weeks before his death. It was during the morning break. My room was full of people, and as I walked towards the door talking to one of them I saw him standing humbly outside.

He was untidily dressed in ancient flannels and a coat and muffler, which had seen very much better days. I know that at least one of my visitors wondered as he passed by who was this slipshod apparition. Although I had not seen Lawrence for some time, and he had aged and lost much of his youth, I recognized him at once and had pleasure in showing him round the College, and of talking to him on all sorts of topics, for about an hour and a half.

I offered to lend him my car to show him round the station, but he would not accept. He had served here with so much happiness that he feared that a return to his old haunts would induce melancholia. I took him first to see the pictures in the Ante-Room, in the choice of which he had played a big part. We talked together of Tuke, whom we had both known at one time. Tuke is the painter of the sailing-ship scene in the first of the cadets' ante-rooms. Lawrence told me he had often been a model for Tuke in his youth; and I had watched him at his easel. [In October 1931 Lawrence gave Clare Sydney Smith *"a very gracious oil-painting of boys bathing by the seashore by* [Henry Scott] *Tuke, . . . "*][14]

After going through the ante-rooms we went to the cadets' quarters and spoke to 'Colonel' Young, who, of course, recognized his visitor, and to two other College servants whose names I cannot recollect.

Then I took him to the main lecture hall, and the library, where I introduced him to Capt. C. W. Pollock and Mr. L. E. Fisk. While he was in the library we showed him the copy of 'The Seven Pillars of Wisdom'. *He studied the book carefully and explained to us the significance of some of the illustrations. He was a modernist in art.*

I asked him why he did not re-engage in the Royal Air Force. He told me that if he signed on for another twelve years he would be too elderly for the ranks. He added with a smile that he had already reached the giddy height of A.C.1. He said that the idea of a man of sixty being in the ranks was preposterous. I suggested that he should apply for promotion, and take the necessary examinations. He said that the educational difficulties were too great.

This was a typical remark made mischievously by a man who was an international scholar in Arabic and archaeology, an unusual linguist and a Fellow of All Souls [Oxford]. *I suppose a Fellowship of All Souls is the highest academic honour in the world.*

I do not know how the train of conversation started, but presently we asked him what he was going to do to balance his budget in the future. He told us he had 25s. a week to live on, and he thought that enough for any man. I remarked that he would never be able to maintain his motor-bike on that. He replied that he was giving up the bike, and he showed me his push-bike on which he had already come a great distance and on which he was proceeding to Cambridge. I felt sorry to see him so worn and, I thought, tired.

He told me that if ever he went short of money he could always translate books from German and French. I urged him once again to translate the Iliad, *and not keep his talents laid up in a napkin.*[15] *We discussed at length my excavation of a Roman Villa at Haceby.*[16] *We talked at some length about what he was going to do when* [sic] *he left the Service. He told me that he was very tired and getting old. In fact, he was 47 years of age, but there was no doubt that he was looking more tired and bleached than when I saw him last.*

I asked him if he would attend our College Library Society one evening, and I think he would have come, but he said: 'For the moment I am "other ranks" and I do not feel happy in the company of officers.' But I gathered he would come one evening; as he was always interested in the College . . . [17] *When I last saw him he was just going off on his push-bike from Cranwell to Cambridge. I offered again to drive him round the camp but he seemed reluctant. I offered to get some food from the Fancy Goods Store, but he was not interested in food.*

He had a long conversation with me on the steps of the College. I remember the last words which I said to him were urging him not to waste his life as a modern Diogenes, but to get down again to a worthy and useful work. But he just laughed in that serene and boyish way of his and pedalled off."[18]

It is highly probable that during one of these conversations de la Bere mentioned that the author Frederic Manning had died on 22 February. As all newspapers were available in the College, de la Bere would have read Manning's only obituary, which was first published in the early editions of the *The Times* newspaper on the morning of 28 February. Final confirmation is established when Lawrence stated that he was *"meaning to call at Bourne and see Manning: but to-day* [28 February] *I turned eastward, instead,* **hearing** *that he was dead."*[19] And *"Manning died as I was on my way to Bourne, to visit him. I turned off and rode down here* [Clouds Hill]*."*[20] Also that Lawrence stated to de la Bere that he was going direct to Cambridge and not via Bourne. Unfortunately a letter and telegram to Lawrence from William Rothenstein conveying

Manning's death and requesting help on his obituary arrived too late at Bridlington.

Rothenstein had been extremely upset that no prompt account of Manning's death had appeared in *The Times* newspaper.[21] Lady Manning, Frederic's mother who lived at Bourne, knowing of their close friendship was hurt at Lawrence's absence.[22]

Lawrence wrote to Manning's publisher Peter Davies on Thursday, 28 February, *"It seems queer news, for the books are so much more intense than ever he was, and his dying doesn't, cannot, affect them. Therefore what has died really? Our hopes of having more from him – but that is greed. The writing them was such pain – and pains – to him. Of late I have devoutly wished him to cease trying to write. He has done enough; two wonderful works* [Her Privates We and Scenes and Portraits], *full-sized: four lesser things. A man who can produce one decent book is a fortunate man, surely? . . . Yet his going takes away a person of great kindness, exquisite and pathetic. It means one rare thing the less in our setting. You will be very sad. . . . Strange to think how Manning, sick, poor, fastidious, worked like a slave for year after year, . . . on stringing words together to shape his ideas and reasonings. That's what being a born writer means, I suppose. And to-day it is all over and nobody ever heard of him. If he had been famous in his day he would have liked it, I think; liked it deprecating. . . . I suppose his being not really English, and so generally ill, barred him from his fellows. Only not in* Her Privates We *which is hot-blooded and familiar. It is puzzling. How I wish, for my own sake, that he hadn't slipped away in this fashion; but how like him. He was too shy to let anyone tell him how good he was."*[23]

Frederic Manning, a chronic asthmatic, was born in Sydney, Australia, in 1882. With little formal schooling he sailed to London at the age of 14 with Arthur Galton, a fine scholar, from whom he received a good education for a number of years. Manning had a natural flair for writing and after experiencing the horrors of trench warfare in France he wrote the classic *Her Privates We*, which was published anonymously in 1930. In November 1930 *Scenes and Portraits* was printed as a larger edition, dedicating one of the new essays *'Apologia Dei – To T. E. Shaw.'*[24] Manning probably first wrote to Lawrence on 7 March 1922, linking an unshakable lasting friendship. Lawrence always maintained that Manning's works were of the highest calibre.[25]

On leaving RAF Cranwell around lunchtime Lawrence avoided Bourne and cycled through Sleaford and Swineshead the 30 miles to Holbeach to stay at the *Talbot Hotel*. This was a public house situated in the High Street (see Plate 22); in 1935 it was run by Andrew Keight. At that time it possessed a large rear yard connecting through to Cross Street. It had been an inn-cum-hotel since the early nineteenth century but was eventually boarded up in the early 1970s, and finally demolished in about 1975 to make way for three modern shops.[26]

After staying the night of Thursday/Friday (28 February/1 March) Lawrence cycled through the morning fog southward to Wisbech, then routing to Cambridge via Chatteris or Ely. Both roads were of similar distance making the journey Holbeach to Cambridge a round 54 miles. This would have taken about six hours arriving at Cambridge around 15.00 hours, when he visited the Fitzwilliam Museum.

In a letter to Sydney Cockerell, Curator of the Fitzwilliam, the previous November Lawrence said, *"I would like to visit Cambridge once more, and perhaps shall venture, after the Great Change: and then I shall search the Fitzw. for you, and console myself with your collected pictures, if you are away,"*[27] which was later confirmed on 6 March when he stated, *"Nice spot, the FitzBilly."*[28]

Unfortunately Lawrence did not meet Cockerell as he was absent with a serious eye inflammation.[29]

Later he arrived at his brother's house (A. W. Lawrence's home) at 31 Madingley Road, Cambridge. He seemed steady, at ease and content, and spoke of passing the time exploring the countryside or printing.[30] Ralph Isham recalled, *"His brother tells me how a day or two after discharge from the Air Force, T. E. stopped to visit him in Cambridge and devoted a great deal of time to the play and interests of his daughter,* [Jane] *aged eight."*[31] As he stayed the night of Friday/Saturday (1–2 March) he wasn't to realize that this would be the last time the two brothers would be together.

After Cambridge, Lawrence cycled to Oxford. He left his brother's house early on Saturday morning, 2 March. It was cloudy with a fine rain and mist. He probably took the slightly shorter route (76 miles) through Bedford and Buckingham. Later in the day the rain became heavier so he must have reached Oxford after dusk. He visited E.T. Leeds, Curator of the Ashmolean Museum, at his home at 88, Woodstock Road, Oxford, where he most probably stayed the night (Saturday/Sunday, 2–3 March). They chatted about old times and all matter of general subjects and in a letter to Sydney Cockerell of 6 March Lawrence wrote, *"I said to Leeds (next day or so)* [the 'next day' was Saturday 2 March.] *that he ought to copy your rug dodge in the Ashmolean. A very few, well worn, good but not excessively rare rugs, I think. They helped uncommonly to break up the oppressive vasty floors which make museums so tiring to the eye."* [32] [Cockerell, as Curator of the Fitzwilliam Museum, Cambridge, had placed loose carpets throughout the museum.]

On Sunday, 3 March, Lawrence visited John Buchan's house at Elsfield Manor three miles east of Oxford. It was cloudy, cool and misty as he push-biked up the long hill into Elsfield village. Buchan fondly recalled the memorable reunion, *"On Sunday morning Lawrence of Arabia arrived on a push-bike. He had finished with the Air Force and is moving slowly down to his cottage in Dorset, a perfectly free man, and extraordinary happy. We had him for the whole day and he has become one of the most delightful people in the whole world. He has lost all his freakishness, and his girlish face has become extraordinary wise and mature. He relies a good deal on my advice, but I don't know what can be done with him, for he won't ever touch public life again, and yet he is one of the few men of genius living. He gave me a piece of good news. He says that the Air Force have decided that land bombing is a wash-out, and that in future bombing must be done on moving targets at sea."* [33]

Buchan's wife also described the visit, *"The last time I saw him was a few weeks before his death."* [34]

A purported later visit by Lawrence to Elsfield towards the end of March must be discounted as Buchan confused the two meetings, referring to Lawrence's journey home south to Clouds Hill. *"I last saw him at the end of March 1935, when on a push-bike he turned up at Elsfield one Sunday morning, and spent a long day with me. He was on his way from Bridlington to his Dorsetshire home."* [35]

Another discounted report appeared in *The Bournemouth Daily Echo* of 2 March. *"An 'Echo' reporter who set out to interview him* [Lawrence at Clouds Hill] *had the greatest difficulty in finding him last night* [1 March], *and when at last he tracked him down he had even greater difficulty in making him talk . . . .*

The cottage was in darkness as the 'Echo' reporter approached and the first he saw of Mr. Shaw was in the light of a torch as Mr. Shaw ducked in order to avoid the possibility of being snap-shotted. He was dressed in mechanic's overalls but he declined to discuss his plans. The only subject he would talk about was the time, and when it was pointed out to him that his watch was 1½ hours fast he merely commented that time did not matter there." [36] The supposed encounter places Lawrence at Clouds Hill on Friday evening, 1 March, but he was definitely at Cambridge.

So Lawrence probably left Oxford on Sunday, 3 March, to

push-bike to his Clouds Hill cottage. The route of about 115 miles was probably through Andover and Salisbury (see Map 4). It would certainly take him two days. With his usual 60 or 70 miles per day coverage Lawrence possibly lodged overnight in the Salisbury area (Monday/Tuesday, 4–5 March). Travelling the remaining 45 or so miles on Tuesday, 5 March, during a beautifully sunny and cloudless sky, he reached Clouds Hill during the afternoon. Unfortunately he found the cottage infested with newspaper reporters and freelance photographers. In disgust at seeing the quietness shattered he immediately left for London – *"The Press were besetting this cottage when I reached it. I went to London for a while: . . . "*[37] Nearly every letter written on 6 March in London mentioned his cottage besieged by pressmen.

8

The Invasion,
6–26 March 1935

After the hasty withdrawal from Clouds Hill he boldly cycled to London, probably via Romsey, and most likely arrived in London late on Tuesday the 5th or early Wednesday, 6 March. To remain incognito he took on a new alias, a Mr. T. E. Smith, and searching for a quiet address he found rooms at 3 Belvedere Crescent (noted as Belvedere Road in 1935 *Kelly's* directory), S.E.1,[1] next door to Howard and Wilton Ltd, a timber merchant.[2] Lawrence usually stayed at Sir Herbert Baker's garret at 14 Barton Street but in January 1934 Baker had sustained a serious stroke[3] leading to the Barton Street property to be put up for sale.

He seems to have roamed about London for most of the 6th, *"so I wander about London in a queer unrest . . . "*[4] and *"went around London feeling quite lost."*[5] During that evening he wrote a large number of letters (eight known to the authors).

With all the upset and tension he was in a low state of mind *"this restless 'lost' feeling I now have has gone dull."*[6] – *"It is a feeling of aimless unrest: and of course I am sorry, while knowing it had to be."*[7] – *"Meanwhile I'm feeling lost – like an evicted hermit-crab!"*[8] – *"and I feel lost and aimless and **cold** somehow. Ah well, that will pass."*[9] – *"I feel lost, now, but everything passes."*[10] – *"wondering if my mainspring will ever have a tension in it again.*

So I'm not cheerful, actually; . . . "[11]

Although preoccupied with despondency and the Clouds Hill problem he still had time to show interest in published works of his friends, *"Exciting news this about the* Indiscretion,*"* he wrote to Florence Hardy, *"I think it must be the reprint of that first magazine serial T.H.* [Thomas Hardy] *wrote in the beginning. It will be very interesting. The apprenticeship of an artist educates others than himself, you see!"*[12]

Similarly he comments to Alec Dixon, *"I hope the book goes well. . . . here you are at Tinned Soldier before the other is accepted,"*[13] and to Ernest Thurtle, *"Thank you for the book. I look forward to reading it when I get home . . . Theodore Powys, . . . is a rare person."*[14]

Lawrence's small printed card was now frequently used to save time and energy in his correspondence, *"I'm sending out dozens of the enclosed* [cards]. *Good idea?"*[15] And writing on the reverse of one of them *"Don't you think this is a good idea? I'm putting them, without comment, into nearly every letter I write!"*[16]

He formulated a strategy of staying away in London for a number of days with the future possibility of moving to the Midlands, including staying at Arthur Russell's house in Coventry, *"For the moment I have to hide here in London; . . . I shall be here for about a fortnight, unless I'm smelt out . . . "*[17] – *"So I will have to keep up in London and the Midlands for the next few weeks. . . . My shiftings about will be many and abrupt, probably: . . . "*[18] – *"When I come* [to Coventry], *I'll suggest my doubling up with you, . . . I'm going to keep gently on the move. . . . But I promise myself a rest at Coventry, . . . "*[19] – *"with an idea of wandering in the Midlands, perhaps, for a while."*[20] – *"Probably I shall wander for most of this year about England."*[21]

Records about Lawrence are scarce during the next week although he proposed to visit his bank [Martin's Bank, 68 Lombard Street, London]*"to find out what my means will be after I straighten everything up."*[22] and we know that he still resided at 3 Belvedere Crescent on 7 March. From here he wrote to Pat Knowles *"shall probably be here another week."*[23]

While in London Lawrence made stringent inquiries as to which appropriate newspaper agencies and individuals to contact with regards to solving the problem of withdrawing reporters and photographers from Clouds Hill.

It was overcast but dry on Thursday, 14 March, when he paid five shillings for a year's membership of the Youth Hostel Association.[24] He also possibly wrote to a poet in Devon (unknown to the authors), *"No, I'm out of tune for lyrics; and such a phrase as 'agate swords' doesn't please me. They were better at that 40 years ago. Sorry you don't think better of Lenin, too. A very great man, probably. However, as I said, I'm no critic of poetry."*[25]

Lawrence left London, on his push-bike, for Clouds Hill arriving there the next day Friday, 15 March. He found the cottage was peaceful with no sign of the Press. Awaiting his home-coming was a letter from Ralph Isham informing him of his London address. Lawrence sent a telegram saying the Press had cleared off and he had returned to Clouds Hill, where he would remain.[26]

Later that day he popped over to Pat Knowles who recalled, *"He arrived one early evening as I was having a meal. He poked his head around the door and said, 'Here is the end and the beginning.'*

We talked for an hour or so and it was well into the night when he went over to the cottage to play some of his new records that had arrived during his absence. It was two o'clock in the morning when I went back to my house. My mind was so full that I did not sleep all that night."[27] This quote does not refer to the first time Lawrence arrived at Clouds Hill, on 5 March. Since the place was infested with Pressmen and Lawrence was in a hurry to leave for London he never even saw his neighbour.

Saturday, 16 March, passed peacefully looking as though, at last, the quietude would persist. Alas, the Pressmen returned the next day, the 17th. Pat Knowles' account is so vivid that his complete recollection is quoted:

"The photographers came early one Sunday morning [17 March]; I heard them talking as they walked along the road past my house. Unseen by them I could see that they had cameras hidden under their coats.

When they had gone a little way, and at an opportune moment I crossed the road behind them and went through the bushes and from there went into the cottage unseen by the photographers, arriving dishevelled and feeling like a character in a low melodrama.

At first Shaw was unimpressed by my warning, in fact he made light of it, joking that we would need to build a tunnel under the road between the two houses, with a small track and trolley so that he could rumble away unseen; perhaps then to pander to me, he suggested I go outside to find out what they were up to.

Doing as he suggested I made as if to go to the bungalow. As I left the cottage they approached me and asked if Lawrence was about.

I said 'No' emphatically, which was not strictly a lie since he had changed his name to Shaw.

*They laughed and said that they knew that he **was** around and that they were going to stay put until they got what they wanted. I warned them that they would have trouble on their hands if they attempted to go into the cottage grounds. I walked away and left them marching up and down the road.*

*By noon when I had seen no sign of Shaw (who should have joined me for lunch) and noticed that the pair **hadn't** given up, I made a second trip across to the cottage with a bottle of milk as an excuse.*

Shaw was sitting on the fender in the downstairs room, chin on his knuckles, his mood a mixture of depression, frustration and anger. He didn't speak at first but at last he said 'Get one of them in and I'll talk to him. I can't stand going on like this.'

I went outside and said, 'Mr. Shaw will talk to one of you. But no cameras.' I took his camera away from him before I let him in. Shaw meanwhile had gone to the upstairs room (the music room, where he always received guests) and I directed the chap upstairs, standing 'guard' at the bottom so as to prevent the other from entering.

After the initial sound of voices there came the more ominous noise of a scuffle followed by Shaw's voice calling me to help him to throw the chap out, which we did. He had already acquired a fast closing and darkening eye.

The two men left shouting that they would be suing for damages.

Shaw, who was nursing a swollen fist was shaking a little from the effects of the scuffle. He said 'It's years since I struck a man in anger.' I left him to calm down quietly on his own and went to see that the two men had really left. I followed them to their motorcycle and watched them depart in the direction of Bovington.

When I returned to the cottage to report that they had left, Shaw had changed into his city clothes. He asked me if I would do a couple of things for him. One; take his push-bike and leave it at a point a hundred yards to the west of the bungalow and then; two, come back and take the Brough for a ride, making a big show of it to draw off any interested onlookers.

Certainly I would, but I pointed out that the two blokes had a motorbike too, and if they caught scent of him on his own [push-bike], he wouldn't stand a chance.

He replied that he had been chased by Turks and had not been caught then and he didn't think those two would do any better. So off I went and off he went too, to London, via Moreton Station, I assumed, though later a letter arrived detailing his progress to London on the bike!

Later that afternoon the two men did indeed reappear. They set up their camera on the little hill south of the cottage, giving a view of the door. They began hurling stones onto the roof thinking to draw Shaw out.

But purely by chance the cottage had another visitor that afternoon, Colonel Isham, a friend of Shaw who was returning to America and had called hoping to see him before he left. [Ralph Isham arrived at Clouds Hill on 17 March after receiving a telegram from Lawrence on 15th stating he was at home – see p. 68.]

I was able to intercept Colonel Isham and 'put him in the picture'. We went over to the cottage and he told them that he was from Scotland Yard, *come to protect Lawrence, and that they'd better clear off or they'd be in serious trouble.*

They left! Whether believing his story or not I do not know. Perhaps his additional presence was enough to discourage them."[28]

Another recollection by Pat Knowles to Michael Yardley was received in spring 1981 but was basically the same.[29]

Pat Knowles' graphic account is further supplemented by Ralph H. Isham's.

"On the 17th [March], *I motored from London to Clouds Hill. As we neared the cottage I noticed a group of, perhaps, four men, talking earnestly together. They carried large cameras. They seemed very curious at my arrival. I knocked, then shouted for T. E., but there was no response. On the few feet of lawn that separated the cottage from the surrounding rhododendrons, I saw fragments of thick old tiles. One could see where they had been broken out of the roof. Then a local man* [Pat Knowles] *came up and said, 'He's gone.' I asked what had happened. He said that a number of Press representatives had arrived, wanting to interview and photograph Lawrence; he had refused but they would not go away, and kept banging on his door and shouting at him, and at last he had given one man a terrific sock in the eye and driven them off. Lawrence had then taken his push-bike through a covered-over path in the rhododendrons and had ridden away on it, only shouting to the man* [Pat Knowles], *'I'll be back when you see me.' The photographers, not having witnessed his departure, had placed some of their number in the bushes facing the door and others had gone to the brow of the steep hill rising immediately behind the cottage, and from there had hurled stones on to the roof, hoping to drive him out into the ambushed cameras of those below.*

I left a letter for him, and drove back to London, . . . "[30]

It is engaging to note Lawrence's later comments on the incident which ironically occurred on St Patrick's Day, *"I blackened the eye of one photographer last Sunday and had to escape over the back of the hedge!"*[31] – *"Their eagerness to find me drove me out: and after I had gone it led them to break the tiles of my roof, split the door and trample all over my patch of land in search of me."*[32] – *"The most exigent of them I banged in the eye, and while he sought a doctor I went off again on my wanderings, . . . "*[33] – *"The Press were very bad, and troublesome again and again; till I banged one in the eye . . . "*[34] – *"The pressmen came here again. There was a brawl, and one of them got hurt."*[35] – *"I gave one of them a beauty, but it rather put my thumb out."*[36]

Lawrence had push-biked to Romsey to stay the night of Sunday/Monday (17–18 March).[37] The Monday morning was dry and cloudy as he cycled from Romsey to London, arriving at his rented rooms at 3 Belvedere Crescent in the late afternoon, *"Romsey on Sunday night; and London by 4 p.m. Monday: 75 miles that second day ! Improving!"*[38]

The following day (19 March) he went to seek advice at the Newspaper Society at Salisbury Square House, London, EC4, and was helped by the General Secretary Edward W. Davies and a Mr G. Leave.[39] He remarked *"Press Association bosses, and Press Photographing Agencies, making quite a lot of ground."*[40] He hoped that by persuading the newspaper chiefs to refuse to accept any stories about him it would dissuade the more menacing freelance photographers. He had made enough progress and expected a complete solution in about three days' time, on the 22nd.

As usual, Lawrence decided to go straight to the top. Unfortunately he did not have the right introduction to Esmond Harmsworth, the new Chairman of the Newspaper Proprietors Association (NPA), although he knew him slightly from the Paris Peace Conference days of 1919. To remedy this on 19 March he wrote to Winston Churchill, to whom he was political adviser in the Middle East Department in 1921, asking his old boss to pull the necessary strings for access to Harmsworth. *"If you can get in touch with him, without embarrassing yourself, I would be most grateful."*[41] A measure of his desperation to solve the Clouds Hill problem can be seen in the letter to Churchill where in putting forth his case he enhances the number of incidents at Clouds Hill, *"and I've since had to run three* [only twice] *times from my cottage in Dorset (where I want to live) through pressure from newspaper men. Each time I've taken refuge in London, . . . "*[42]

Lawrence cycled through the early morning fog, on Wednesday 20 March, to Sir Herbert Baker's flat at 2 Smith Square, Westminster, to inform him of the likely telephone call from Winston Churchill.[43] It would seem that a positive call from Churchill was received as Lawrence telegraphed a reply.[44] As a result *"I also saw Mr. Esmond Harmsworth* [at the NPA, 6 Bouverie Street, EC4], *and have at his request written him a letter to lay before the N.P.A. If they do not rear up and fall over backwards with rage at it, then I am likely to be ignored by the entire London Press hereafter."*[45]

He later visited the house and studio of Lady Kennet at Leinster Corner (see Plate 23) on the corner of Bayswater Road, opposite the Round Pond in Kensington Gardens, *"Ned Lawrence turned up early, saying he was not stopping to lunch, and of course he did stop till five, when I had to make him go. He was disappointed because the slump in America has prevented the second edition of his* Homer *from selling.*

He was a bit cynical and depressed at first, and then as the day wore on childlike, lost, and infinitely pathetic. I was so wretchingly divided between my work [sculpturing], . . . sick to finish, and Ned, who so clearly needed me. He was trying to see the Press-men in order to get them to stop harrying him. He said that I had suffered from it too, and what could be done? I said to let them do what they like, and then it will die in a week. When he arrived there were others there, and I didn't mention his name in introducing them. Ned began a tasteless tirade about royalty, and they were shocked and more or less turned their backs. I said, 'You musn't take Colonel Lawrence too seriously,' and they came round immediately, and one of them asked him to stay with him in the country.

As Ned left I saw him out of the gate, and as he turned away, I asked him where he was going, and he replied 'I don't know. It's of no importance where I go.' He's in great need of care. Oh God! I wish I had time for them all."[46]

Around Thursday 21 March Lawrence made an abortive attempt to visit William Rothenstein at his home, 13 Airlie Gardens, Holland Park, London W.8., *"I had to go to London and I called at Airlie Gardens: vainly, as usual."*[47]

Also about this time he accidently met E. M. Forster, *"The last meeting of all was by the turnstiles of the National Gallery. He was in civies – a stocky quizzical figure, turning his head slightly until I recognized him. He was out of the service at last and had been hurting his hand against a reporter's face at Clouds Hill [on 17 March]. He invited me to stay there again – we hadn't met for a couple of years. We went on to see Epstein's 'Christ' which he remarked would be publicly convenient for birds and then we ate an omelette in a French restaurant in Wardour Street. Our talk was of the impending prosecution of James Hanley's novel, Boy. I think that he allowed me to pay for the omelette and that we parted for ever outside the picture gallery, but our last moment together held no more significance than the first moment at Berkeley Square."*[48] Later Lawrence recalled *"I saw E. M. F. while the case [James Hanley's Boy] was pending and talked to him about it."*[49]

For most of the week he had been involved with visiting old friends and acquaintances. On Friday, 22 March, he called on Ralph Isham at his London hotel suite:

"March 22nd, 1935. At 9.30 the valet woke me up with a note from Lawrence to say that he would be back at eleven. I was shaving, when he suddenly appeared in the door, . . . and we talked. He said he was sorry to have missed me at Clouds Hill, but the photographers had driven him out. I said I knew full well, as I had seen them and the damage they did to

his roof . . . We spoke of the cottage . . . The swimming tank across the road was more a reservoir against fire, which saved him insurance on his valuable books. He said the whole business had been made possible and paid for by the fee for translating the Odyssey *and the one-third royalty from the American edition, on which he had received about £450. His income was now £2 a week. He had not served long to get a pension. He said he was now 46 and had probably 20 good years ahead of him, which he planned to spend reading and seeing England on a push-bike. 'England is the most beautiful spot on earth. You who dash through it in motor cars never get to see it properly.' I made the suggestion that he come to America first for a visit. He answered, 'Yes, I'd like to, but you see I have not got time. England is a much bigger place than you think.'*

I told him that Simon & Schuster wanted him to do a life of Mohammed – as a modern biography. After considering a while, he said, 'No', because to do it would take his mind back to the East which he wished to forget. Besides, he couldn't bear the thought of work, was looking forward to complete idleness and didn't need money . . .

We spoke of the apparent threat of European War. The thing that worried him more was the possibility of war between Italy and Ethiopia. He seemed to think it very likely as Mussolini had to do something to turn people's minds from home realities. Having nourished their ego and their dramatic sense, he dared not stop. This war, if it came, would be the beginning of a conflict between dark and white races that would spread over the world. Every coloured race would be incensed at the arrogance of Italians (whites). In the end they would regard all whites as one.

We spoke of a mutual friend whose wife had let him down. He said, 'But women's emotions are too strong and various to permit them to hold to a course. Their dishonesty is not fundamental or conscious, as with men; it is the result of emotional sickness and there is no dealing with it.'

God is something one feels. Destroyed by intellectuality. He believed, but had no religion. Organized religions attempt to justify man's urge to God. It is silly and dangerous to try to justify natural feelings. Religions are mainly over-thought.

Leachman – brave as a lion – used to keep treacherous tribes in order by threatening and beating their chiefs. Got away with it by sheer courage and spirit. Lost his nerve six months before he was killed. So wrote to his family, but carried on. One day drove up to tent of disaffected chief. Cursed him, then seized him and spat in his face. Turned to leave. Chief shot him in the back before he got out of the tent, which was violation of Arab hospitality.

– (the author of a recent book on the East) had persecution complex.

73

In Arabia they did all they could to help him but he complained bitterly.

[Hilaire] Belloc's The Jews – 'good book, but I don't agree with him. I am very fond of the Jews. Belloc has real genius, but the necessity of keeping the pot boiling has strangled it.'

I spoke of the Tanks Corps. 'Royal Tanks Corps,' he corrected. 'Don't you like the idea of royalty?' I asked. 'Yes, I think it is very valuable for Boys' Books.'

How the miracle of harmony was achieved in a man who was once prophet, poet, jester, crusader, I am at a loss to understand. Yet I find it difficult to think of him as anything but a very simple, lovable and charming companion whose wit and comprehension made the hours with him delightful and memorable. Indeed, when he got going on some subject that particularly interested him (and there were many) he talked with such a rush of brilliance, and with such a force of comprehension of men and matters, that I, at times, experienced a sense of elation comparable to that which music can give."[50]

The morning conversation and exchange of opinions would seem to suggest that both parties were friendly, but the following letter, written by Lawrence to W. Merton, shows otherwise, "*Isham turned up suddenly in London and asked to see me. He had various book and film projects, but all of them I turned down. The man breeds a suspicion always in my mind, he tries so constantly to earn the money.*

In the course of our talk it transpired that he had not had a copy of our Odyssey. *This rather horrified me. Of course it is really B. R's [Bruce Rogers] business, but he and Isham did not get one: eventually B. R. took over Isham's share of the project, not in cash but in part payment of his bill for arranging the format of the Boswell Papers. B. R. probably reckoned that Isham was rich enough to buy his copy: and he is. Perhaps* amour propre *forbade. Anyhow he hasn't one, and ought to have. He was the first begetter of the whole undertaking.*

So I rang your office up and learnt that you were away ill. Wherefore I had to act on my own. I rang up Wilson of Bumpus [London bookshop] *and told him to send Isham a copy by taxi, as he was leaving that afternoon [22 March] for the States. I told Wilson that you would send him another copy, from your stock, in replacement. Please do. I told Isham this was not a gift from me (the idea of putting him under an obligation to me is repellent: as I say, I don't trust the man or like him, to my regret) but from the firm, to repair the remissness of their American agent. I want you to charge me for the copy, and send the bill here: . . . and lastly and worse (but you do not know Isham, which makes it easier for you) will you please type him a letter saying that the firm of Emery Walker . . . their pleasure in sending him a gift copy of the* Odyssey *which he helped to produce in its early stages, the said copy having been handed him by me during his recent visit to England? . . .*

I don't want to appear to give it; . . . it must be at my (secret) charge: . . . "[51]

Lawrence also called on Liddell Hart at 60 Gloucester Place, W1, during Friday 22 March. In the Liddell Hart's diaries they talked about the 1935 RAF budget for fast boats, *"If T. E. had stayed in the service he would have taken The Air Council round the fleet in one at the Jubilee Review at full-speed, ensconced in armchairs!*

Suggested I should write a book, Fifteen Decisive British Defeats.*"*

The most important subject discussed was a job Lawrence had been offered by the Government, helping to reorganize Home Defence by serving as the deputy and eventual successor to Lord Maurice Hankey, *"Said he had received approaches to become successor to Hankey, but had replied that he would only do so if the normal Cabinet side was removed from the C.I.D.* [Committee of Imperial Defence] *side- . . . "*[52] Liddell Hart added more specific detail in 1967 clarifying that Lawrence would agree to the post *"if the posts of Secretary of the Cabinet and Secretary of the C.I.D. were separated."* Liddell Hart had been offered the same post in 1932 to which *"T. E. was not surprised, and remarked: 'Hankey is careful to avoid having anybody who could replace him. He thinks he can go on forever, although the Cabinet realises he cannot.' I said that I had always found Hankey most pleasant and helpful. T. E. agreed, but added: 'Neither you or I are the sort of people Hankey would like to have as deputies – and thus potential successors.' T. E. said this rather wistfully, . . . "*[53]

It must have been on Saturday 23 March that Lawrence called in on his old pal H. S. Ede: *"Lawrence's last visit to me was towards the end of March 1935 . . . .*

I thought he was a little tired, showing it for the first time; . . . And he had had to give up his motor-bike, and so could not easily get away.

I asked him what his bicycle [Brough] *would cost per year and he said £18, so when he had gone I sent him a cheque for twenty – knowing that of course he could raise the money if he wanted to, but felt that he might accept it from me, from whom it was so absurdly accidental, if only to give me pleasure . . . .*

For the first time in our friendship he became personal, saying that now he was free he hoped that we could meet more often and for longer."[54]

Sunday, 24 March, was a balmy day with moderate south-westerly winds and temperatures in the upper 50s (Fahrenheit) – a perfect time for cycling the 20 miles or so to Winston Churchill's large house at Chartwell in Westerham, Kent. *"The last time he came was a few weeks before his death. He was riding only a 'push-bike'! He was going, he told me, to get rid of his motor cycle. He could not afford such luxuries. I reminded him that he had the purse of Fortunatus. He had but to lift his hand. But he tossed his head disdainfully. Such a thing as a motor cycle was beyond his means. Alas, he did not stick to his opinion!"*[55]

Lawrence's real motives for visiting were both social and to thank Churchill for his quick intervention allowing the approach to Harmsworth and hence the resolution of the newsmen nuisance at Clouds Hill.

Presumably he returned to London on the same day. Monday, 25 March, was cloudy but dry as he cycled from 3 Belvedere Crescent aiming for Clouds Hill. It is certain he arrived there during the dry evening of Tuesday, 26 March, *"I hurl another autograph recklessly towards you* [Edward W. Davies], *in thanks for your letter of the 21st which I found waiting for me here last night* [26 March]."[56]

9

The Omen,
27 March–24 April 1935

Upon returning to Clouds Hill Lawrence finalized the letter he had started in London, which Harmsworth had requested to place before the NPA.[1] He wrote to thank Edward W. Davies, of the Newspaper Society, on Wednesday, 27 March, for his co-operation in the Harmsworth saga.

During the rest of the week Clouds Hill was free of pressmen and the secluded peace Lawrence so longed for seemed to have begun at last. On Monday, 1 April, he wrote, *"Now I am hoping to stay here quite a while, finishing off my cottage after my own liking. There is pleasure (and engrossment) in arranging and fixing one's surroundings. I find I spend nearly the whole day, beginning job after job and laying them aside, part-done. The sense of infinite time, all my own, is so new."*[2] – *"I am back here again in precarious peace, and liking a life that has no fixed point, no duty and no time to keep."*[3] – *"Now I hope to have continuing peace. The cottage is a great success, and I am liking the aimless life."*[4]

John Buchan's laudable letter of 12 March praised Lawrence's writing of *The Mint*, *"I have read your Air Force notes with acute interest and great admiration. It is the kind of document which has never been produced before about any service. One thing is clear to me, that you are a great natural writer.*

. . . it is an amazing picture of the beginning of a new service,"[5] Lawrence's elated reply was penned on 1 April, *"I had banked a good deal on your opinion, you being a discreet and exquisite bookman, and that you should say such good things delighted me."*[6] Buchan suggested writing fiction or a biography, *"for you can see a long way into the human heart, and you have an amazing power of imaginative construction."*[7] Lawrence thought the biography a good idea, *"A*

biography – yes, I had wanted to write Casement, Sir Roger; . . . "[8]

Similarly he communicated to Sir Evelyn Wrench on 1 April about Wrench's book *Uphill* (published in 1934 – the first volume of his autobiography), *"which had a poignant directness of impact that I found somehow very gracious."*[9] In his proposed second volume called *Struggle* (published later in 1935), Wrench wanted permission to include Lawrence, *"Need I be in the new one? . . . However what you say will not be vulgar: and therefore it may serve to correct (at least in my own esteem) some of what others have said."*[10]

Lawrence had obviously tried to find a job for a neighbour by asking Buchan, *"It was kind of you to try the National Trust for Knowles* [Bill Knowles]. *I have sent him the message, and told him to call on them when he next visits London. The unfortunate man wants badly something other than his present life, obviously. If only he knew what!"*[11]

Congratulations were in store for Buchan's appointment as Governor of Canada but Lawrence was sad that something would be missing *"round Elsfield way."*[12]

In this first week of April Lawrence began to improve his cottage by building a bunk bed with drawers in the smaller upstairs room: *"so I built into it a bunk, of ship-cabin type, with drawers beneath for my clothes. A rough job I made of it, but it works."*[13]

During 2–3 April the pressmen returned again to annoy Lawrence and desecrated the brief peace at Clouds Hill. By cross-referencing it is possible to date this third interference. In letters of 1 April to Wrench and Buchan he talks of the aimless life but never refers to any Press appearance. But 5 April to Ede: *"The Press have still been troublesome,"* but the final clinchers are, 13 April to Buxton: *"The Press have not troubled me for* **two weeks."** and 22 April to Florence Hardy: *"The last* **three weeks** *have been* **almost** *unbroken peace."*

For safe measure he persuaded the local police to patrol Clouds Hill.[14] This annoying incident with the Press was probably the main reason behind Lawrence's decision to motorcycle into Dorchester and road tax his Brough Superior SS100 (*George VII*), as a means to get far away from Clouds Hill whenever he wished. This Dorchester trip probably took place on Wednesday, 3 April, when he also registered his change of address in the logbook (see Appendix 2). Unfortunately the date frank is unreadable but under high magnification is most likely *"3 AP 35"*. Another factor was undoubtedly Ede's cheque for £30 (not £20 as originally stated), which had arrived, reminding him that funds were available for the Brough – although it was never cashed and was found, after his death, laid in a book.[15]

During these early fine and warm days of April he went *"almost wholly in wandering about the south-country."*[16]

On Thursday, 4 April, he motorcycled *"into Poole to buy some necessary fittings for the house. It goes like stink and is altogether a marvellous machine."*[17]

George VII did not always run smoothly however. Around this time he took a trip to Sandbanks, a narrow spit of land jutting south off Bournemouth and immediately east of Brownsea Island in Poole Harbour, to test the Brough for speed on the seashore.

He probably overheated it with sand entering the engine which in turn led to a burnt-out coil. Lawrence pushed the heavy machine from near the *Haven Hotel* (see Map 5), where it broke down, along Banks Road to Louie Dingwall's garage. She (see Plate 24) related the incident many years later to Alan Bennett.

"One spring afternoon in 1935 there arrived at Louie's Garage a rather disconsolate motor cyclist. His machine had apparently broken down somewhere near the Haven Hotel *and, directed by one of Harvey's boatmen, he had pushed his heavy Brough motor-cycle to the garage in the hope of having it repaired.*

The man was an unexceptional looking individual, quite slimly built, wearing rather ordinary clothes with his riding goggles slung around his neck.

Louie examined the motor-cycle and, at length, traced the fault to a burnt-out coil. However, although she had diagnosed the malaise she had to confess that she could not affect a repair.

Louie commented that he must have been riding the machine hard and that the fault had probably occurred through overheating, possibly because sand had got into the engine. The man replied laconically that he liked to get about quickly.

. . . She suggested that, if his destination was not too far distant, he might like to avail himself of her break-down service. She would gladly transport him and his machine to wherever it was that he wished to go, within reason. The offer was accepted with alacrity. The man mentioned that he was bound for Bovington, a journey of about fifteen miles.

It proved to be quite a struggle to lift the Brough into her van but, thanks to their combined strength, they eventually succeeded in the task.

Louie was impressed.

'You're pretty tough, aren't you?' she commented.

'I ought to be tough,' came the reply.

'Why's that? You don't look particularly strong,' was Louie's frank appraisal.

'Well, I am Lawrence of Arabia,' the figure replied. Louie was sceptical.

'Don't tell me such a whopper!' she exclaimed. 'Of course, you're not.'

The pair of them clambered into Louie's vehicle and set off.

She enquired of her passenger where precisely it was that he wished to go. The man replied that he had a cottage near the army camp at Clouds Hill.

. . . Louie and her passenger began to talk about their respective lives. He seemed to be especially interested in her wartime activities. [Lawrence was probably enthusiastic about her exploits as an ambulance driver and despatch rider on Harley-Davidson and Indian motorbikes.]

'You know, you should be doing something better with your life,' he commented.

. . . She asked Lawrence what he had been doing at Sandbanks. He replied that he had been riding his motor-bike about on the dunes. [See Plate 25].

'They remind me of the desert,' he commented wistfully.

The journey through Wareham and Wool to Bovington lasted about three quarters of an hour. Arriving at Clouds Hill the struggle with the motorcycle was resumed, although it fortunately proved easier to remove the bike from the van. Nonetheless, both of them were rather breathless by the time the job was over.

Lawrence invited Louie into the cottage for refreshment. A high, dense rhododendron hedge virtually hid the cottage from the road. The broom in the garden was almost in flower and the oak trees wore a mantle of pale green. Yet the cottage struck Louie as a forbidding and profusely lonely place.

Inside it was small and cramped, and Louie thought it looked a mess although she did not say so. She accepted his offer of a glass of milk but was rather embarrassed when he suggested an especially handsome present for her service in getting him and his motorcycle safely back home. She explained that she had thoroughly enjoyed the journey and the conversation and insisted that she would accept just a modest renumeration. Lawrence expressed his gratitude, they shook hands and said goodbye.

It was a brief encounter but Louie was struck by the modesty and agreeability of her distinguished passenger."[18]

Apart from this minor upset *George VII* was running well and

THE LAST DAYS OF T. E. LAWRENCE : A LEAF IN THE WIND / PAUL MARRIOTT AND YVONNE ARGENT.

NTAS

I S B S (OR)   1996   1 VOLS

1-898595-16-X   45.00 USD CLOTH
N8-959312

                        QTY ORDERED: 001
                        QTY SHIPPED: 001
                                      710709/0457

BLACKWELL BOOK SERVICES

FLORIDA STATE UNIV-BACKRUN | 112980023| JUTA-B

Lawrence was reluctant to exchange it for the new *George VIII* promised in the near future. He wrote to the manufacturer and designer George Brough, *"I have wondered of late how the new engine was shaping. You were going to make a new angle of inlet for the mixture. Now you are working on the timing gears! Please tell Mr J.A.P.* [JAP engine manufacturer] *for me that if I had his sized firm and couldn't get an aircooled twin right in 18 months, I'd eat my test-bench and wash it down with my flow meter!"*[19] adding *"Meanwhile I've only ridden the ancient-of-days twice this year. It goes like a shell, and seems as good as new. . . . I had half-thoughts of a touring sidecar, for long jaunts, with the push-bike for leisured local trips, but we shall see. The old bike goes so well that I do not greatly long for its successor. If only I had not given up my stainless tank and pannier bags and seen that rolling stand!* [These parts on *George VII* were transferred to *George VIII* on 30 August 1934.] *But for those gadgets my old'un would still be the best bike in the S. of England."*[20] The letter also discussed Brough design problems, calling on Lawrence's vast and accurate knowledge of different engines.

He continues to pursue his new life-style and as often as possible the authors have purposely included descriptions to monitor his ever-changing state of mind. On Friday, 5 April, he was *"full of cottage-duties, very empty in mind, tired-out, and futile-feeling."*[21] – *"an endeavour to enjoy idleness. That is (by modern standards) not a very moral aim. I do not care . . . .*

The golden rule seems to direct me to live peacefully in my cottage."[22] – *"I think I am going to be happy and comfortable here."*[23] – *"Finishing off, or rather fitting up the cottage is the only pursuit that interests me, at the moment. I am grateful for its quiet and the loneliness: but lost, all the same."*[24] Similarly he penned to T. E. Willis, *"I sleep in a sleeping bag, anywhere on the floors: and go to Bovington for a daily meal. That is called the simple life. I think I shall like it, but for the moment the place is in an awful mess, and I have so many odd jobs to do that I can finish nothing. So the general confusion grows. By midsummer I hope to be tidier and cleaner and more comfortable."*[25]

Back in early February he had advised the publishers Boriswood Ltd on their forthcoming prosecution for James Hanley's book *Boy*. The case had recently concluded with Boriswood fined £400 for printing an obscene publication. On 5 April he wrote again to C. J. Greenwood, a partner in the firm, furious at the result, *"It seems to me monstrous. To say that every publisher is at the mercy of the discretion of any Police Chief, at any time – why, it makes publication almost an impossibility."*[26] Even a book called *Economic Nationalism* by Maurice Colbourne sent by H. S. Ede to him for opinion about the Douglas Credit Scheme received the same sharp judgement, *"Your book. I can't settle to it. These claims are distracting. So I sent it back. Economics are like tides. We fail to harness them, yet they ebb and flow. The right thing would be to chart them, but nobody can distinguish their moon."*[27]

To complete the nautical theme of his small bedroom upstairs, containing his ship's bunk bed, he decided to insert a porthole. On Saturday 6 April he wrote to T. B. Marson asking for one, *"It is for a slip of a roomlet upstairs in my cottage – . . . A window is not desirable, just there: but a ship's port-hole would be perfectly in keeping . . . It should be the gunmetal frame (circular) and hinged glass: size – largish, if possible . . . I would like it cut out complete with a square of plating . . . My notion is to cement the four edges into the brick wall and so have the job complete . . .*

I hope this eccentric proposal will not lead you into great trouble: abandon it, if it offers to become arduous. Only the notion of a real port-hole by my imitation bunk in my simili-cabin strikes me as happy in the last degree. Should they be cutting up some ship or other in the harbour, it might be easily obtained."[28]

Tuesday, 9 April, was dry and windy but the south-westerly gales did not prevent Lawrence from motorcycling to RAF Farnborough. There he probably met *"a little man (name unknown: certainly a naval officer: probably Fleet Air Arm: doing a course at the R.A.F. School of Photography at Farnborough, now; and destined for the Leander soon."*[29]

Into the third week at Clouds Hill his mood is more relaxed: *"The place is natural, somehow: and I feel as if I might stay in it always: . . . There are enough pottering-about jobs to fill a whole working day."*[30] – *"Life here is pottery; I think in time I will get used to the feeling that nobody wants me to do anything today. For the moment it is a lost sort of life . . . I do not like civil life, nor leisure. . . . What ails me is this odd sense of being laid aside before being worn out. However I musn't bore you with that, and Time is on my side."*[31]

Help was proposed by one-time Air Force comrade Ira T. 'Taffy' Jones who seems to have suggested that the *News of The World* newspaper was prepared to pay well for a series of articles about Lawrence, *"Your letter and motives were very kind. I am grateful, and sorry not to be ready to take advantage of you. But I am not starving yet, not nothing less than starvation, I hope, would induce me to make money out of myself and the Press. . . .*

Please explain to your News of The World *friend that my attitude towards newspapers is not founded on anything the* News of The World *has ever-done. I had a great liking for Lord Riddell, and the paper has always been decent in keeping quiet about me."*[32]

Lawrence goes on to congratulate him on his book about Maddock, saying *"how surprisingly well – to my mind – you wrote it. . . . Your book was excellent I thought."*[33]

On the same day, 13 April, writing to Robin Buxton, he had high hopes that a portrait of his mentor, D. G. Hogarth, sent by Buxton to Hogarth's family in Oxford, would this time, be liked and accepted: *"Things point that way, I think, but I shall hear for certain in ten days or a fortnight."*[34]

With surprise and delight Lawrence couldn't believe his luck when a porthole arrived on Wednesday, 17 April. Nearly two weeks before he had asked T. B. Marson if he could possibly obtain one. Marson had come up trumps in a naval scrapyard in Donibristle, Scotland, purchasing a porthole from the demolished *H.M.S. Tiger.* In a reply on 5 May Lawrence wrote, *"It is cleaned up trimmed and only waiting for a guest to go . . . before building into the wall. It is a good porthole. I have inscribed your initials on its brass rim, in memory."*[35]

Marson was feeling generous, also offering a chair for Clouds Hill, but Lawrence refused on the grounds of overcrowding an already small cottage.[36]

During the second week in April he motorcycled to visit his old Scott Payne works at Hythe, *"and scrounge a lot more screws."*[37]

Over the Easter holiday period (19–22 April) Lawrence continued with domestic chores, letter writing and pottering. On Saturday, 20 April, he was troubled by a bird constantly flapping its wings against his Bookroom west window. It annoyed him all day with its tapping noise. *"The cottage has become quiet, now: except for a beastly tit, which flutters up and down one window-pane for six hours a day. First I thought it was a bird-pressman, trying to get a story: then a narcissist, admiring his figure in the glass. Now I think he is just mad, and know him to be a nuisance. If he goes on to next week I shall open the window some day and wring his silly neck."*[38] John Evelyn Wrench later recalled *"Mrs Hardy was at his cottage a few days before the accident. She says he was very nervous and depressed, and almost driven wild by a blue tit which kept hammering at the window."*[39] Pat Knowles also recalled the feathered intruder: *"There was a small bird – a robin probably – which had taken to hammering eerily on the windows, protecting its territory from its own reflection. Mrs. Hardy told me afterwards that they were in the downstairs room first of all and were so distracted by the insistent tapping that they went to the upstairs room where the pestilential bird followed them and continued its attack.*

The persistent creature continued its frenzied mating tap-tap-tap right up to the day of Shaw's accident when a superstitious friend went and shot it."[40] It was certainly still pecking the Bookroom window during Lord Carlow's visit on 4 May.[41] Apparently the bird persisted with its activities for many weeks until it was finally shot after Lawrence's death.[42] There is an old Dorset adage which states that a bird tapping on your window is a sign of death. In fact superstitious people still maintain, quite seriously, that the bird was an augur foretelling Lawrence's end.

Apart from this feathered interference and the Press incident of three weeks ago, a precarious peace seems to have returned to Clouds Hill. *"My time passes between swearing at him* [bird], *cutting brushwood, and inventing odd jobs. No letter-writing any more, except under extreme need, and no duty. A queer lapse into uselessness, . . . "*[43] – *"My bikes are both well, and myself. The many little jobs incidental to settling into a new place distract me and fill my days. So all is well as could be expected."*[44] – *"It feels so queer and aimless here. I potter about all day, picking up jobs and laying them down, to keep myself in an attitude of busy-ness. Already it is getting better, and soon it will be natural."*[45] – *"Clouds Hill is going to be all right as a living place, I fancy. . . . I feel very indisposed to do anything more; and very tired . . . and I potter with job after job."*[46]

During this peaceful period Lawrence often motorcycled to Wareham to visit his friend Percy Spiller who lived in a cottage next door to St Martin's church. At the time he was repairing the church roof. Lawrence would arrive and park his Brough against the cottage railings, often in time for tea. On one occasion John Spiller, Percy's son, had to motorcycle to the Ramsden Estate between Corfe and Studland to buy two replacement church roof ridge tiles. Immediately Lawrence offered his own Brough for the trip and with delight John snapped up this golden opportunity. Lawrence, a lifetime appreciator of church architecture, admired St Martin's so much that he made a donation towards its restoration.[47]

Two photographs of Lawrence (taken by Reginald Sims during one of Lawrence's weekend visits during February 1935) were dispatched on to Ian Deheer and P/O Manning on 20 April.[48] Lawrence also intended to motorcycle again to Hythe, the following Wednesday, 24 April, to meet Flt. Lt. H. Norrington and Flt. Lt. Beauforte-Greenwood to accept and *"collect the artwork* [a pair of stainless steel candlesticks], *which will be a very good reminder of our long spell together."* [49]

By Easter Monday, 22 April, he had read and appreciated *An Indiscretion in The Life of An Heiress* by Thomas Hardy recently published by Florence Hardy. "The Indiscretion *proved charming. I like the appealing simplicity of the prose . . . like, and yet a very poor relation of, the sweeping sentences that made up* Jude. *I understand why he kept it unprinted, . . .*

You have made a beautiful little book of it. I have enjoyed the reading, and enjoy the possession." [50]

On Wednesday, 24 April, Lawrence met Norrington and Beauforte-Greenwood over lunch in Hythe. They talked over old times and presented him with a pair of stainless steel candlesticks to commemorate their recent working time together, *"They look lovely . . . in exact keeping with their upper room. By day they sit on a brown oak mantel shelf above a S.S. [stainless steel] fender. By night they move to my writing table (as at present) or to my reading chair. They clean easily; stand solidly and feel good. I only wish they had not been possible – in other words that our association had not ended. I try to cure myself of the habit of saying 'we' when I mean the air."* [51] They are both inscribed *"A souvenir of a very happy partnership 1930–35 from B. G. & Norry."* It is also possible that Lawrence gave to Beauforte-Greenwood an exchange present – his wallet-cum-purse inscribed *"TEL"*, which he had carried in Arabia and all through his time in the Army and RAF (see Plate 26).[52]

10

Pottering,
25 April–12 May 1935

Between 25 April and 4 May very few letters (possibly none) were written, implying that Lawrence was busy, probably with travelling. Certainly another mild visit by the Press is indicated as *Daily Mirror* camera-man Dixie Dean was supposed to have interviewed Lawrence in early May: *"He found a small, slight man of 46 in oily overalls, tinkering with the latest 100 m.p.h. Brough motor-bike. He lent a hand and although Lawrence could see he was a camera-man, he was friendly. Dixie recalls; 'he talked about life in Dorset. He was fascinated by the thought of being able to do whatever he liked. He let me take several pictures of him with the bike, and asked me to send him copies.'"*[1]

This is possibly confirmed by E. T. Leeds' account: *"So comes the last memory of him three weeks before his death, when driven from Clouds Hill a third time* [probably the fourth time] *by the gadfly torment of an insatiable and inconsiderate Press, he escaped to Oxford. There he made one of his never omitted, however short, calls, – to a favourite haunt of other days, to learn how the Ashmolean* [Museum] *still fared. A restatement of certain facts surrounding an archaeological conundrum for which he himself had been largely responsible over twenty years before, a brief discussion of the ways and means to solve it, the smile and jest of farewell, and quietly he was gone for ever."*[2]

This motorcycle trip to Oxford was most probably on Friday, 26 April, coinciding with a visit to John Buchan's home at Elsfield Manor (3 miles east of Oxford).

William Buchan, son of John Buchan, thought that Lawrence motorcycled to their home on Friday, 10 May. *"I cannot give an exact date, but I think that it was late in the previous week, perhaps Friday the 10th, . . . "*[3] Although his mother, Susan Buchan, stated *"The last time I saw him was a few weeks before his death."* [4] The two references recall the same visit as both mention Lawrence visiting Alaister Buchan (sixteen and a half years old) in his sick-bed down with a bad cold. So Friday, 26 April, can be accepted as the true date of the two recollections because of reference to 'three' and a 'few weeks' before Lawrence's death and the insistence of a 'Friday'.

Susan Buchan recalled, *"No one could have been more charming . . . He seemed somehow older than when I had last seen him, lines had deepened on his forehead and around his mouth, but he looked as always, both hard and fit."* [5]

William, then 19 years old, remembered, *"Lawrence made one of his surprise visits to Elsfield. My father was away on that day, but my mother and I were at home, . . . I can only tell of that morning's encounter as one of memorable charm and easiness which has left a recollection, stronger than most, of something at once pleasurable and deeply sad. . . . I see him standing by the tall window in the library, facing me when we talked and giving me every strand of his attention . . .*

He was full of enthusiasm which was almost boyish, an excitement which clearly possessed him completely and gave him a youthful, a holiday air. What he was doing, in fact, was setting out to start on a new way of living.

We sat in the library, in the mild light of that late spring day, and listened to the plans which Lawrence was about to put into effect. He told us of the bothy in a thicket of rhododendron which from then on was to be his home, his place of retreat, where he hoped to think and read and write in utter peace, free from disturbance by any but his most cherished friends . . . .

He planned a daily round of the utmost simplicity, . . .

When that unforgettable visit was over, Lawrence mounted his fearsome machine and with a roar up the village street, leaving behind, for memory to lay hold of, the dying growl of a powerful motor and a whiff of castor oil." [6]

Florence Hardy wrote to Lawrence, on Thursday, 2 May, mentioning that his mother and brother Bob, Dr R. M. Lawrence, would probably soon be home from their missionary work in China. Florence had kindly made inquiries into possible hospital work for them at the Children's Hospital at Swanage, by speaking to the Dorset County Hospital Chairman, *"the **influence** of Dr. Lawrence would do the hospital good, his absolute unselfishness would be an example."* [7]

During the first sunny week of May Lord Carlow visited Clouds

Hill,[8] and during the only wet day, Saturday 4 May, Pat Knowles recalled, *"he [Carlow] and Shaw went off to Portland to get some gelignite to blow off the top of a tree near the cottage which was unsafe and liable to hit the corner of the building if ever it came down during a gale.*

Shaw made a poultice of the gelignite and lashed it to the tree with an old puttee, about thirty feet from the ground. I insisted on lighting the fuse and he relented when I said that I would rather be the **subject** *of an inquest than the witness at one.*

We waited for the bang at a safe distance. The tree top came down just where we wanted it to, but the glass in the skylight blew in with a musical tinkle. We looked at each other without a word until Shaw said, 'Blast!' – with wry humour, for the weather looked uncertain with the chance of rain.

I left them sawing up the branches and went down to Bovington Camp to Bill Bugg's workshop to get glass."[9]

During a mammoth-writing session (at least eight letters) on Sunday, 5 May, Lawrence covered all manner of subjects. Ernest Rhys (1859–1946) had inquired if he would give his consent to include *Revolt in the Desert* in his editorship of *Everyman's Library* (begun in 1906), *"about* Revolt in the Desert. *I ought not to speak for it, as I parted with all rights in it before publication. It was a financial expedient, rather than a book, and of it I am heartily ashamed. Its present owner is a lawyer, The Hon. Edward Eliot . . . You may write to him, if you please: but I think it will be in vain, for I own the master-copyrights of the* Seven Pillars *(from which text the* Revolt *was extracted) . . . "*[10]

Similarly his aircraftman pal, G. W. M. Dunn, who Lawrence helped in getting his book *Poems – Group One* published with Jonathan Cape in 1934, had inquired about the possibility of commissioning Augustus John, *"John like Gore, Cezanne and Epstein is rather deaf and quite formidable. He usually gets £50 for a drawing. If I see him before you do, I shall prepare him for canteen prices, instead. He is a great figure. Poor John."*[11]

Another portrait, a photograph taken by Reginald Sims in Hornsea in February 1935, was also in demand, *"By all means a photograph to Ian Deheer, if you feel so generous."*[12] Also wood specimens were discussed, *"Alas: Baker [Sir Herbert Baker] had had to change offices, and in the move all his rare wood samples were left behind or lost. I could only find those few rubbishy bits of ordinary wood. Sorry. He has promised to collect all that . . . but I'm not there* [Baker's offices at 14 Barton Street, Westminster] *to jog the matter on."*[13]

Lawrence's mood is still peaceful although tinged with an underlying melancholic nature, *"I shall stay here indefinitely, till I've forgotten that I ever had anything to do."*[14] – *"It is quiet here now, and I feel as though I were fixed in my cottage for good. It is as I thought . . . something is finished with my leaving the R.A.F. . . . It gets worse instead of healing over.*

When I see the little latch-key in my pocket I get sorry for having troubled you without cause. Am I to send it back? [to Lady Astor] *I am most sorry."*[15]

"Life here is quiet and good enough, but a very second best. . . There's such a blank afterwards."[16] – *"Something has gone dead inside me, now."*[17] – *"so that I no longer have the mind or wish to do anything at all. I just sit here in this cottage and wonder about nothing in general. Comfort is a very poor state after busyness."*[18] – *"[he feels] queer and baffled."*[19] – *"Also I work enough at wood-cutting and gathering,* [see Plate 27] *pipe-laying and building to tire me out thoroughly by each early afternoon . . . and then follows a heavenly laze, in the sun, if available, or by my fires if not."*[20]

Lawrence's famous leaf description – inspiring the title of this book – first appears on 6 May in letters to close friends, *"'You wonder what I am doing?' Well, so do I, in truth. Days seem to dawn, suns to shine, evenings to follow, and then I sleep. What I have done, what I am doing, what I am going to do, puzzle me and bewilder me. Have you ever been a leaf and fallen from your tree in autumn and been really puzzled about it? That's the feeling."*[21] – *"and sitting in my cottage rather puzzled to find out what has happened to me, is happening and will happen. At present the feeling is mere bewilderment. I imagine leaves must feel like this after they have fallen from their tree and until they die. Let's hope that will not be my continuing state."*[22] He also wrote parts of a proposed addition called *Leaves in the Wind.*

Lawrence must have just finished fitting the ship's porthole in the small upstairs bedroom with the help of Pat Knowles and 'Jock' Chambers at the time he sent one of his printed cards to T.B. Marson thanking him again for such a magnificent purchase.[23]

On Monday, 6 May, a perfect cloudless day, with temperatures reaching the mid-seventies the country celebrated the Silver Jubilee of King George V and Queen Mary, *"All over bonfires, the beautiful Dorset, to-night. Twenty six, I think, so far, from my window. Ah well, poor George!"*[24]

It seems that Lawrence and Eric Kennington had recently been working together on some drawings but because of the artist's bad health and Lawrence's low spirits he thought it best to *"Leave it a little while till I revive my humanities and come up to see you."*[25] But on hearing that the American publisher Bruce Rogers was in England, he offered to motorcycle anywhere for a rendezvous, *"We must meet: . . . So tell me where and when you will be somewhere (London and Oxford are equi-distant from here)* [Rogers was staying at *Anderton's Hotel,* 162 Fleet Street, London, EC4] *and I shall do my best to arrive."*[26]

In answer to E. M. Forster's letter of 4 May asking if he could stay for a few days at Clouds Hill around the 20th, Lawrence replied, *"Your arrival will be marked by the setting of a white stone into the new wall* [a Victorian practice, especially at Oxford, often recorded by Lewis Carroll (Charles Dodgson) in his diaries to remember a happy visit by saying he'd mark the day with a white stone]. *Wool Station: taxi to here: any day after the 14th superb."*[27]

Also on 7 May, Lawrence ends the long saga about James Hanley's *Boy;* writing to K. W. Marshall, *"I couldn't do just as you suggested: it is very dangerous to come between a carnivore and its prey. But I have made guarded enquiries. My friend* [possibly Lord Trenchard] *knew nothing about the 'drive': and after he had sniffed round to find out, he knew there was no drive, so far as his minions were concerned. Nor is there any connection between Bury and London. They regard Lancashire* [the prosecuting Police county] *as rather foolish to have done what it did . . . .*

I hope Boriswood is unbowed and bloody, under these stresses. It is the right mixture . . . .

Commend me to Greenwood, and say that I'm sure my interventions have not harmed him: and hope they may help. But they were very indirectly done."[28]

Marshall had also sent Lawrence their new publication *Daughters of Albion* by Alec Brown, *"Thank you for the new Brown monster. I have not tackled it yet."*[29]

One of the most intriguing sentences Lawrence ever wrote appeared in the Marshall correspondence of 7 May. It occurs after he describes his busy tiring days at Clouds Hill followed by well-slept nights, *"The noble weather and various causes have kept me outdoors from dawn till dark, and sent me dead-beat to bed immediately it was decent to sleep.* **But that ceases in ten days."**[30] Was he contemplating a totally different style of life from 17 May? Or was it possibly connected with the proposed visit of E. M. Forster when they probably intended to enjoy a lazy holiday.

The proposed visit to Lady Astor, when her *"last ride* [on the

Brough] *with him was only a fortnight before his fatal accident*"[31] seems most unlikely. On Wednesday, 8 May, he wrote to her in answer to her letter of the 7th stating "*No: wild mares would not at present take me away from Clouds Hill. It is an earthly paradise and I am staying here till I feel qualified for it. Also there is something broken in the works, as I told you* [in a letter of 5 May]: *my will, I think.*"[32] Throughout all of these last letters no meeting was mentioned. Lady Astor was most insistent that he stay for the following weekend at Plymouth or at Cliveden on Saturday 25 May, " *The room is ready* [at Plymouth]. *I believe when the Government re-organizes you will be asked to help re-organize the Defence forces. . . . Please, please come* [to Cliveden]. *Lionel* [Curtis], *Pat* [Mrs Curtis], *Philip* [Lord Lothian], *and, for the most important, Stanley Baldwin. Please think about this.*"[33]

As we know (see chapter 8, p. 75) Lawrence had been offered the job, was holding it open with certain restrictions, but it was clear now that he had completely put any such role out of his mind.[34]

Around Wednesday, 8 May, an old friend appeared at Clouds Hill. It was Regimental Sergeant Major H. H. Banbury who knew him from his Tank Corps days. Lawrence recalled, "*HHB was here two days before your letter* [from E. 'Posh' Palmer] *and has returned to Perham Down. He leaves the Army in January next, is jerky but not much altered in face or mind.*"[35] Banbury remembered his short visit, "*At that last meeting he was a changed man; he was showing signs of age, and expressed disappointment at leaving the R.A.F. 'I wish I could go on for another twelve years,' he said in a sad tone. He was restless and tired, he knew he needed rest before recommencing writing. He busied himself with his hands, building over with brick and tile the wooden bungalow* [Knowles'] *which so nearly opposed his own cottage, without plans, to make it different from any other house, jesting at the difference, and hoping to surprise the county surveyor when he came.*"[36]

On Friday, 10 May, Lawrence replies to his army friend E. 'Posh' Palmer on hearing that he was contemplating suicide – apparently because of personal, financial and marital problems. With positive and cheery words he advises 'Posh' by saying, "*Many people oh excellent P, would like to make a complete break with the past – but pasts are unavoidable facts. You can (by the aid of a gas oven) make a complete break with your future – but that's all!*

And at Clouds Hill there are no gas ovens, so I shall look forward to seeing you this summer as soon as all the plants have been watered. . . . You will be a marvellously welcome person as and when you please to come.

You will be an abused and conscience haunted major if you fail to come soon.

Beethoven's Violin Concerto in D Major (Op 61) we had and have, it is 'it' . . . But DON'T MISS CLOUDS HILL. I put an S on the envelope to show how seriously I intend you to visit the Hill this summer. Bring your worst clothes and few of them, I'm as scruffy as ever."[37]

Equally Lawrence was also keen for G. W. M. Dunn to stay at the cottage, *"Not yet, please: everything here is ready for you, and the country beautiful but E. M. Forster . . . has written to suggest himself for some time 'about the 20th'. I cannot do two people together . . . .*

I will write to you again as soon as E. M. F.'s plans have precised themselves . . .

E. M. F. will not probably stay more than four or five days, but once he endured a fortnight. . . . Nothing more till I can give you a sure date."[38]

In answer to a request to attend the Royal Review at Duxford, Cambridge, Lawrence pointed out, *"No. I shall not see the fly past. My leaving the R.A.F. is too recent. It's all an ache, still. If only I could have gone on!!"*[39]

One of his sustained joys was the reading and involvement with books and authors. The 'boys hero' book writer R. H. Kiernan had approached him during autumn 1934 to seek his help to create a stirring story for youngsters to be called *Lawrence of Arabia* (published in July 1935). Lawrence wrote to him about 10 May explaining that, *"Most children are fed up with the War and the inclination (among its survivors) to treat it as a matter of significance. I sympathize with them: the last war is always a bore for the next generations."*[40]

Lawrence became furious with another printing venture that an American University (probably Stanford University, California) had published. They had sent him a copy of the printed works which contained a letter written by Lawrence to another party. He strongly objected as they had *"published it without even attempting to ask my permission first."*[41] He wrote to Ralph Isham on 10 May asking if he could find a lawyer to pursue the matter but cautioned him that cost was a problem *"So please don't involve me in any expense greater than the income of one week . . . say seven dollars the limit."*[42]

Henry Williamson also penned a letter to him on 10 May declaring that he planned to visit London on Tuesday, 14 May, and asked if he could call at Clouds Hill to lend him the typescript of *Winged Victory* by V. M. Yeates for criticism, *"I'll call in anyway on Tuesday* [14th May] *unless rainy day."*[43] Williamson intended to collect the manuscript a few days later.

In Lawrence's last known letter of Sunday, 12 May, to K. T. Parker (Keeper of the Department of Fine Arts, Ashmolean Museum, Oxford and the Hope Collection of Engraved Portraits 1934–62), he is glad that at last the Hogarth drawing by Augustus John (mentioned in chapter 9, p. 83) had finally found a rightful place of rest, *"I am delighted that your expert scrutiny has pulled the John. To me it has always seemed a powerful and characteristic drawing: but ownership blinds the judgement, and then I liked both Hogarth and John as people. So I couldn't trust myself. However if it is a decent drawing, there is only one fit home for it, and that's in your place. Hogarth was so much the Ashmolean, for his last years.*

In my letter to Leeds I asked that it should be classed as a drawing, not hung on the back-stairs among the former Keepers. This is in accordance with a wish of Mrs. Hogarth's. She dislikes it as a portrait – which is the side that most pleases me!"[44]

According to Sir Mortimer Wheeler, Lawrence travelled to Maiden Castle, an ancient hill fort just south-west of Dorchester, on the evening of the 12th. *" It is, I think, fair to say that the excavation of Maiden Castle – of such small part of it as came within our compass – touched the imaginations of others than ourselves. T. E. Lawrence stood shyly watching us at work on the eve of his sudden death."*[45]

Pat Knowles recounts Lawrence's last evening at Clouds Hill. *"On the evening* [Sunday 12 May] *before the accident, after we had had our evening meal* [Joyce Dorey also ate at the table] *we went and sat on the hilltop and talked, our conversation ranged from Maiden Castle to Bridport and from Culliford Clump to Hardy's* Dynasts, *which was one of Shaw's favourite epic poems . . . .*

Shaw had news for me about which he had mixed feelings. It seemed that our plans to start up our small printing press would have to be put on hold for a year or two because he was expecting to be asked to undertake work of national importance, work relating to Home Defence [see p. 75].

Whilst I was greatly disappointed I wasn't surprised.

From our hilltop vantage point we enjoyed an excellent view of the heath [see Plate 28]. *On one occasion we saw a white deer follow the track below the hill to a spring, where it drank its fill. It then turned in our direction towards the road and towards the east.*

It had nearly reached the road when it caught our scent. It stopped still, looking in our direction momentarily, then galloped off north-eastwards and on out of sight.

When the sun had set we went into the cottage. Amongst the most recent additions to his gramophone record collection was Smetana's Ma Vlast. *I had already heard parts of it but on this occasion he decided to treat me to the whole waltz. He seemed really contented and happy and I later went to my house with the feeling that he had at last settled down to an easy stretch of living."* [46]

11

Brough Superior,
GW 2275 – *George VII*

Lawrence had a passion for speed, *"The burble of my exhaust unwound like a long cord behind me. Soon my speed snapped it, and I heard only the cry of the wind my battering head split and fended aside. The cry rose with my speed to a shriek: while the air's coldness streamed like two jets of iced water into my dissolving eyes. I screwed them into slits, ...*

The next mile of road was rough. I braced my feet into the rests, thrust with my arms, and clenched my knees on the tank till its rubber grips goggled under my thighs . . . .

The bad ground was passed and on the new road our flight became birdlike . . . .

A skittish motor-bike with a touch of blood in it is better than all the riding animals on earth, because of its logical extension of our faculties, and the hint, the provocation, to excess conferred by its honeyed untiring smoothness. Because Boa loves me, he gives me five more miles of speed than a stranger would get from him."[1]

To stimulate this emotional experience, Lawrence had owned six of the most powerful motorbikes on the market during the period 1922–35, namely a series of Brough Superiors sold by the manufacturer George Brough at his Nottingham works. He was particularly choosy to whom they were sold, often personally interviewing a potential customer for suitability. This was the case of Lawrence's first purchase in 1922. George would use Lawrence's fame in advertising the new Brough. Lawrence named them all *Boanerges* ('son of thunder'), and called them *George I* to *VII*.

The mechanical complexity of GW 2275 can be seen from the back jacket illustration.

A brief chronology of his three year, three month ownership of *George VII* begins in early February 1932 when George Brough offered him a new one in exchange for his old Brough UL 656, *George VI*, which the Shaws and friends had purchased for him on his return from India in January 1929. George Brough offered an attractive trade-in price, *"Thank you very much. I have £80 already, and can get the balance shortly, I think."*[2] Lawrence insisted on transferring his stainless steel petrol tank from his old Brough (*George VI*) to the new machine.[3] Knowing that collection was due, he registered the new Brough in his log book on 27 February 1932 at the London County Council, Road Fund Licence Office, County Hall, Westminster Bridge, London, SE1 (see Appendix 2).[4]

On 3 March he collected *George VII* from the Brough works in Nottingham.[5] After only three days Lawrence fell in love with the mechanical maiden calling it *"the silkiest thing I have ever ridden: . . . and at 50 she is a dream . . .*

I think she is going to be a very excellent bike."[6] Technically he approved of its perfect timing due to the high gear and spring sprocket. It geared down to 16 m.p.h., pulled fairly at 30 m.p.h. and sounded so sweet that the revs could be counted.[7]

By the middle of April 1932 the beloved female was performing well, *"She is extraordinary fast, with a following wind and downhill. I got over the hundred on Easter Monday in the New Forest."*[8] Also it could be kick started from the saddle and through experiment Lawrence introduced his own technique of starting the machine – two cold kicks followed by a third exploding the engine into life. By now he had completed 1,100 miles.[9]

Of his many trips during that summer and autumn regular visits to the Shaws at Ayot St Lawrence, Herts., was a common route, and once he journeyed from Plymouth to Birmingham and Cranwell, returning to Plymouth.[10]

Perhaps a trivial observation, but from the summer of 1932 until his death in May 1935, *George VII* was most often referred to as *"it," "him"* or *"the ancient-of-days"* or some similar phraseology, but rarely *"her"* or *"she"* which was the case during the early spring days of ownership.

He often travelled the long journey from Plymouth (Mountbatten) to London during the autumn.

By early January 1933 he had notched up 6000 miles. He recorded, with meticulous care, average speeds over long distances (in the past he had calculated similar measurements on his push-bike in England, Wales and France as a young man in

1906–8). He was however honestly cautious when commenting, *"I find myself a little 'windy' on wet roads, now a days."*[11]

Although the Brough performed extremely well with power and handling and was comfortable over 35 m.p.h., minor faults were common. At slower speeds the carburettor had a tendency to affect its performance by bumping or hunting a little.

His love of clean, white pure items features throughout his life. The white robes of Arabia, stainless steel fixtures at Clouds Hill and his stainless steel petrol tank. The latter *"is still spotless, whereas all the plating is going west, by degrees. I have never had such a good tank before."*[12]

During March 1933 he comments on his deliberate intention of riding slower at night.[13] By the end of May he had patent black oilskin motorcycling overalls made, copied specially from his working ones.[14]

Repeated changing of sparking plugs was a regular feature of pre-war motorcycles and on long journeys Lawrence always carried five spares and regularly dried and rubbed old ones for re-use.[15]

During August 1933 he raced from Hythe to Otterbourne keeping well ahead of Liddell Hart in his car, *"the way he shot through traffic led me to chide him about the risks he ran."* Lawrence argued that with its immense power of acceleration it minimized the risks but ended by saying *"It'll end in tragedy one day."*[16]

With such a large engine (nearly 1,000 cc) magneto timing was often a problem. During September *"As I was buzzing along at 60 he suddenly missed badly, picked-up, missed again, and began to clank."* It turned out to be a badly chipped magneto timing bevel.[17]

Lawrence's mechanical know-how and command of technical language were of a high standard and throughout his long letters to George Brough most of the content was connected with some specialized detail of the Brough.

In late December 1933 he was in London and taxed the machine for 1934.[18]

The familiar story of the Brough's powerful performance, slightly marred by its minor electrical and cable faults, continued. On 10 April 1934 it had completed 19,000 miles *"and is running like stink."* but *"the speedometer died on me, between Andover and Salisbury: . . . Other needs:– New electrical wiring*
> *New control cables*
> *New windscreen*
> *New head-race . . .*

These things are trifles. The engine sounds to me as healthy as possible:"[19]

Lawrence called at Nottingham in May 1934 to view and praise the new *George VIII*. By now he had totalled 20,000 miles and was still achieving exceptional speeds, ironically recalling, *"It looks as though I might yet break my neck on a B.S."*[20] Another faulty part developed with a troublesome headlamp which he replaced with an inferior Lucas.[21]

Lawrence was insured for third-party cover with policy no. 3121573 issued by the Motor Union Insurance Company of 70 Cornhill, London.[22]

In the summer of 1934 he related to Liddell Hart the sensitive kind of rider he was at high speed by once trying to avoid running over a hen despite the risk of swerving. This acute awareness to perceptive safe motorcycling remained throughout his life. Although consideration for others on the road was commendable it magnified the disregard for his own safety, which in the end resulted in his death.

By July he had clocked up 25,000 miles and the *"Changes to rear plug stand at 86 to date."*[23] Further faults developed, with a gas leak in the exhaust, a frame coil spring had broken on 16 July, and a more serious need to reline the back brake.[24] He had purposely delayed fixing these defects locally, taking dangerous risks, in the expectation of soon receiving the new machine and knowing that he could get expert help and spares at the Nottingham works during the summer.

Lawrence had extensively ridden the Brough in August and September, *"In the last month it has been Wolverhampton, Kent, Nottingham, London, Plymouth."*[25] In September *George VII's* dynamo failed to charge.[26]

There is a very strong doubt that not all defects were repaired, and that for this reason Lawrence stored the machine on two stands in his thatched garage at Clouds Hill (see Plate 29) for the first seven weeks of his posting to Bridlington from 15 November 1934.

During Christmas 1934 at Clouds Hill he must have made some temporary repairs to the Brough as he foolishly journeyed to London on 27 December and, on a dangerous wet road, motorcycled the next day to Bridlington (see p. 29).

In January 1935 he stated that *"My Brough goes like unholy smoke, when I turn its taps on."*[27]

On 12 January 1935 he motorcycled to Birmingham to stay the

weekend with his old pal Corporal Arthur Hall, his wife and family (see p. 37). The following day Lawrence journeyed to London on *George VII* and eventually arrived at Clouds Hill on 24 January. By now it was plainly obvious to him that the machine was a potential mechanical hazard, so he decided to catch the train to Bridlington via London on 25 January (see p. 43).

After another nine to ten weeks of storing the motorbike at Clouds Hill he rode it to Dorchester on 3 March to register his change of address from London to Clouds Hill in the Brough log book. No visits had been made to the Nottingham workshops since 30 August 1934, as George Brough later confirmed, *"I shall be very pleased to see you when you can spare the time to run up to Nottingham and whilst you are here we can give* George VII *a look over."*[28]

Around early April he test drove the machine on the beach at Sandbanks only to overheat the engine and burn out a coil (see p. 79).

George Brough had design problems with *George VIII* and it was never ready for collection during Lawrence's lifetime, even though various proposed exchange dates were always promised throughout the spring of 1935.

Although *George VII* was operational, Lawrence seems to have only made local trips, except for a trip to Oxford on 26 April.

The background of motorbike faults prompts the authors to strongly suggest that, although possible repairs were made to the Brough at Nottingham on 30 August 1934, on the day of his accident, 13 May 1935, the mechanical imperfections were a contributing factor to the horrible crash and its consequences. A better maintained machine could have given the edge towards a less major incident.

Plate 30 shows Lawrence sitting on his beloved GW 2275 which was photographed in the summer of 1934 by young Bill Knowles, *"His* [Lawrence's] *arrival one evening coincided with mother and Bill who had spent the day at Lulworth Cove. Bill, who had been taking photographs, had a film or two left on the roll. He was reluctant at first but then relented and took a photo of Shaw who said, ' It will be a long time before you can catch one with a camera in your hand.'*

In less than 12 months Bill was the only one alive out of them."[29]

The authors have dated the photograph on the following evidence. Henrietta Knowles died on 20 November 1934 and Lawrence on 19 May 1935, also young Bill must have been on his summer school holidays, so *"In less than 12 months"* dates the photograph between June and September 1934. Lawrence's stainless steel petrol tank and pannier bags can be seen in Plate 30. In May 1935 he wrote, *"If only I had not given up my stainless tank and pannier bags and seen that rolling stand!"*[30] The last visit to Nottingham was on 30 August 1934 where he most likely had these items transferred to the new *George VIII* – so the photograph must have been snapped between June and August 1934.

The final words are perhaps very apt from the mouth of the man, G. B. Shaw, who partly gave the Brough to Lawrence as a gift: *"He told of his young friend's* [Lawrence] *mania for speed and confessed that the demoniacal motor cycle which led to his death was provided by him.*

'It was like handing a pistol to a would-be suicide,' he said."[31]

BROUGH WORKS RECORD SHEET FOR GW 2275

Supplied to:	*T. E. Shaw.*
Model:	*S.S. 100. 1932. Spring frame.*
Engine No:	*22000/S.*
Engine Symbol:	*JTO/Y.*
Frame No:	*1041.S.*
Gearbox No:	*SB. 181.*
Tank No:	*Stainless steel.*
Fork:	*Castle (Brampton).*
Rear Wheel:	*Enfield 19 × 2½. John Bull rim. Wired on.*
Front Wheel:	*Enfield 21 × 2½. John Bull rim. Wired on.*
Carb:	*Amal 1¼ inch. One float. Muffler. Lever.*
Chains:	*Coventry. ⅝ inch × ⅜ inch.*
Mag. Dyno:	*Lucas MSV 50 degrees anti-clock.*
Headlamp:	*Lucas S.40 AS c/with ammeter, dipping beam & B.S. dipper.*
Horn:	*Lucas 6v Altette.*
Speedo:	*Jaeger 120 m.p.h. Rear wheel drive.*
Oil Pump:	*Pilgrim. Anti-clock. Variable oiling.*
Saddle:	*Lycett Aero with enclosed 96 springs.*
Sprockets:	*Engine: 22T. Rear Wheel: 45T.*
Clutch:	*34T. Axle: 22T.*
Front Tyre:	*28 × 3.50 Ribbed. Wired on. Woods valve.*
Rear Tyre:	*26 × 3.50 Fort. Wired on. Woods valve.*
Reg. No:	*GW 2275.*
Date Desp:	*3rd March 1932.*
Route:	*Collected.*
Advice Note:	*B. 7821.*
Invoice No:	*M. 1624.*

Remarks:

Tank top switch.
Battery on front platform.
Separate oil tank c/with
Bowden control.
Tank gate control – short vertical lever.
Large Alpine Carrier and bag with valises.
Amal R and L.H. external twist grips.
Propstand.
Shock absorber engine sprocket.[32]

12

On the 13th Day of May

And so we come to the day of the crash, Monday, 13 May 1935. It was a fine and calm early morning. By mid-morning the sun had warmed the heath to produce broken cumulus cloud accompanied by a moderate east to north-east breeze blowing in the clear air. Pat Knowles remembered, *"he came across to my house earlier than usual. It was one of those bright, still, early spring mornings, and the bird-song, clear and vibrant in the still air had awakened him soon after five, so, seeing the smoke from my fire he came across.*

Whilst I was getting breakfast the postman came. Shaw opened his mail and said that Williamson wanted to see him [Williamson's letter written on 10 May]. *Over breakfast we discussed his letter* [see Plate 31]. *Shaw felt that it would be as well to let him come as soon as possible as he might not have the time to spare later. I said why not the next day? He thought it a good idea, and so it was decided* [despite the fact that Williamson had already suggested this in his letter!]; *he would go down later and send off a telegram telling him to come for lunch the following day.*

We even thought up a few ideas for lunch. We came to the conclusion that Joyce [Pat's intended and later wife, also present that morning] *would make an attractive addition to the occasion and that we would ask her to be hostess. If she could be available we thought to leave the details to her but thought that the meal ought to include fresh bread and butter, cheese and pickled walnuts . . .*

After breakfast Shaw brought out the Brough and I heard him running it up. I guessed that he was cleaning and polishing and servicing it. About mid-morning he came across to ask if there was anything he could get for me whilst he was in Bovington.

I was working in the garden and heard him leave and heard the sound of the Brough's engine all the way to Bovington. The wind was light and from the south, and, believe it or not, but I could even hear the sounds of the parade-sergeants on the square and, by their cadences, almost recognise what they were shouting." [1]

Lawrence took some books on his Brough to Bovington, roughly parcelled in brown paper, to post on to his pal 'Jock' Chambers. He went direct to the *Red Garage*, parked his motorbike by the petrol station, then walked back across the road to the Post Office (see Plate 32 and Map 6).[2] He addressed the parcel to *"The Sorter?, Padd. D.O., London W"* (see Plate 33). Lawrence first met A. E. 'Jock' Chambers in 1922 at the RAF School of Photography, Farnborough. Although Chambers was highly intelligent he lacked formal education, and Lawrence, over the years, had taken it on himself to provide books by post to improve his tuition. On 13 May Chambers was working as a clerk at the Paddington District sorting office in London. The parcel Lawrence sent also contained a humorous letter to Chambers and amongst the many books was a copy of *Don Juan* by James Elroy Flecker.[3]

At precisely 11.25 a.m. a telegram (see Plate 34) was dictated and the Post Office assistant wrote it out and sent it to Henry Williamson which read:

> *"Williamson Shallowford Filleigh*
> *Lunch Tuesday wet fine cottage 1*
> *mile North Bovington Camp*
> *Shaw"* [4]

The telegram would have cost Lawrence one shilling – the address was free and the charge for the first 12 words was 1/-. It was received at Filleigh in Devon at 12.20 p.m. and franked as *"Filleigh, Barnstable."* From the Post Office Lawrence walked the short distance back across the road to the *Red Garage*. Walt Pitman, the pump attendant, asked him if he needed any fuel; Lawrence replied, *"I'm alright, thanks,"* then he climbed on to his Brough.[5]

Lawrence then went through the complicated task of starting up the Brough. He sat astride the bike checking that the three-gear-lever on the right side of the petrol tank was slotted into neutral in its gate, i.e. opposite to the forward tooth (see Diagram 2). Next the push-slide in the petrol tube from the petrol tank was pushed in to allow the fuel to flow down to the carburettor below. Then he set the ignition lever control – just off left centre on the handlebar, to half way. He then positioned the valve lifter on the extreme left of the handlebar. The next stage was to utilize the right-hand throttle twist grip (see Plate 41 and back of jacket).

As soon as these complicated procedures were completed, Lawrence kick-started the machine with two cold preliminary attempts followed by the third successful kick which fired up the Brough into action. The complete operation was the normal procedure for starting a 'cold' Brough, but since he had already ridden about a mile the engine was relatively warm and therefore some of the individual actions may have been omitted.

With his left hand Lawrence pulled in the clutch lever on the left-hand handlebar and engaged first gear with his right hand and pushed the gear lever forward. Then with a gentle twisting of the throttle and a slight loosening of the clutch *George VII* started its journey home to Clouds Hill and changed into second and third (top) gears. He had only travelled about 350 yards when he recognized some army soldiers at the Camp gates on the eastern side of the road. He pulled in and chatted to the group. One of them was Frank Gordon who recalled that he only stayed for a minute or two. Lawrence then restarted the bike and moved towards the lonely, narrow road leading to Clouds Hill (see Plate 35).

It is now important to familiarize oneself with the layout of the road between Bovington Camp and Clouds Hill. The revised 1934 Ordnance Survey map (25 inches to 1 mile) is reproduced in Map 7. At first glance one can observe the slight bend in the road just south of Clouds Hill which was straightened by American soldiers, during the second World War, into its present straight alignment.

During the summer of 1992 the authors reconnoitred the terrain. The area was dense in greenery and rhododendrons but it was easy to find the old concrete post and wire that denoted the Frampton estate boundary, south of the Knowles' land, which appeared in Lawrence's 1934 sketch map (see Map 10).

Using this as a marker the old road was discovered as it wound south (just to the west of the modern road) amongst thick foliage with an elevated ridge as its western banking.

Using the four 1935 photographs (Plates 36–38), especially Plates 37A and 37B, and finding the old road's western embankment the accident site was easily pinpointed. At the time a white line with "421" was painted across the road surface at the accident spot (see Plates 37B and 38B). Opposite stood a temporarily erected wooden sign denoting a slippery road. The distance between the crash point and Clouds Hill garage entrance was measured as 410 yards.

Today the hills and dips of the old road south of the accident spot have vanished. So two methods were used to reconstruct their positions and distances from Clouds Hill. The first system incorporated the siting of each telegraph pole visible in Plates 36–38 (see Map 7) with their known distance apart of 70 yards. Secondly, contour cross-sections of contemporary maps were constructed and together the final measurements calculated.

Six major dips and hills have been noted with their distances south of Clouds Hill:

Dip (a) – approximately 650 yards from Clouds Hill garage,
Hill (a) – about 580 yards,
Dip (b) – about 510 yards,
Hill (b) – 440 yards,
Dip (c) – 380 yards,
Hill (c) – 100 yards.

Dips (a) and (b) are deep enough to hide any traffic to the north and dip (c) is open and clear.

Lawrence's eye level, sat on his motorbike, was about 3½ feet above the road surface. As he travelled north in top gear around 50 m.p.h. he dropped into dip (a) having already travelled 580 yards from the *Red Garage*. Hill (a) ahead was blind to traffic beyond and no vehicles had passed him in any direction. He negotiated this and descended into dip (b) having covered about 710 yards of the journey.

Now came the crucial stage. As Lawrence moved up hill (b) north out of dip (b) he automatically changed down into second gear (his usual procedure during hundreds of similar trips) till viewing hill top (b) blind to traffic beyond. As his vision cleared the hill he suddenly came face to face with a push-bike on the left-hand side travelling the same way (ridden by young Albert Hargraves) with another push-bike immediately in front (ridden by Frank Fletcher) in single file. There was no oncoming black car or any other vehicle or person. Also a very steep bank on the western side of the road at this point (see Plate 38A) caused the cyclists to be much further into the road than in normal open country.

This sudden million to one encounter on an extremely narrow (16 feet or so) section of the road caused Lawrence to instinctively perform an emergency stop. To execute this he jammed on both front and back brakes with right hand on the front-break lever (at right end of handlebar) and right foot on back-brake lever (by right-front footrest) respectively.

Plate 37A facing north shows the accident spot (about 410 yards south of Clouds Hill garage entrance) with disturbed gravel and flint caused by the skid marks of the Brough as it careered to the right.

Lawrence tried to swerve to the right (east) to avoid the rear push cyclist but caught the back wheel of the cycle. This gave the necessary jolt to send the Brough on to its right-hand side skidding across the road, which in turn threw Lawrence into the air, also to the right.

A newspaper reporter inspected the crash site on Tuesday, 14 May, and recalled, *"the accident, . . . occurred in a dip in the road leading to the camp. Marks in the road suggest that Mr Shaw braked hard to avoid the accident and indicate that he was thrown a considerable distance . . . "*[6]

The Brough finished up about 20 yards beyond the accident spot on the right-hand side of the road and Lawrence a little further beyond. The damage to Hargraves' push-bike (see Plates 39A–C) is consistent with a frame that has been shunted or given a sudden jolt from behind, and **not** a case of having the Brough running over it. The abrupt impulse from the motorbike caused the back wheel and back right side of the frame to buckle, locking the damaged wheel in its forks. Hargraves' bike, after hitting Fletcher's, fell to the ground immediately on the left-hand side of the road. Hargraves was simultaneously thrown in the air and sustained minor injuries, and eventually became unconscious. Fletcher was only shaken when he fell on the left side of the road slightly further north.

Lawrence, not wearing a crash helmet, had launched head first on to the gravelled road, skidded along it and ending in a position just north of his motorbike on the right side of the road.

Naturally, Fletcher walked to his pal Hargraves to see how he was, and found him still semi-conscious. Hargraves handed Fletcher his butcher's book. Fletcher even found three pennies lying in the road but by the time he enquired if they were his friend's, he had become unconscious. Fletcher was close enough to see Lawrence's face covered in blood as he lay in the road just to the north but was too scared to venture near him. A minute or two later a civilian cyclist arrived and told Fletcher to run for the field ambulance which was attached to a tented field hospital in an army summer camp of bell tents situated immediately east of the road on open heathland (see Plate 40).

Fletcher recalled in his first statement to the Press on 15 May 1935 that *"a man came up on a cycle and asked me to get the ambulance."* The significance of "came up" implies that the cyclist came from the Bovington direction.[7]

Before Fletcher could go for the ambulance, soldiers from the summer camp arrived on the scene. The accident spot was becoming a hive of activity.

The cyclist hastily returned to Bovington to inform the military hospital of the crash. This man was observed by John B. Connolly who at the time was in the hospital waiting room to receive a knee dressing. He remembered that someone ran in and said to the orderly, or the officer, that there had been a serious accident just **up** the road involving several people.

Connolly and Captain Geoffrey Anderton, an officer in the RAMC (Royal Army Medical Corps), drove the hospital ambulance to the crash scene, where an army lorry had already been stopped to assist in the emergency. Immediately Captain Anderton carried out a thorough medical examination of Lawrence, then ordered him to be carried on a stretcher into the ambulance along with Hargraves, to return to the hospital.[8]

The newspaper reporter mentioned earlier also confirmed that *"The accident was witnessed by soldiers of 6E Tank Corps, stationed at the* [summer] *camp, who promptly conveyed Mr Shaw to the military hospital in a lorry."*[9]

The doctor at the military hospital, Captain C. P. Allen, said that the two injured persons were admitted between 11.30 and 11.45 a.m.[10]

We have previously suggested (see chapter 11) that if Lawrence had properly maintained his Brough, particularly his back brake, the accident may not have had such a tragic ending.

The protruding components of the Brough, registration number GW 2275, that caused the skid marks on the road, can be seen in Plate 41, with its sideways position well demonstrated in Diagram 3A and the resultant damaged parts in Diagram 4.

In Diagram 3B marks are observed on the road surface. Three of them curve to the east and were caused by the skidding of GW 2275. The other irregular mark on the western side was due to the collision between GW 2275 and the two push-bikes.

The right-hand handlebar and knobbly handle gear lever gouged the road surface and produced the first skid mark (nearest to Bovington Camp). To bend back the handlebar and twist the gear lever and gate, punching multiple dents into the petrol tank, emphasizes the tremendous impact experienced in the crash.

The second skid mark contact was made by the footbrake pedal (severely bent back), foot rest (broken off) and kickstart lever (slightly bent).

The third and most northerly skid mark was created by the rear pannier toolbox which ended up crumpled with its top lid bent down.

Other incidental damage included a detached front headlamp rim and glass, grazing to the nose of the front mudguard and a slight scrape on the right rear of the saddle edge.

Analysis of the length of the motorbike skid marks enables the speed of Lawrence's Brough on impact to be calculated between 30 and 35 m.p.h. The gear lever was found to be in second gear. Skidding along on that right-hand side it would certainly have been impossible, for surface contact with the road, to cause it to jump into any other gear position in the gate.

Plate 37A and Diagram 4, the undamaged left side of the Brough and the continuous long skid marks confirm that the Brough was not *"twisting and turning over and over along the road . . . "* as stated by corporal Ernest Catchpole, one of the main witnesses. Also the calculated slower speed contradicts Catchpole's adamant estimate of the speed of Lawrence's motorbike at the time of the accident as *"50–60 m.p.h . . . "*[11] Therefore Catchpole's other major suggestion – that a black saloon car caused the accident – must be regarded as highly doubtful. Frank Fletcher always maintained that there were no vehicles at the time of the accident.

Pat Knowles gives an insight into the minutes after the accident, *"The next thing to disturb my peace was an R.A.M.C. [Royal Army Medical Corps] sergeant who came running down my garden path. He said that there had been an accident and asked me to come and identify the injured man. He had been 'sent' and did not know much more.*

With my mind in a whirl of questions I followed him to his Austen Seven car. He drove me to the hospital and I went to the casualty department. Shaw was laid on the table with his eyes closed. His head was bandaged leaving only a little of the forehead showing. There was no sign of injury on the parts left uncovered except a small red mark over his left eye.

The medical officer in charge was anxious and questioned me closely but hurriedly. He then reached for the telephone. I don't know to whom he was speaking but whoever it was evidently asked how he knew it was T. E. Lawrence, for he said that Lawrence has been identified by 'some sort of servant' – evidently that was what he thought I was.

I didn't bother to put him right on that but went back to the casualty room and stayed for a while although there was nothing I could do. I asked the sergeant whether he thought there was a possibility of him regaining consciousness.

He looked at me closely for a few moments and then asked whether I was a relative; I said that I was not. He then explained that the injury was severe and that there was no hope of even a partial recovery.

He led me away, gave me a glass of water and then drove me back to Cloud's Hill. I was totally at a loss as to what to do. Before nightfall however the bad news had evidently reached London, for the whole area became alive with reporters, and the curious. My concern then was to make the cottage secure. It became my main task for some while."[12]

Colonel Etherington, who had an appointment with an officer at Bovington Camp around lunchtime, was kept waiting for quite a while after his arrival. The officer he had come to see explained that the Camp was in some turmoil, as an extremely important person, known under a pseudonym, had just then been admitted to the camp hospital after a serious motorbike accident.[13]

As the news spread and reached London later on 13 May, the Air Ministry contacted various friends of Lawrence to ascertain the next of kin and their whereabouts. Liddell Hart recalled that evening:

"On Monday, May 13th, returning home about 7.30 p.m., I was told by my secretary that the Air Ministry, first, and Alan Dawnay, later, had telephoned to say that T. E. had met with an accident when riding back, on his motor-cycle, to his cottage at Cloud's Hill from Bovington Camp, and that he was lying gravely injured with a fractured skull in the Military Hospital there. The Air Ministry had asked whether I knew the whereabouts of his next of kin. I got through to them at once, and gave them such information as I had. T. E.'s mother was in China, with his eldest brother [Dr Robert M. Lawrence], while his other surviving brother [A. W. Lawrence], the younger of the five, who held a University appointment at Cambridge, was on holiday in Majorca. I was not able to get in touch with Alan Dawnay until later, but put a call through to the hospital and found that Lord Carlow, another friend of T. E., had arrived there; he had come on a visit to Cloud's Hill only to be greeted by the news of the accident, and was remaining on the spot to look after things. T. E. had pitched on his head after a violent swerve in trying to avoid a butcher's boy. . . . Thinking that Newcombe ought to be informed, I sent him a message, and he arranged to go down to Bovington as soon as possible to relieve Carlow; these two kept vigil by turns till the end."[14]

13

The Long Wait,
14–19 May 1935

The following day the whole area was a scene of extraordinary activity. All military personnel, soldiers' wives and police constables were ordered not to say anything about the accident. No one was allowed near the crash site where a mounted member of the military police was on duty.[1] Even visitors to the military hospital were refused admittance – Mrs Agnes Hargraves, young Albert Hargraves' mother, was denied access to her injured son on the evening of the 13th and only allowed to see him for the first time on the 15th.[2] The clampdown extended to Frank Fletcher's house where on the 14th both military and civil police told his father that on no account was his son to be interviewed without authority.[3]

Major General J. W. West, Honorary Surgeon to the King, arrived at the hospital Monday night (13 May) to consult with the medical staff over Lawrence's condition. He returned to London on the 14th.[4]

Early on Tuesday, 14 May, Captain Knight, staff captain at the hospital, stated that Lawrence was suffering from concussion and a fractured skull was feared. By late afternoon he was still unconscious and *"fairly critical"*[5] (unconscious for 28 hours). This contrasts with a hospital official who stated on the 14th, *"All I am permitted to tell is that we have in the hospital a Mr Shaw. We have strict instructions to give no other information. No I cannot say how he is."*[6] Also *"We have a Mr Shaw here after a motor cycle accident, but we can give no report about his condition. We are definitely forbidden by higher authorities to discuss it."*[7]

A cable was sent on the 14th to Lawrence's mother and his eldest brother Dr R. M. Lawrence on missionary work in China informing them of the bad news.[8]

Sir Farquahar Buzzard, Physician-in-Ordinary to the King, and Mr H. W. B. Cairns, brain specialist at the London Hospital, also attended Lawrence early in the week.[9]

On Wednesday afternoon, 15 May, Lawrence was reported as still unconscious, his condition unchanged but he still had *"a fighting chance"* of recovery.[10] (Unconscious for 50 hours).

When reporters attempted to gain access to the hospital on the 15th they were apprehended by a military policeman who requested that they leave as they were trespassing on War Department property. However, this restriction was soon relaxed and they were told that information could be obtained in bulletin form from the hospital.

During Wednesday afternoon his brother A. W. Lawrence, Reader in Archaeology at Cambridge, arrived at Bovington Camp after a quick flight from holidaying in Majorca. He went straight to the small room where Lawrence lay.

At 10.15 hours on Thursday, 16 May, the hospital bulletin stated *"Mr. T. E. Shaw is still in an unconscious condition. He has passed a fair night. His general condition is, if anything, a little weaker, but he is holding his own well."*[11] (Unconscious for 70 hours).

However, during the afternoon (16th) his condition deteriorated and serious concern for his recovery was expressed. Shortly before 15.00 hours it was stated that his situation was critical. Even Arnold Lawrence, moved by the hopelessness, decided to talk to the Press for the first time, *"I am afraid the chances of my brother's recovery are very slender. There is nothing we can do except to wait and hope he will pull through."*[12]

A special guard was sent to Clouds Hill, where A. W. and his wife Barbara were staying, to protect them and Lawrence's valuable book collection from reporters and sightseers.[13] Although many years later A. W. said *"We stayed in Clouds Hill till after the funeral, seeing and hearing nothing of the security services. If they had already searched the cottage they would not have left the two typescripts of* The Mint *and the hundreds of letters – some in very difficult handwriting – that I found there."*[14] Publication of *The Mint* in Lawrence's time would not have been welcomed by the RAF. They had known of it for years and kept a secret file titled *"Precautions For Preventing Publication of The Mint"*.[15]

The inevitable rumours circulated; Air Ministry officials were searching for secret papers at Clouds Hill; Lawrence was involved in secret Government work; the accident was a murder attempt by foreign powers, and so on.

111

At 10.30 hours on Friday, 17 May (Unconscious for 91 hours) *"Mr T. E. Shaw is still unconscious. There is no change in his condition."* At 13.00 and 16.00 hours there was also no improvement. A slight optimism emerged with A. W. remarking *"I think his chances of getting through are better than those of the average man in a similar condition."*[16]

Lawrence was still fighting with super-human strength but further complications soon occurred. The 15.00 hours (unconscious 119 hours) statement on Saturday, 18 May, read *"Still unconscious, strength being well-maintained, some congestion of the right lung."*[17] This was enough to bring in a chest specialist.[18] The situation worsened and in the evening a relapse set in with the later report stating his condition as *"very grave".*[19] (Unconscious for 126 hours). Oxygen was administered. Three specialists rushed to the bedside, Sir Farquahar Buzzard and Mr H. W. B. Cairns from Oxford and Arundel respectively arrived just after midnight (19 May) quickly followed by Dr Hope Gosse, the London chest and lung specialist. With the resident army doctor, Captain C. P. Allen, they remained in attendance all night.

At 03.30 hours on the 19th a bulletin reaffirmed the overall anxiety felt. The original X-rays taken of the skull fracture were re-examined in hope of an emergency operation, but the situation was impossible. Shortly before 0700 hours Lawrence's pulse had almost gone and his breathing was weak. Adrenalin injections and oxygen were administered in the effort to revive him and artificial respiration was tried.[20] But the attempts failed. Shortly before 08.30 hours on Sunday 19 May he died after 140 hours of being unconscious. Captain Allen entered the little waiting-room where friends and others were gathered and simply said *"I suppose you have heard, gentlemen, that is all over now."*[21]

As the news was announced at the Sunday morning parade service in the camp church by the Rev. G. H. Heaslett, a genuine sadness was felt by all.[22]

With the consent of A. W. a post-mortem was immediately carried out by Captain Allen and Mr Cairns. It revealed a large fractured fissure, 9 inches long, extending from the left-hand side of the head backwards. There was also a small fracture of the left orbital plate. The brain was severely lacerated, especially in the left temple. The cause of death was fracture of the skull, with severe cerebral damage, congestion of the lungs followed by heart failure. If he had lived Lawrence would have been unable to speak; he would have lost his memory and been paralysed.[23]

Even more macabre was the removal of Lawrence's brain, which was taken by Cairns and eventually placed, pickled in a jar, in the old Radcliffe Infirmary Hospital in Oxford. It remained there till March 1971 when a fire demolished the area in which it was housed.[24]

It is somewhat surprising that the two civilian nurses, who were quickly summoned after the accident from Bournemouth to Lawrence's bedside, did not know the fame of their patient, only that his name was Shaw.[25]

To put the record straight, although certain restrictions were imposed by the military just after the accident not to speak to the media, at no time was there any stringent security placed around Lawrence's bed, "*In none of my visits to the military hospital did I pass through a 'maximum security cordon'. Nor see plain-clothes men at the bedside or sleeping outside the door.*" A. W. Lawrence explained.[26]

A cable was sent on the 19th to the Chinese Mission at Hangkow to his mother and eldest brother with the news of his death. News was received on the 18th, reporting that they were journeying to England and had reached the coast of the Chinese mainland.[27]

The King and Queen were also informed of the sad news.[28]

Later in the morning (the 19th) the body was wrapped in a Union Jack and taken in gentle falling rain from the hospital the hundred yards to the little slate-roofed mortuary which stands beside the main camp road.[29] There, before an altar with a small crucifix, Lawrence laid in state.[30]

Lawrence's own obituary, sent to Robert Graves in February 1935 (see p. 50), appeared in the *Evening Standard* on 20 May 1935 headed "*Myself, by Lawrence.*"[31]

14

Inquest and Funeral, 21 May 1935

The inquest and funeral were planned for Tuesday 21 May, only two days after his death, with the inquest in the morning. The afternoon funeral was organized by Arnold Lawrence on the Sunday[1] and Liddell Hart suggested *"on Sunday night to quench the idea of donning top-hats . . . "*[2]

The civilian inquest was held in a dining room by the military hospital. Just prior to its commencement the damaged *George VII* motorbike and Hargraves' buckled push-bike arrived in an open lorry (see Plate 42) as evidence for the hearing. The seven jurors consisted of S. C. Patrick (Foreman), G. Mason, R. Dulleston, W. G. Bugg, W. Burke, Thomas Shaw and Jesse Rawles, who noticed that the right handlebar of the Brough had been wrenched back, its front lamp glass broken, and that there were slight dents on the right-hand side of the petrol tank and front lamp.[3]

A. W. arrived with Colonel S. F. Newcombe (see Plate 43). At the back of the court sat Sir Ronald Storrs; there were only 30 people in the room, including representatives of the Press[4] – *"barely 30ft. long and less than 20ft. wide. The Coroner sat at a small, baize-covered table with his two fellow officers seated on either side of him.*

Three wooden benches and five rows of chairs were the only accommodation available for witnesses and members of the public. A plain wooden form about 15ft. long served as a jury box."[5]

In an unprecedented opening speech, the East Dorset coroner R. Neville Jones prejudiced the court and jury by telling them that he had already made up his mind as to the verdict of the inquiry. From this one must come to the unhealthy conclusion that there was a strong need to hasten Lawrence's earthly disappearance as soon as possible. He began:

"I very much regret the necessity for calling you together to-day to inquire into the circumstances which have led up to the death of someone who was known to you at the time of death as Thomas Edward Shaw, but who was much better known to the world in general as Col. Lawrence of Arabia.

The facts are very simple. I do not propose to go through them, but you will gather just what took place from the witnesses. The accident occurred on May 13. Mr. Shaw was removed to the Military Hospital at Bovington where, despite the skill and devotion of eminent medical men who attended him and the hospital staff, he died on Sunday last.

The cause of death you will hear from Capt. Allen and Mr. Cairns, who performed a post-mortem. I shall first call Mr. Arnold Walker [should be Walter] *Lawrence."*[6]

Only the chronological order of the inquest follows; the full text of witnesses is covered in more detail in chapters 15–17.

After A. W. Lawrence, Corporal Ernest Catchpole took the witness chair and was cross-examined, followed by Frank Fletcher and Albert Hargraves; Fletcher and Catchpole were recalled; Inspector Drake of the Dorset Constabulary made a statement; Captain C. P. Allen, the army doctor, told the medical story.

Finally the coroner summed up, addressing the jury, saying that the only conflicting point in the evidence seemed to be with regard to the car. It did not necessarily mean that it had anything to do with the accident, but the fact that Corporal Catchpole was certain that he had seen it, and the two boys equally adamant they had not, was rather unsatisfactory. Apart from that he did not think the jury would have any difficulty in arriving at their verdict. The court inquest then ended, having lasted two hours.

After the inquest Lawrence's will was revealed by A. W.:

"'He has left the estate to me with certain private instructions as to its disposal which I do not think will be of public interest.

The estate comprises about £200 in his current account, certain investments, his cottage, Clouds Hill, Moreton, his motor-cycle and books, documents, private papers, and furniture in the cottage.

The will is written on a small slip of paper and was drawn up by a lawyer. It makes me and a lawyer the executors, and I have been made the literary executor. I do not think, however, that he will be found to have left any works of importance.'

Mr Lawrence added that he did not intend to dispose of the cottage."[7] [*The Times* of 9 September 1935 disclosed that Lawrence *"left estate of the gross value of £7,441, . . . "*]

After the inquiry the coroner came to view the body in

the coffin to find Sir Ronald Storrs, with the permission of A. W., photographing Lawrence.[8] Storrs was an inexperienced photographer with little idea of the exact exposure required. He stood on a trestle astride the coffin and took six exposures with his camera – one came out reasonably well. He even asked if Kennington or John could sketch Lawrence but time was short.[9]

In a flowery manner Storrs describes the scene: *"I stood beside him swathed in fleecy wool; stayed until the plain oak coffin was screwed down. There was nothing else in the mortuary chamber but a little altar behind his head with some lilies of the valley and red roses. I had come prepared to be greatly shocked by what I saw, but his injuries had been at the back of his head, and beyond some scarring and discolouration over the left eye, his countenance was not marred. His nose was sharper and delicately curved, and his chin less square. Seen thus, his face was the face of Dante with perhaps the more relentless mouth of Savonavola; incredibly calm with the faintest flicker of disdain. The rhythmic planes of his features gradually became the symbolized impression of all mankind, moulded by an inexorable destiny. Nothing of his hair, nor of his hands was showing; only a powerful cowled mark, dark-stained ivory alive against the dead chemical sterility of the wrappings. It was somehow unreal to be watching beside him in these cerements, so strangely resembling the* aba, *the* kuffiya *and the* aqal *of an Arab Chief, as he lay in his last littlest room, very grave and strong and noble . . . "*[10]

Hundreds of the important, and ordinary, flocked to the little village church of St Nicholas at Moreton in the sunny afternoon. A simple service with no mourning or flowers had been requested – just as Lawrence would have wished it. A train with three coaches left Waterloo at 09.30 hours and arrived at Moreton station at 13.58 hours, and was met by motorcars to transport friends to the church. Their first return train after the funeral was at 17.05 hours.[11]

After the inquest the coffin was carried into a small black van (see Plate 44) which drove almost unnoticed through Bovington Camp passing the tank hangers where one or two soldiers stood to attention and saluted.[12] Ironically, it travelled quickly and alone along the road to Clouds Hill, motored over the accident spot and passed Lawrence's retirement cottage of eleven weeks and on to Moreton church.

Liddell Hart recalls, *"The setting was perfect in its pastoral charm – the church beside the banks of the Frome, and the hall near by, at the end of the drive. May sunshine brought warmth, . . . The path up to the church and the wall was lined with spectators, but most seemed to be from the near-by villages, and the only discordant note was the crowd of cameramen like a swarm of black flies . . . and only one man present had disregarded the notification of 'no formal dress'. . . . Only a few, even, wore black lounge suits. Most of the friends went into the church, but I waited till the hearse arrived, and then followed it in with Jack Salmond and Scott-Paine."*[13]

Indeed only few were in mourning – only black ties, two policemen and one aircraftsman in uniform, and one silk hat worn. The black hat was worn by Mr Atta Amin of the Iraq Legation.[14]

Six pallbearers, representing six facets of his life, carried the coffin from the motor-hearse to the church. They were Sir Ronald Storrs, representing British officials and colleagues in the East; Eric Kennington who illustrated *The Seven Pillars of Wisdom*; Aircraftsman W. Bradbury for the Royal Air Force; ex-private Arthur Russell for the Royal Tank Corps; Colonel S. F. Newcombe for his Arabian life; and Pat Knowles representing Clouds Hill.[15]

It is of interest to note some of the people who attended the occasion. In alphabetical order: Captain C. P. Allen, Mr Atta Amin (Chargé d'Affaires of the Iraq Legation), Lady Nancy Astor, Gunner H. W. Bailey, Sergeant T. W. Beaumont, Flt. Lt. Beauforte-Greenwood, Mr C. R. R. Bell, Captain Samuel H. Brodie, Mr J. A. L. Brown, Colonel R. Buxton, Mr Jonathan Cape, Mr and Mrs Winston Churchill, Major Colin Cooper, Colonel and Mrs Lionel G. Curtis, Colonel W. A. Davenport, Colonel and Mrs Alan Dawnay, Captain Dixon, Mr Alec Dixon, Joyce Dorey, A/C G. W. M. Dunn, Mr Phillip Graves, Captain Green, Mr and Mrs Ben Godwin, Mrs Thomas Hardy, Mr Augustus John, Canon M. W. Kinloch, Captain Knight VC, Mr and Mrs A. W. Lawrence, Captain and Mrs Liddell Hart, Lord Lloyd, Colonel H. F. Newcombe, Flt. Lt. H. Norrington, Captain Philpott, Major I. J. Pullar, Mr Bruce Rogers, Mr R. C. Rolls, Mr St. Leger (representing Sir Herbert Baker), Sir John Salmond, Mr and Mrs Seigfried Sassoon, Mr Raymond Savage, Mr Hubert Scott-Paine, Sir Ronald Storrs, General A. P. Wavell, General Sir Archibald Weigham, Mr C. F. Wheeler, Rev. R. H. White and Earl Winterton.[16]

General Wavell had flown in by autogiro from Aldershot.[17] No representatives were sent to deputize for the Chapman family (Lawrence's paternal family name).[18] Villagers, soldiers and navvies working on the Wool road were present.[19]

Those absent included Charlotte and Bernard Shaw, who were on their South African holiday. Clare and Sydney Smith were in Singapore.[20] Feisal had died in Switzerland in 1933. In 1968 John Bruce claimed he attended[21] but obviously wasn't present as A. W.

explained, *"I was there and I did not see him; moreover I have a letter from him written from Aberdeen two days before the funeral in which he regrets his inability to be present."*[22] Tom Beaumont also confirms he did not observe him at the occasion.[23]

Winston Churchill, looking grim, with his wife and party arrived and walked between the assembled crowds into the church (see Plate 45).

As the pallbearers bore the coffin from the hearse along the small pathway to the church one of the two policemen on duty, PC 26 Sidney Frank Loader, saluted.[24] The coffin was followed up the steps into the church by the familiar figure of Augustus John in Tweed jacket and scarf (see Plate 46).

The church service began at 14.30 hours led by Canon M. W. Kinloch. The church was packed to its 170-person capacity and many could not gain admittance, including Sir John Salmond and Major Colin Cooper.[25]

The order of service was short and simple:

1. Psalm 121 – "I will lift up my eyes unto the hills."
2. Lesson read by Canon Kinloch from Revelations, chapter 7, verse 9.
3. Hymn 193 – "Jesu, lover of my soul, Let me to my bosom fly."
4. Prayers.
5. Nunc Dimittis.[26]

On reading the lesson the canon was overcome with the occasion and faltered. The singing of Lawrence's favourite hymn, *"Jesu lover of my soul"*, led by the choir, cascaded outside as the many throngs joined in.[27] Ironically the beautiful hymn was played by Mr A. P. Shaw, an organist from Dorchester.[28] Even nature provided a blackbird to sing in a tree during the service.[29]

After the service the procession slowly left the church led by Canon Kinloch followed by the choir, in two's, of six choirboys (Arthur Lillington, Reginald Greening, unknown, John Caleh, Sydney Churchill, and William Harvey) and four choirmen (George Lillington, Arthur Pride, Harold Pitman and Samuel Pitman).[30] Behind followed the coffin on a trolley attended by the six pallbearers, immediately in front of A. W. Lawrence and his wife. (see Plates 47, 48).

Storrs commented, *"As we carried the coffin into and out of the little church the clicking Kodaks and the whirring reels extracted from the dead body their last 'personal' publicity."*[31]

PLATE 1   The Ozone Hotel, Bridlington, *c.*1920.

PLATE 2   RAF birthday party at the Ozone Hotel in 1930s.

PLATE 3   Hilda Barchard, proprietor of the Ozone Hotel, *c.*1940.

PLATE 4   Clare Sydney Smith and Lawrence in his boat *Biscuit* in Plymouth Sound during early 1930s.

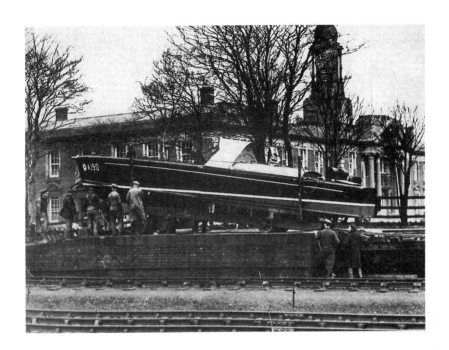

PLATE 5 Armoured motorboat A190 at Bridlington railway station, 1930s.

PLATE 6 Lawrence in RAF uniform in the garden of *The Cuddy*, Flamborough, *c*.1934. Photograph taken by Ian Deheer.

PLATE 7 Flt. Lt. Reginald G. Sims taken in Iraq, 1931.

PLATE 8 *The White Cottage*, the Sims' home at Hornsea, East Yorkshire.

PLATE 9   Rough seas at Bridlington, 1935.

PLATE 10   Clouds Hill with woodshed.

PLATE 11 Pat Knowles at Clouds Hill, May 1935.

PLATE 13 Leslie Howard — one of the many actors chosen to portray Lawrence in the proposed film *Lawrence of Arabia*, May 1934.

PLATE 12 Lawrence and Arthur Hall at Birmingham, January 1935.

PLATES 14 AND 15   Two views of the interior of Augustus John's new studio at Fordingbridge, Hampshire, 1934.

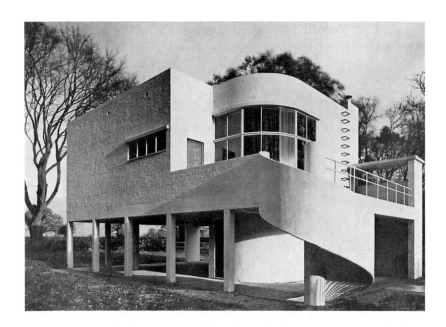

PLATE 16   Exterior view of Augustus John's new studio at Fordingbridge, Hampshire, 1934.

PLATE 17   Augustus John's January 1935 portrait of Lawrence destined as the frontispiece to his proposed printing of *The Mint*.

PLATE 18   James Hanley *c.*1930.

PLATE 19 Lawrence, photographed by Reginald G. Sims at *The White Cottage*, Hornsea, February 1935.

PLATE 20 Film
advertisement for
Cleopatra, in the
Bridlington Free Press,
16 February 1935.

Phone 3012.   SUPER CINEMA   Manager: G. F. Mundy.

THIS WEEK-END

GIVE HER A RING (U)

Starring CLIFFORD MOLLISON and WENDY BARRIE.
Also a PAGEANT OF VARIETY STARS in

PATHETONE PARADE (U)

Times and Prices as usual.

MONDAY, FEBRUARY 18th, and ALL THE WEEK:
A Mammoth Historical Spectacle of Thrilling Magnificence, founded on the
Love Story that altered the History of the World!

Also Pathe S.S. Gazette, etc.

Continuous daily 6.15 to 10.30 p.m.   Matinee Daily at 2.30
Admission 2/-, 1/4, 1/- and 9d.
All Children half-price to Matinees. Monday to Friday evenings if with
adults. Seats booked for Matinees and 6.15 performances, 2/- seats any
performance

PLATE 21 Lawrence on his push-bike leaning against Bridlington harbour wall
prior to cycling south on 26 February 1935.

PLATE 22 Talbot Hotel, Holbeach, Lincolnshire, 1930s.

PLATE 24 Louie Dingwell on top of a coach in the 1930s.

PLATE 23 Lady Kennet in her studio, Leinster Court, London, 1939.

PLATE 25   Seashore and dunes at
Sandbanks, Bournemouth.

PLATE 26   Lawrence's wallet/purse.

PLATE 27   Lawrence's log basket and saw
trestle, Clouds Hill, late 1935.

PLATE 28   Hill-top view looking west from Clouds Hill.

PLATE 29   Lawrence's motorcycle garage at Clouds Hill.

PLATE 30 Lawrence on GW 2275 in summer 1934.

PLATE 31 Interior of Pat Knowles' bungalow, Clouds Hill.

PLATE 32 Bovington main High Street, mid-1930s.

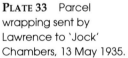

PLATE 33 Parcel wrapping sent by Lawrence to 'Jock' Chambers, 13 May 1935.

PLATE 34 Lawrence's telegram to Henry Williamson, 13 May 1935.

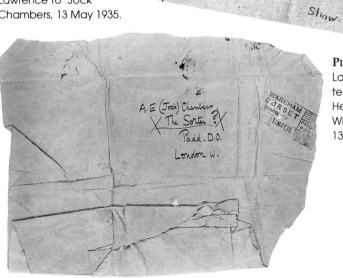

PLATE 35 Road to Clouds Hill looking north from Bovington Camp, *c.*1930.

PLATES 36A AND B
Two similar views
of crash site
during mid-May
1935.

The lonely road where
the fatal accident to
Mr. T. E. Shaw
occurred.

PLATE 37A   Crash site looking north, 14 May 1935.
       B   Same view taken in summer 1992.

PLATE 38A   Crash site looking south, 14 May 1935.
   B   Same view taken in summer 1992.

PLATES 39A, B AND C
Three different views of
Albert Hargraves'
damaged push-bike,
21 May 1935.

PLATE 40 Wool Camp or Clouds Hill army summer training camp with the old Bovington to Clouds Hill road as a footpath, *c.*1920.

PLATE 41 Front view of Lawrence's Brough Superior GW 2275 today showing the protruding components responsible for skid marks at the crash site.

PLATE 42 Damaged Brough GW 2275 and Hargraves' push-bike on lorry as exhibits for the Inquest of 21 May 1935.

PLATE 43 A. W. Lawrence and Colonel S. F. Newcombe arriving at the Inquest, 21 May 1935.

PLATE 44 Lawrence's coffin lifted into hearse, 21 May 1935.

PLATE 45 Winston Churchill, wife and group at Lawrence's funeral, 21 May 1935.

PLATE 46 Pallbearers, Augustus John with scarf and PC 26 Sidney Frank Loader saluting the coffin as it enters Moreton church, 21 May 1935.

PLATE 47 Procession from Moreton church to the graveside, 21 May 1935.

PLATE 48   Six pallbearers with coffin on wheeled bier followed by A. W. Lawrence and wife in procession to the graveside, 21 May 1935.

PLATE 49   At the graveside, 21 May 1935.

PLATE 50   Lawrence's last resting place.

PLATE 51   Ernest Frank Catchpole just before attending the Inquest, 21 May 1935.

PLATE 52   Frank Fletcher with Albert Hargraves at the time of the Inquest, 21 May 1935.

PLATE 53   Albert Hargraves at the time of the Inquest, 21 May 1935.

PLATES 54A AND B   Two views of Clouds Hill music room in late 1935.

PLATES 55A AND B Two views of Clouds Hill book room, late 1935.

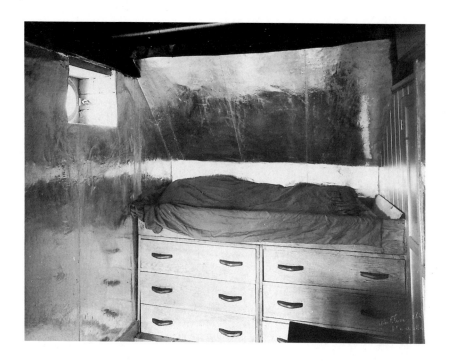

PLATE 56 Clouds Hill bunkroom (smaller upstairs room), late 1935.

PLATE 57 Clouds Hill, showing the pivoting western window in the book room which Lawrence had fitted in September 1932.

PLATES 58A AND B
Two views of Clouds
Hill bathroom in late
1935.

PLATE 59 Fred Way with his grandson Anthony Franklin at Clouds Hill in 1937.

PLATE 60 Lawrence's Jedda doors fitted as the north entrance to his study in the water tank building erected in Knowles' garden in spring 1934.

PLATES 61A AND B   Two views of Clouds Hill water tank building incorporating Lawrence's study, May 1935.

PLATE 62   Clouds Hill — Lawrence's carved lintel over the front door, late 1935.

The normal churchyard surrounding the church was full and in 1930 a new annexe had been added some 400 yards away in a fresh field on the edge of Moreton village. The procession eventually arrived at the new cemetery where Lawrence's last resting place was lined with evergreen. The grave was next to two others – two old friends, Arthur Knowles aged 49 who died on 1 April 1931 and Henrietta Knowles who recently passed away on 20 November 1934, aged 52 – another Clouds Hill in a Dorset meadow.

Already inside the coffin with Lawrence was some grass sent from Akaba.[32] As the coffin was lowered and dust sprinkled on it the pathetic figure of Pat Knowles, the unashamedly tearful Winston Churchill, the commanding presence of Augustus John with other friends, and hundreds of people, sang the Lord's Prayer (see Plate 49). Seigfried Sassoon recalled, *"(As I stood by T. E. Lawrence's open grave, a man tried to photograph the coffin. I knocked the camera out of his hand, God forgive me!)"*[33]

As the gravediggers filled in the hole with earth a little girl ran forward and threw in a small bunch of violets.

Immediately after the funeral the nasty and greedy side of mankind emerged. Hordes of reporters and photographers descended on the Post Office in nearby Dorchester, where, in a caravan parked outside, photographs were developed of the proceedings. These appeared for sale the next day Wednesday, 22 May (see Plate 50). Also various bits and pieces went missing from the graveside, plundered by souvenir hunters.[34]

The local squire, Henry Rupert Etherstonhaugh Frampton (1862–1955), distantly related to Lawrence, entertained guests at his nearby home, Moreton House, opposite the grave.

Arthur Russell, one of the pallbearers, recalled many years later (1988) *"I don't know how I came to be chosen. Even now I don't know how I got through it. Normally things like that don't affect me. I couldn't go to the gathering afterwards."*[35]

15

Crash Witness –
Corporal E. F. Catchpole

Although the hospital issued short bulletins of Lawrence's condition from the late afternoon of Tuesday 14 May, no official statement from a witness, with permission of the authorities, was allowed until Frank Fletcher gave his interview to newspaper reporters on Saturday, 18 May. He had volunteered an unofficial interview to the local *Dorset Daily Echo* on Wednesday, 15 May, which is the first really lengthy account available.

As soon as the news of Lawrence's accident became known, swarms of reporters descended on Bovington. It is obvious that they carried out their usual sleuthing and interviewing of army and civilian personnel directly involved with the crash.

Before any communique concerning the accident was issued most of the details were common knowledge.

Take the *Oxford Mail* reporter who penned the following on the evening of Tuesday, 14 May, *"The accident occurred about midday yesterday while Lawrence was returning after a visit to the camp, to his home at Clouds Hill, about a mile to the north of the camp.*

He was riding a powerful motor-cycle and was thrown heavily. After the accident he was picked up by the driver of a lorry and taken to the military hospital. Albert Hargreaves, aged 14 (employed by a Bovington firm of butchers, for whom he started work three weeks ago), with whom Mr. Shaw collided, is also in hospital, suffering from concussion.

Lawrence, it is understood, made a supreme effort to avert the collision and only just failed to do so."[1]

Having come to the conclusion that the crash, like the official coroner's report, was due to accidental circumstances, let us look at the contemporary and later statements provided by the known and unknown witnesses. Statements are recorded in their entirety with final comments added separately. In our view contemporary reports are always the best evidence as later statements tend to become less accurate as the time gap increases.

Although copies of the statements of three official witnesses, signed after the inquest, have been used, the best unbiased and first-hand statements needed for our investigation are those produced by provincial and national newspapers. For our case the *Daily Telegraph* reporter, who was present at the inquiry, provided the most accurate information.

The first official hint of a motorcar at the scene of the accident occurred on Saturday, 18 May, when A. W. Lawrence let it slip to a *Daily Mail* reporter.

"'*A vanished motorist who was seen at the spot where Mr Shaw crashed into the two boy cyclists is being sought.*

The car was seen travelling towards Mr Shaw, who was just about to pass the cyclists on his motorcycle.' I was told today. Apparently, he swerved to avoid the car, and he wrenched his machine into the banking to minimise the impact with the cyclists."[2]

(A) *Daily Telegraph* inquest report published on Wednesday, 22 May

"*Cpl Ernest Catchpole* [see Plate 51], *of the Royal Army Ordnance Corps, stationed at Tidworth, who was on the camping ground* [east of the accident spot] *about 100 yards from the road at Clouds Hill on May 13, said that when he heard Shaw's motor-cycle coming from Bovington Camp he estimated the speed at between 50 and 60 miles an hour.*

Asked by the coroner if he saw any other vehicle, he said, 'The motor-cycle passed a black car when it was about level with the camp. The car, which was a private one, was going in the opposite direction, and the motor-cycle got past it all right.

Then I saw the motor-cycle swerve across the road to avoid two pedal cyclists coming from Bovington. It swerved immediately after it had passed the car. The next thing I heard was a crash. I saw the bike twisting and turning over and over along the road.'

The coroner: Did you see anything of the driver? – No, sir.

Asked if the motor-cycle appeared to be dragging the rider along. Cpl Catchpole replied, 'I cannot swear that the driver was then on the motor-cycle.'

Witness said that he ran to the scene of the accident and found the motor-cyclist lying on the right side of the road.

'His face was covered with blood, which I tried to wipe away with hand-

kerchiefs,' he added. 'I sent to the camp [summer camp on east side of road] for a stretcher. Then an Army Service Corps lorry came along, and I stopped the driver and asked him to take the motor-cyclist to hospital.'

The coroner: Did you see anything of the pedal cyclists? – One of them was lying some distance down the road.

You did not actually see the accident happen? – No, sir.

Cpl. Catchpole was then questioned by Inspector Drake, of the Dorset Constabulary, who asked, 'You cannot describe this car except that it was a black, private one?' Witness replied, 'No, sir.'

The Inspector: Can you estimate its speed? – It was not going very fast.

Did you see Mr. Shaw pass this private car? – Yes.

How far after he passed this private car did the collision take place? – Fifteen to twenty feet.

Inspector Drake: You are quite sure about this distance? – Yes . . .

The coroner: Did you notice whether the pedal cyclists were riding behind each other or abreast? – I could not say.

Was there sufficient room for the motor-cyclist to pass between the car and the pedal cyclists? – There would have been if the motorcyclist had not been going at such a speed . . .

Mr. G. D. Ridge (for Albert Hargreaves, one of the cyclists), asked Catchpole, 'Did you actually see the pedal cyclists before the crash?' – 'No,' was the reply.

Mr. [A. W.] Lawrence [Shaw's brother] asked whether it would have been possible for the motor-cyclist to see the cyclists before passing the car. Catchpole replied that it would have been possible if he were on the right side of the road. The road was straight.

Mr. Lawrence: I should like to ask you whether the car was on its proper side? – It was . . . .

Inspector Drake said in consequence of receiving a statement about a motor-car being on the road at the time, inquiries had been made in the district of a number of people. No other person than Cpl. Catchpole could say that they saw a car, and the Lieutenant in charge of the Camp could not say he saw a car . . . .

Catchpole was recalled, and the coroner asked: 'You have heard the evidence of these two boys that they saw no vehicle pass them on the road. Is it possible you were mistaken?'

The Corporal: No, sir.

Witness said that he saw the car when he was alone. It was a black four-seater saloon.

The Coroner: How far away were you at the time? – About 100 yards. I could not see how many people were in it. It was going about 30 miles an hour.

122

Cpl. Catchpole added: 'I actually saw the motor-cycle swerve after it passed the car.'"[3]

(B) 21 May 1935

Official Deposition taken at the inquest on view of the body of T. E. Shaw. Signed Ernest Catchpole. Corporal No 7581979 Ernest Catchpole.

"R.A.O.C. stationed at Tidworth states: –

At about 11.20 am on May 13th 1935, I was at Clouds Hill Camping Ground and about 100 yards from the road.

I heard the noise of a motor cycle coming from the direction of Bovington Camp. I saw the motor cycle which was going between 50 and 60 miles per hour.

Just before the motor cycle got level with the Camp it passed a black car – it was a private car and the motor cycle passed that safely. I then saw the motor cyclist swerve across the road to avoid two pedal cyclists going in the same direction. The motor cyclist swerved immediately after he passed the car which was going in the opposite direction.

I then heard a crash and saw the motor cycle twisting and turning over and over along the road.

I immediately went to the road and called for help.

I found the motor cyclist on the right side of the road – his face covered in blood and I sent to the camp for a stretcher.

An army lorry came along and I asked them to take the injured persons to Hospital which they did.

One of the pedal cyclists was lying some distance down the road on the left side.

I did not actually see the accident happen.

Cross-examined

By the Police: *The car was not going very fast. I actually saw the deceased pass the car.*

I should say the collision occurred about 15 to 20 feet after the motor cyclist passed the car.

By the Jury: *I do not know whether the pedal cyclists were riding one behind the other or abreast.*

There would have been sufficient room for the motor cyclist to pass between the car and the pedal cyclists if the motor cyclist had not been going at such a speed.

By Mr Ridge: *I did not see the pedal cyclists before the crash.*

By Mr Lawrence: *The car was on the proper side of the road.*"[4]

Conclusion: It seems that Catchpole did not give any earlier statement other than his co-operation as a witness at the inquest.

Frank Catchpole was attached to the Royal Ordnance Army Corps (RAOC) stationed at Section 2 at Tidworth on Salisbury Plain. Later he rose to the rank of Staff Sergeant and through mysterious circumstances shot himself in his NCO's quarters in Egypt,[5] presumably in Cairo, on 10 July 1940. He is buried in Plot P, Grave 236 in Cairo War Memorial Cemetery, Egypt.[6]

As explained in chapter 12, major parts of Catchpoles's statement are open to question. The authors have discounted the Brough's speed of 50–60 m.p.h. just prior to the crash, as it was only travelling at 30–35 m.p.h. In our view, and in light of this major discrepancy, the black car must be eliminated.

It is highly questionable that Catchpole observed, in detail, the whole chronological sequence of the crash, albeit that he adamantly states, possibly through convenience, that he did not view the crash itself.

16

Crash Witness – Frank Fletcher

(A)   15 May 1935

Frank Fletcher (see Plate 52) told the reporter of the *Dorset Daily Echo* on Wednesday, 15 May, that he and Albert Hargraves were cycling to visit a bird's nest at Warwick's Close [Waddock Cross], two miles from Bovington.

"'We were riding in single file. I was leading. I heard a motorcycle coming from behind and then I heard a crash. Bertie's cycle hit mine and I fell off. When I looked up I saw Bertie lying in the road. The motor cycle had skidded on the other side, and the man who had gone over the handle bars had landed with his feet about 5 yards in front of the motor cycle which was about 5 yards ahead of where I fell. I got up and went to Bertie to see if he was all right. He gave me his butcher's book. I found three pence on the road. I asked Bertie if that was his money but he never answered. He seemed to go to sleep. I waited a minute or two, being afraid to go to the man, because his face was covered with blood. Then a man came up on a cycle and asked me to get the ambulance. But before I could go some soldiers came and he went to get it himself. A lorry came up. The men got two stretchers from some camp at the roadside [Clouds Hill summer camp] and the injured man and Bertie were put on them and taken into the lorry.'

The boy said that there was no motor car or other vehicle on the road at the time. 'I heard the noise of the motorcycle and then the crash. I did not hear any sound as if possibly a tyre had burst . . . . '

The day after the accident military and civil police called on the father and told him that on no account was the boy to be interviewed by anyone without authority."[1]

(B)   An interview given to a newspaper reporter on 18 May 1935

"Fletcher told me that there was no one else within several hundred yards when the collision occurred. With Hargreaves he was cycling along the road leading past Shaw's cottage at Cloud's Hill, Moreton. They were on a bird-nesting expedition.

'We had gone about half-way towards Mr. Shaw's house,' he said, 'and were half a mile from the camp [Bovington Camp], when I heard a motor-cycle coming up from behind. Albert and I were in single file, myself in front.

The next thing I knew was that there had been a crash. Albert's cycle hit against mine and I was knocked to the ground. At the same time, the motor-cyclist [should be motorcycle] skidded past and fell on the road in front of me. The rider went head over heels over the handle-bars. When I looked up I saw that he had landed five yards ahead of his cycle, with his feet pointing in the direction to which he was going.

I got up and went over to Albert to ask if he was all right. Soon after he had answered me he fell unconscious. I was afraid to go over to the motor-cyclist, for his face was covered with blood. I did not know until afterwards that he was Mr. Shaw.

Soon afterwards a man came up on a bicycle. A few minutes later some soldiers who had been taking down tents a short distance away and who had heard the crash also arrived.

The man, after looking at Mr. Shaw, went off to fetch the ambulance, but before he could get there an Army lorry came along. The soldiers fetched two . . . [rest missing]'."[2]

(C)   Interview also given on 18 May

"A first hand account of the accident was given today [18 May] by 14-year-old Frank Fletcher, who told how the crash occurred while he and Albert Hargreaves, another boy (who is still in hospital), were cycling on their way to visit a bird's nest at Warwick's Cross, 2 miles from the camp.

'We were riding in single file,' he said, 'I was leading. I heard a motor cycle from behind and then I heard a crash. Bertie's cycle hit mine and I fell off.

When I looked up I saw Bertie lying in the road. The motor-cycle had skidded on the other side and the man, who had gone over the handlebars, had landed with his feet about five yards in front of the motor-cycle, which was about five yards ahead of where I fell.'

The boy said there was no motor-car or other vehicle on the road at the time.

'I heard the noise of the motor-cycle,' he said, 'and then came the crash. I did not hear any sounds as if possibly a tyre had burst.'"[3]

(D) Inquisition No 160 of the inquest signed by Fletcher 21 May 1935

"Frank Fletcher states; – I live at 50 Elles Road, Bovington Camp, and I am 14 years old.

On 13th May 1935 at about 11.20 a.m. I was riding a pedal bicycle from Bovington Camp towards Clouds Hill and Albert Hargraves was with me.

I was riding in front and Hargraves was riding at the back.

I was riding on the left of the road.

When opposite Clouds Hill Camp I heard a motorcycle coming up from behind – I then heard a crash and Bert's bicycle fell on top of me and knocked me off my bicycle. I got up and saw Mr Lawrence go over the handlebars of the motorcycle and fall about 5 yards in front.

I went to Bert who gave me his butcher's book and I saw 3 pennies lying on the road. He then seemed to fall asleep.

I saw a lot of men running over from the tents.

Cross examined by the Police:

There were no cars on the road then.

I did not pass a car from the time I left Bovington Camp and the accident.

Cross examined by the Jury:

We did not leave the road at all.

Cross examined by Mr Ridge:

I was riding close to the left hand side – between one and two yards.

Cross examined by Mr Lawrence:

When the crash occurred the other boy was not at my side.

I do not know what part of the road the motor cyclist was on at the time of the accident.

After Bert's bicycle struck me I looked up and saw the motor cycle about five yards in front in the direction in which I was going and the rider going over the handle bars.

We had been riding one behind the other for about 100 yards."[4]

(E)   An exact account recorded at the inquest by the
***Daily Telegraph* reporter on 22 May 1935**

*"Frank Fletcher, Elles Road, Bovington Camp, a 14-year-old boy cyclist,
who was riding with Albert Hargreaves, said that Hargreaves was cycling
behind him. They were on the left of the road, and opposite Clouds Hill
[summer camp] he heard a motor-cycle coming from behind.*

*'I heard a crash, and Bert's bicycle fell on top of me,' he said, 'I was
knocked off. I got up and saw Mr. Lawrence' – that was how he described
the dead man – 'go over his handlebars.'*

*The Coroner: Was the motor-cycle still careering about the road?
– No.*

*Fletcher added that he went to his companion and saw three pennies on
the road by him. He asked if the money were his, but Hargreaves 'seemed
to fall asleep.'*

Fletcher said that he did not see a motorcar on the road.

The Coroner: You are quite clear on this point? – Yes.

No car passed you going in the other direction? – No.

*A juryman, who said, 'It seems a funny thing how the car was not
seen,' suggested that the boys might have left the road and ridden for a
way across the common. When the coroner asked if they had left the road,
Fletcher answered, 'We did not leave it at all* [This phrase 'at all', a
personal trait of Fletchers, was constantly used in the author's 1991
interview with him – another reason to accept this inquest account
as authentic and probably taken down in shorthand.] *from the time
we left Bovington Camp.'*

*Mr. A. W. Lawrence . . . said, 'We are told the second boy was riding
behind. Is there any reason to suppose he was still behind when the
accident happened, or had he swerved to the side?'*

The boy replied, 'I did not look behind, but he was not at my side.'

*Mr. Lawrence's next question was whether the boy knew where the
motor-cycle was at the time of the accident, whether it was still on the
left of the road or if it had swerved. The boy said he did not know.*

*. . . the coroner asked the boy, 'Whose bicycle fell on you?' The boy
replied, 'Bert's.'*

The Coroner: Did the motor-cycle come on top of you?

Fletcher: No.

*Mr. Lawrence said that he would like to ask Fletcher for further details
of how his brother went over the handlebars.*

*Fletcher, in reply to questions by the coroner, said: 'After Bert's bicycle
hit me I looked up and saw the rider of the motor-cycle going over the
handle-bars. He was about five yards past me.'*

Mr. Lawrence: What happened to the other bike? — It fell on top of me.

It was not pushed forward much? — No.

Was your bicycle much damaged? — Only the pedal and mudguard.

Mr. Lawrence asked how long the two boys had been riding one behind the other.

Fletcher: Not very long — about 100 yards.

What happened in that 100 yards to make you change? — I overtook him.

The Coroner: For any particular reason? — No. [We infer that although they were in single file for the last 100 yards, they changed order, i.e. Fletcher from behind moved and changed positions to the front.]

. . . The coroner recalled Frank Fletcher to ask him if, as his friend had said, it was the sound of the motor-cycle that caused them to go one behind the other.

'I did not hear it myself until just before the crash,' said Fletcher, who added that he went ahead of his companion but could give no particular reason for having done so."[5]

(F) Interview given to Harry Broughton in 1960s

"Frank Fletcher concerned in the accident told me, 'The idea did not come from me. There was not a black car on the road in front of us or behind us. The road was clear. Bert and I would have seen it if there had been one.'

. . . After seeing the film 'Lawrence of Arabia' Frank Fletcher's comment was, 'In the film the two errand boys on bikes were wrong. We were not facing him when he came up the road. I only wish we had been for he might still be living today.'"[6]

(G) Interview to the *Bournemouth Evening Echo* in early 1985

"The road wasn't like it is now at that time. They've widened it since then, added a lot to each side —

Then you've got the straight bit of road first of all and then it dipped down a bend [dip (a), p. 105] a wee bit more then up again.

The second dip [dip (b)] we were above that — a few yards along, he wouldn't have seen us like.

When he came up he hit my mate's bike. But as for the black car that they talk about there was definitely no black car around at all.

My mate heard the motorbike coming up behind us. We were riding side by side at the time then I moved in.

And then we only went along 20 yards or so when – wooff it hit the back of my mate's bike and then that hit mine, though there was no damage to mine and I went over to one side. The motorbike itself skidded along the road – I thought it was going to explode – I straightened myself up and looked around I saw my mate unconscious. Then I looked across the road. I saw Mr Lawrence go over the handlebars and the bike skid across the road.

It wasn't very wide a road, more like a track then, and he was sitting up against a tree facing Bovington Camp. So I went across to him and saw this blood on his face.

The next thing I knew that the soldiers came and an ambulance, which must have come from the camp [tented summer camp] *. . . But* [Bert] *was definitely behind me – because he was the one that told me to get to the side of the road in front of me."*[7]

(H)   Extracts from an interview between Frank Fletcher and the authors Paul J. Marriott and Yvonne Argent on Tuesday, 13 August 1991

"So as you go along a bit more there's two more hills, one down and one up, and then you get your flat road again.

Well, we [Hargraves and Fletcher] *must have been on the second hill about 150 yards along the road at the time. When the, um, when we heard this motorbike come along. Like Bertie said we had better get inside the road. So we must have, as he* [Lawrence on his Brough] *was coming up the road. He must have seen us too late. That's the way I looked at it. And then, uh, he didn't have time to pull out.*

Well the next thing I knew, I heard Bertie's bike go down with a wallop at it [Brough] *hit the back wheel, like you know, and then, uh, when I looked round, Bert was laying flat on the road. And this old motorbike was skimming along the road., sparks all flying from it. And they, ah, the next thing, I went over to Bertie first of all and asked him if he was alright. I picked up his butcher's book and I went over to Lawrence of Arabia, and, uh, when I go there he was facing Bovington Camp way. I weren't there two minutes when these people, the soldiers, were in a camp on the hill at the time. They were in tents, like you know. Well they came over and, um, after that about two minutes after this an ambulance must have come from the camp, cos they picked him up, and picked my mate up. Then they took them off to Bovington Hospital.*

They all went away and left me on my own.

So, um, I had to look around like you know, saw a few orders [Bert's parcel orders] *on the ground, and all that , and I couldn't ride the bike or nothing a'tall and the wheel was smashed – I picked them up* [orders] *and put them in the basket* [on Bert's bike] *and got on my own bike and went home . . .*

PJM: . . . I have . . . , your original statement, at the inquest.

And, it's very interesting in as much that, . . . it says that you and Bert were going bird's nesting at Waddock's Cross.

FF: No.

PJM: That's what it says . . . it says that you were in single file.

FF: That's right . . .

PJM: Where the summer bell tents are, you heard a motorbike.

FF: Hmm. Hmm.

PJM: And then you hear the crash, when the motorbike hits Bert's back wheel.

FF: That's right.

PJM: . . . then Bert's bike hit yours and you came off.

FF: I went over one side. Yea.

PJM: And when you saw the motorbike skidding along the road. Now had Lawrence come off before the side-skidding or was he sort of still hanging on?

FF: No. No, no, no, no. He went over his handlebars before the bike went along there. . . . Over like that, there, and then the bike skidded straight along the road. That's how I found him sitting up against the tree with the blood coming down his face.

PJM: . . . which way did the bike skid? Do you remember which way the wheels went forward?

FF: Yes, er, the wheels was out towards the road and the saddle was in towards the kerb.

PJM: And the saddle was towards the left.

FF: Hmm, hmm . . .

[PJM realizes that the recording tape had ended and thinks that he has lost some of the conversation. Inserts a new cassette and requests a repeat.]

. . .

PJM: Right. According to the original signed statement at the inquest, you stated that you were going with Bertie bird's nesting to Waddock's Cross, whereas later on you said you were just going on a butcher's errand.

FF: I don't know where this bird's nesting comes from! . . . We were only just trying to deliver his errands that was all, . . . we had to turn left at Clouds Hill. . . . But I didn't know what address we had to go to, 'cos, he had the addresses on the parcels, like you know, . . . meat parcels . . . .

PJM: Now you heard the motorbike or was it in fact that Bertie told you there was a motorbike?

FF: Bert told me there was a motorbike.

PJM: So you never heard it then?

FF: We heard it. But Bert told me to get inside the road in front. Because we were riding like that (indicates with arms riding abreast). . . . Then he told me to get to the side. Which I did do. . . . He [Bert's push-bike] hit mine a little bit and I went over . . . .

PJM: . . . And as you were falling over, Lawrence came off the . . .

FF: He went in front a bit and I saw him go over, then the bike came to him and skidded like that there (demonstrates side skidding).

PJM: It didn't actually go over.

FF: No, the bike fell over afterwards.

PJM: Did it twist?

FF: No. It just went straight along. Straight across.

PJM: And it went with its wheels facing the same side as the camp.

FF: That's right. And the handlebars were on my side . . . .

PJM: . . . . So then you went over to Bert . . . ..He was lying in the road. He gave you his butcher's book, he said.

FF: Ah, no, no butcher's book. . . . I picked the butcher's book up myself. . . . Yea. . . . No pennies. (FF laughs).

PJM: No, but you mentioned three pennies, so that's fine. You said that was wrong.

FF: Hmm.

PJM: Then you went to speak to Bert. . . . And he seemed to go to sleep. You use that phrase all the time.

FF: That's right.

PJM: So he was obviously semi-conscious, then he went unconscious. And then you looked at Lawrence but you were scared 'cos you saw his blood and you didn't go to him. You say that's wrong, don't you?

FF: Yes. Wrong, yea.

PJM: And you actually say you went to him.

FF: I went to him, yea.

PJM: . . . Then there was a couple of minutes delay, and then these army chaps came onto the scene.

FF: That's right. From the camp, . . .

PJM: . . . and a chap on a bike appeared, that's what you say.

FF: No. . . . That's wrong.

PJM: So, was Catchpole amongst these guys?

FF: No. Catchpole was only out walking his dog. Not on the road a'tall, he was behind bushes at the time so I hear, with the dog. And he must have been looking through the bushes at the time when he hear the crash.

PJM: So he never actually came, as far as you know he never actually joined the soldiers. I mean it would have only taken him a couple of minutes to get there, wouldn't it!

FF: Yea.

PJM: But you wouldn't know him anyway!

FF: I wouldn't know him. No.

PJM: So he could have been there.

FF: He could have been there, yea.

PJM: But there was no dog there!

FF: No dog.

PJM: . . . OK. These guys came and they sent for an ambulance. Which presumably is the field ambulance which the camp used to have.

FF: From the camp, that's right.

PJM: From the summer camp we're talking about.

FF: Yea.

PJM: And then a lorry came along the road.

FF: No lorry.

PJM: No lorry. Soldiers went to the tents to get two stretchers.

FF: No, they took them out of the ambulance.

PJM: So the ambulance came, um, took the stretchers out of the ambulance. The two casualties went into the ambulance and then they went to Bovington Camp.

FF: That's right. . . . The way I remember it is because you remember them old box affairs ambulances at the time, that year. . . . It's one of those with a red thing on it. Instead of the stretchers they use now, they were just ordinary canvas stretchers.

PJM: Yes.

FF: With big poles, you know, they put them on them.

PJM: So they could actually pull the poles out of them.

FF: That's right. Yes, hmm.

PJM: Yes. . . . Do you remember, say near the crash sight on the left, there were some water towers . . . .

FF: I know every inch of them moors round there when we were kids, and I never noticed any water towers.

PJM: So there were no water towers.

FF: No. . . . You must remember, the road what they're on now, is much wider now.

PJM: What sort of road was it?

FF: It was a rough kind of road where the tanks used to go along. They used to go on the moors, like you know, then they used to cross this road on to the other moor. The roads were not very wide in them days 'cos of the trees, you see, on the right and on the left.

PJM: What sort of surface was the road? . . . I mean, you were laying on it.

FF: Yea, I know. (Both laugh) It was a kind of rough road like, you know. It was tar, a kind of tarry but was rough with the tracks of the tanks.

PJM: Was there any gravel, any chips?

FF: Oh yea, there was chips 'cos the tanks used to go along there and cross that road. . . . They still do now . . . .

PJM: . . . Did your father or you ever go back to the site of the accident?

FF: No. We didn't. No. We didn't go there a'tall . . . .

PJM: . . . What happened to your bike and Bert's bike, do you remember?

FF: Well, there weren't a scratch on my bike a'tall. Not a scratch. But Bert's bike, you saw it was . . .

PJM: We saw the squashed back wheel. And what ever happened to it? I mean . . .

FF: No idea what happened to it, 'cos I just left it there and went back on me own . . . it [Lawrence's blood] was coming from the top of his head all the way down through here (shows face).

PJM: On the right-hand side?

FF: He was sitting up against a tree with his legs out like that there facing Bovington Camp itself.

PJM: And the blood was coming on his right-hand side – you show me!

FF: Up here.

PJM: From the top.

FF: Yea. . . . All over his face.

PJM: . . . And was there anything else?

FF: No I didn't see anything else.

PJM: I mean when he skidded he must have cut his clothing, surely!

FF: I never noticed it. . . . All I know is this [blood] coming down here. I didn't look at his clothing, nothing a'tall.

PJM: No.

FF: No.

PJM: No there were no bits of motorbike over the place or anything?

FF: Only the markings of the pedals where it skidded along the road, that was all.

PJM: Oh! That's interesting, that. So there was a score mark?

FF: Yes.

PJM: *One or two score marks, were there?*

FF: *Yea, yea.*

PJM: *. . . I've got some maps here of the road. . . . That (shows photograph) might help you – that was taken a few days later – that's where the accident occurred. Unfortunately you can't see the dip behind there.*

FF: *No.*

PJM: *Do you remember these telegraph poles as a matter of interest? Can you see them?*

FF: *Yea, I can see them now. . . . Them telegraph poles was there alright. . . . But, um, they must have cleared this up all here, 'cos there's all bushes and bits of trees and what about along these, along here then. They must have kind of widened the road at the time. That's the way I look at it . . .*

(PJM gets FF to draw a map of the accident scene.)

. . .

FF: *And, ah, as he* [Lawrence on Brough] *came out of the dip and onto a straight road he couldn't possibly have seen us because the hill's that steeper you know. He must have come up and saw us too late along there. . . . And then Bertie's bike caught mine there. . . . We're on the side of the road.*

PJM: *It was mangled. Was it mangled with yours, or where did Bert's bike finish?*

FF: *No, his front wheel just touched my back wheel, that was all.*

PJM: *So they were very close.*

FF: *That's right. . . . He went over the bar* [handlebars] *there. . . . Straight across the road there and ended up against the tree there.*

PJM: *Right off the road.*

FF: *Hmm, hmm. . . . And his bike skidded along there with his wheels on the right-hand side and his saddle and bars on the left-hand side.*

PJM: *The bike was in the middle of the road or to the side?*

FF: *Yea. On the left-hand side. Now, there was nobody around a'tall, only, when these, you know, tent people.*

PJM: *Soldiers from the camp.*

FF: *That's right. Well they came across to Lawrence there – I'll put an 'L' there* [see Map 8] *. . . . And, uh, the um, ambulance must have come from the camp 'cos it came very quick . . . .*

PJM: *The ambulance was on the side, was it?*

FF: *Yea. Pulled in the side here. And, ah, they picked up Mr Lawrence there and, uh, Bertie was, um, let me see, by, near his bike here.*

PJM: *. . . Can you put an 'A' there Mr Fletcher. Just put a 'A' for ambulance then I shall know what that is for, you see. . . . Now your push-bike is here 'FF push-bike'. Alright!*

135

FF: Yea. . . . Bertie's [bike] *is just at the back.*

PJM: *And Bert is going to be back here. On the side of the road was he?*

FF: *He was over this side of the road. . . . He was halfway between.*

PJM: *. . . The centre . . .*

FF: *From the road. Yea.*

PJM: *Opposite his bike. So there's 'Bert Hargraves'. He's there, OK. According to you Lawrence is over here. It's where he finished up that I'm interested in. The tree is what about here?*

FF: *Yea.*

PJM: *He's a bit further on.*

FF: *A bit further on up to here, yes . . . .*

PJM: *His motorbike has gone further on. Is it in the middle or on the side?*

FF: *On the side.*

PJM: *But its totally in the road, is it?*

FF: *Yea.*

PJM: *He's there, and the handlebars are there. So that's Lawrence's bike. The ambulance comes and it ends up between Bertie and Lawrence. And the ambulance is parked there.*

FF: *That's right. . . . Yea:*

PJM: *Is it possible that Lawrence could have fallen against a telegraph pole?*

FF: *There weren't a telegraph pole, a'tall. There was just an ordinary tree. A fir tree.*

PJM: *But there were telegraph poles.*

FF: *There were a couple along there.*

PJM: *Remember you saw them.*

FF: *Hmm. They were on the left-hand side, you see, the poles were, not on the right.*

PJM: *No, the poles were on the right. Let me show you a minute.*

FF: *No, just a tree and bushes on the right-hand side.*

PJM: *Let me show you this photograph. . . . Alright. Now obviously Lawrence ended up on a tree somewhere. There's the telegraph poles, look how close they are to the side of the road. That's the right-hand side of the road – that's where the camp is.*

FF: *They must have been . . . I've got some idea they must have been put there afterwards, because . . .*

PJM: *No. This was taken two days afterwards.*

FF: *No it couldn't be.*

PJM: *'Cos it appears in the newspaper. It's dated you see. Dated 23 May 1935. So that photograph's got to be taken on that day or before.*

FF: *We never noticed any of them . . .*
PJM: *Getting back to the black car. You never saw anything at all.*
FF: *Nothing.*
PJM: *Until you saw the ambulance.*
FF: *That's the only car we seen.*
PJM: *You saw nothing on the way from Bovington Camp?*
FF: *No. Not a thing. No.*
YA: *And a lorry didn't turn up to take the bikes away?*
PJM: *No lorry, army lorry?*
FF: *They left everything as it was.*
YA: *The motorbike and the cycle.*
FF: *That's right. I don't know what happened to the motorbike, or nothing a'tall. All I know I was left on my own. I got on my bike and went home . . .*
PJM: *Thank you Mr Fletcher that's excellent."*[8]

(I) Correspondence with Frank Fletcher 1991

"*I met Bertie out side of the shop* [Dodge and Son, butchers, Bovington Camp] *about 10 o'clock in the morning* [Monday 13 May], *we moved off about 10.15. There was no motorbike behind us on the way out at that time of the day.*[9]

It must have been about 10.50 a.m. and we did not stop for bird nesting, and we did not see a motor bike.[10]

If nothing else the mammoth collection of Frank Fletcher interviews and statements show the distortion and invention thirty or more years can play on the memory. The substitution of delivery meat parcels for bird's nesting at Waddock's Cross; the misplacement of the final position of the Brough on the western side of the road instead of the earlier eastern; the latter denial of the three pennies; the later absence of a man on a push-bike and the arrival of an army lorry; the more important change from being too scared to approach Lawrence to the later bravado act of going to him to find him crouched against a tree looking south. The only important consistency is the absence of the black car or vehicle.

It is a true lesson for all researchers – contemporary statements are the only serious important key to obtaining the truth.

Frank Fletcher lived at 50 Elles Road, Bovington Camp, in 1935. Later that year the family moved to Wareham. Frank then joined the army when 17 years old. He was till living in London in 1992.[11]

17

Crash Witness –
Albert Hargraves

(A) An exact account recorded at the inquest by the *Daily Telegraph* **reporter**

"Albert Hargreaves [should be Hargraves] [see Plate 53], *who said that he was 14 and was employed as a butcher's errand-boy, described how he was riding from the camp. As he and Fletcher were passing Crownhill Camp* [Clouds Hill summer camp] *he was four to five feet behind Fletcher on his own side. He heard a motor-cycle coming from behind him.*

The Coroner: Did a motor-car pass you at about this time? – No.

Did any vehicle of any sort pass you? – No.

What happened after you heard the noise of the motor-cycle? – I do not know. I do not remember anything afterwards. I did not know anything more until I found myself in hospital.

Do you not remember, giving Frank your butcher's book? – No.

The Foreman: Were these boys talking about anything to cause their attention to be distracted?

The coroner put the question to Hargreaves and he replied, 'No.'

Mr. Lawrence: How long had you been riding one behind the other? – About 10 minutes.

The Coroner: When you heard the motor-cycle what kind of noise was it making? – It sounded high-powered.

When you heard it did you change your position? – No. I did not look round. I was on the left, two or three feet from the verge. I do not remember anything. I do not even remember being thrown off my cycle.

Mr. Lawrence asked: 'What speed were you going' and Hargreaves replied, 'A normal pace.'

The Coroner: 'Had you both hands on the handlebars?' – Yes.

Mr. Lawrence: How does this bicycle fit you? – Is it the right size?
– Yes.

The Coroner said he thought that they had better see the bicycle. A police officer carried into the court a black delivery bicycle. Its rear wheel and mudguard were damaged.

Mr. Lawrence: 'May I suggest he gets on it?'

The Coroner: Yes, certainly.

Hargreaves then rose from the witness-chair and while a police officer and a civilian held the bicycle erect he mounted it. [The damaged bike remained in the area until about 1986 when it was buried in a dump just to the north of Lawrence's cottage.[1]]

The coroner said that it seemed rather too big, and that Hargreaves had to reach a little for the pedals.

Mr. Lawrence asked if there was any reason for the boys riding one behind the other, and the coroner put to Hargreaves the question: 'After riding abreast, why did you suddenly change positions?'

'Because of the noise of the motor-cycle,' was the boy's answer.

The coroner: I want you to be very careful. You tell me you had been riding in single file for about ten minutes, but did you hear the motor-cycle for as long as that?'

Hargreaves replied that they were riding slowly and were in single file for about 80 yards.

At the suggestion of Mr. Lawrence Hargreaves went outside the court room to indicate his ability to judge distance. When he returned the coroner said that he had estimated the distance from the court-room to a telegraph pole in a field outside as 80 yards. The coroner thought it would be agreed that the estimate was about right.

The boy, in answer to the coroner, said that he was sure about the distance they travelled single file, and he was not about to regain his position when the accident occurred. The road was very uneven at the sides, but was not uneven at the point where they were cycling."[2]

(B) Original statement signed after the inquest on 21 May 1935

"Albert Hargreaves states: –

I am 14 years of age and live at 56b Somme Rd, Bovington Camp. I am employed as an errand boy by Dodge & Co, Butchers, Bovington Camp.

On 13th May 1935 I was cycling from Bovington Camp to Warwick Cross, Tonerspuddle [Turnerspuddle] and Frank Fletcher was with me for company.

Opposite Clouds Hill Camp I was riding 4 or 5 feet behind Fletcher and on the left side of the road. I heard the sound of a motorcycle coming from behind.

No motor car passed me about this time nor traffic of any sort.

I do not remember any more until I found myself in Hospital.

Cross examined by the Jury: *We were not talking.*

Cross examined by Mr. A. W. Lawrence: *We had been riding one behind the other for about ten minutes.*

We were riding at a normal pace with both hands on the handlebars. The bicycle is the right size for me but I have to reach a little for the pedals.

We changed positions because of the noise of the motorcycle.

We had been riding single file for about 80 yards.

Cross examined by the Police: *When we left Bovington Camp we were riding abreast.*

Cross examined again by Mr. A. W. Lawrence: *I slowed up and got behind Frank, I did not wobble at all.*

The road was not uneven at the side where I was riding.

[Signed] *Albert Hargraves."*[3]

(C)   Interview between Albert Hargraves and Stewart Rigby in 1982 at his home in South Reddich, Stockport

"You don't go round telling people about it. Besides, I'm not that sort, . . . My father knew him because he used to serve him petrol at the camp.

But to me he was just a soldier. I did not know he was some great man. That particular day I was out with my friend Frank Fletcher. We were cycling up Tank Park Road, him in front and me behind.

It was a very narrow road and we could hear a motorbike coming up from behind. The next thing I remember was waking up in hospital with a lot of nurses and soldiers around me.

One of them said: 'You have had an accident with Lawrence of Arabia,' and I said, 'Who?'

It was well afterwards that I realised just how important he was. I was questioned a lot by the police. A lot of people, especially the Arabs, wanted to be sure that we had not been put up to it – you can understand that, but obviously we had not been put up to it . . . .

It must have been some crash. Apparently we both [Lawrence and Hargraves] went up in the air. I was in Wool Military Hospital for 11 days. I've got deep, brown gravel scars on my arms and back which have been with me ever since."[4]

(D) Interview with Mrs Agnes Hargraves, Albert's mother, in May 1966

She stated: *"Fletcher ran in to me and said Bert had been knocked down. I rushed off to the hospital with my hair in curlers. He was in there for 11 days. He had brown marks on his arms and back which will be with him for life."*[5]

The only notable conclusions here are the inconsistency and muddled explanations of the positions of the two boys on the bicycles, whether abreast or single file, and when or if they changed over. The first hearing of the Brough engine is also very contradictory.

That Hargraves could not recall any incident after the crash must be accepted.

Albert Hargraves was born in 1921, the son of Agnes and Albert Hargraves. His father served in the British Army for 38 years,[6] and in 1935 was a bandsman in the Tanks Corps at Bovington Camp with Fletcher's father, ending up as a sergeant.[7] He finally worked for the last 14 years in the Bovington workshop. He died in 1965.[8]

In 1935 the Hargraves family lived at 56b Somme Road, Bovington Camp. Young Albert took a job in late April 1935 as an errand boy with a local butcher, Dodge and Co at Bovington Camp.

After Lawrence's accident he was admitted to Bovington Military hospital suffering from shock and concussion. His parents were barred from visiting him until 15 May, even though he was stated as being 'comfortable'. On 20 May the hospital said he was 'making good progress'. Bert left hospital after 9 days (13–21 May) well enough to attend the inquest on 21 May.

He returned to Dodge and Co until called up for the Navy in 1939. After action in the Mediterranean Bert was discharged in 1945 as a leading seaman. The same year he married Tess. After various moves they finally settled down in Stockport in 1952 where he worked for a number of years with Ellis Jones, a local chemical company. Bert died in the 1980s after a long illness.[9]

18

Indirect Witnesses

John B. Connolly

John B. Connolly was a young soldier in the Tank Regiment based at Bovington in 1935. In early May he suffered a painful knee injury and had made several visits to the military hospital for treatment.

Connolly was recently interviewed by Bob Hunt, who published the following account.

"The approach to midday [13 May 1935] *found him* [Connolly] *seated waiting to have a fresh dressing put on his knee. As he waited someone ran in and said to the orderly, or to the officer that there had been a serious accident just up the road involving several persons* [see chapter 12, p. 107]. *As he was the only spare 'body' available he was detailed there and then to go along to help out as extra hands could be needed.*

In the event, he said, all that he was called upon to do was to hold the door of the lorry open. He described the vehicle as being soft-sided but with doors at the rear.

He said that the piece of road near where the crash accident took place had been resurfaced by the usual method at the time, namely, sprayed with tar and stones simply thrown on the top.

*Connolly described the area of the accident as a death trap. He also said that he hadn't realised who the injured man was. 'None of us knew,' he said, 'And even afterwards they didn't bother to ask anyone. There were dozens of blokes about, but it was just as if no one **wanted** to know what had happened.'*

Connolly said that the officer in charge of the ambulance was a Captain [Geoffrey] *Anderton, a regular soldier of about 40 years of age. Anderton, says Connolly, carried out a thorough check of the injured man before having him moved onto a stretcher and into the ambulance.*

Connolly observed skin and blood on the road 'for several yards' and that 'When they arrived the man was unconscious' and also 'that there were several soldiers standing around'.

Connolly also noticed that the injured man had a 'terrible injury with the brain exposed.' When they got back to the hospital Connolly followed the stretcher bearers and saw Captain [Charles Phillip] *Allen lift the edge of the blanket to look at the injury. Captain Allen shook his head as if to say that there was little or no hope.*

Catchpole and the black car were mentioned to Connolly . . . he became slightly vexed. 'All this talk of black cars annoys me,' he said, 'All cars in those days were black. It would have been odd to see one that wasn't black!'"

In a recent interview with Connolly, Hunt asked him about the presence of an army lorry at the accident site. *"He replied indignantly 'well an army ambulance is an army lorry !'"*

The standard 1935 British military ambulance was the Morris Commercial 30 cwt 6 × 4, which had double rear doors and wooden frame sides with stretch canvas.[1]

Conclusion: Although this recent report evolves after half a century, the authors cannot find any fault with it. It has therefore been incorporated in the accident recreation.

Joan Hughes

Mrs Joan Hughes (née Way), now deceased, was the younger daughter of Charlie Way. Lawrence knew the family well as they used to live in a caravan north-west of Clouds Hill.

In an interview with Roland Hammersley in February 1986, Joan Hughes stated that she (then 15 years old) arrived on the scene of Lawrence's accident just after the crash.

"Mrs Joan Hughes, tells me that on the day of the accident involving T. E. Lawrence, and the two boys Hargreaves and Fletcher (13/5/1935), she was riding/pushing her bicycle from her home at Clouds Hill, towards Bovington village. [Her sisters were bathing in one of the tanks of the three water towers on the west side of the road opposite Clouds Hill summer camp.] *She had to get off the bicycle several times as one tyre had punctured, she tried to maintain the air pressure by using the hand pump without success. As she walked, she came in sight of the three water towers on her right* [west] *with the bell tents, etc, on her left* [east] *at Wool Camp* [Clouds Hill summer camp]. *Just before the water towers were a number of soldiers in the road, there was a lorry and an Army Ambulance which looked like the one that usually stood by the*

Medical Tent at Wool Camp. A motorcycle was lying in the road and two cycles, one of which was a delivery cycle from Bovington village.

She stood by the crowd of soldiers as the ambulance door was closed. It was driven off followed by the lorry. A soldier by her said, 'The poor sod, if it hadn't been for those water butts he would have missed that tree.' The soldier added that he saw it happen.

At no time from leaving her home at Clouds Hill did any vehicle, car or otherwise pass her in either direction.

A sketch – not to scale [see Map 9] – is attached of how she remembers the accident site.

Feb. 1986
R. H. Bovington."[2]

Conclusion: A recollection fifty years old presents difficulty in deciphering fact from fiction – the modern belief that Lawrence ended up by a tree on the western side of the road still prevails.

Lyall Chapman

Lyall Chapman was a teenager and on the day of the accident was working with Mr O'Conner, a local lorry driver. The army contracted them to *"clear the gear"* from an army training camp at Clouds Hill summer camp.[3]

Michael Yardley in his book *Backing into the Limelight* states, *"While L. C. and Mr O'Conner were loading the lorry, they heard the crash and ran to the spot, arriving just after Catchpole. They saw an overturned motorbike on the side of the road . . . . a little way in front of the bike a man was lying in a pool of blood. L. C. recognized him and said, 'It's Lawrence.' O'Conner, noticing the blood pouring from the side of the victim's head, remarked, 'He's done for.' At this point Lawrence, who had appeared unconscious, opened his eyes and, looking directly upward towards L. C., O'Conner and Catchpole, brought up his hand and held out a finger as if to indicate the number one – then he lapsed back into unconsciousness."*[4]

Bob Hunt interviewed Joyce E. Knowles in his book *The Life and Times of Joyce E. Knowles*. She stated that Lyall Chapman was her cousin and records the following information.

"Lyall Chapman was a workman at Bovington working close to the road on the 13th May. He was aware of the Brough travelling from Clouds Hill to Bovington but did not look up from his work. Much later he heard the Brough return but again did not glance up until a loud noise from the

revving engine suddenly alerted his attention. Anticipating an accident Lyall Chapman and his working companion ran to the road. They found Lawrence laying on his back with his face a mask of blood which a soldier, corporal Catchpole, was attempting to wipe away.

'Why it's Mr Lawrence,' exclaimed Lyall Chapman. Whereupon Lawrence raised his eyes and attempted to focus on the speaker. He then smiled and raised one hand with pointed finger moving it unsteadily from side to side. Without uttering a word he relapsed into unconsciousness.'"

The authors accept that Chapman and O'Conner were in the vicinity of the accident spot and also that they raced to the scene and saw Lawrence. However it is highly unlikely that the remainder of the accident concerning finger theatricals ever occurred. Contemporary reports do **not** mention Lawrence crashing into a tree or regaining consciousness.

Margaret Montague

On 5 September 1985 the following letter was published in the *Bournemouth Evening Echo*.

"Sir – as I was clearing away some old Echoes *I saw an article about Lawrence of Arabia, and it stated: 'There was no car.'* [involved with Lawrence's accident – proposed by witness Cpl Catchpole]

I can assure you there definitely was a car, and it was a black one. It was a Hillman. The registration number was COW 41, and I know who was driving it.

The driver and Lawrence waved at each other as they passed.'

Margaret Montague.
Address supplied. Wimborne"[5]

Later she told a *Bournemouth Evening Echo* reporter that the driver was her late husband, Lionel.

"I know it has been a mystery – that's why I thought I would lay this one for good and all if I can.

I don't know whether he was on his way to, or coming back from, Bovington Camp, as he waved to Mr. Shaw. He had told me before that that bike would be the death of Mr. Shaw. It was an awful looking thing, sinister looking.

My husband and he were quite friendly, they used to talk to each other.

When my husband got back to the garage at Sandford he spoke to Mr.

Hope and they had just heard about the accident. My husband said: 'I don't think so – because I've just waved to him.' It must have happened seconds after my husband waved to him.

My husband always said that Mr. Shaw swerved to avoid that butcher's boy, . . .

It was a treacherous bit of road in those days." [6]

Interview between Margaret Montague and Andrew Simpson in November 1985.

"When the present author of this article talked with Mrs Montague she stated that she couldn't recall anything in detail as it was over 50 years ago. Surely if Shaw had passed the black Hillman before the accident he would have raised his right hand in salute to a car that would have been passing him on the right side.

When Lionel Montague arrived in Sandford Garage, north of Wareham, having passed through Wareham, Mr. Douglas Hope, the then owner of the garage, or one of his employees, told Montague that Lawrence had had an accident. Montague replied (in the vein of) he didn't believe it as he had just waved to him on the road near Clouds Hill. Mr Montague died 10 years ago [1975], and Mrs Montague has no photograph of him. Mr. Hope has also died and Mrs Montague does not believe there is anyone left alive who knew her husband. She wrote to the Bournemouth Evening Echo *and another publication to try and dispel the myth about the black car once and for all. The car, she says was a black Hillman 10. The D.V.L.C. computer has no record of a registration COW 41 at any time. However the present owner of the Sandford Garage, Mrs Millington confirms that she bought the property from Mr Douglas Hope. An old resident remembers him as a former Shell salesman from Devon."* [7]

Conclusion: The authors are convinced that no black car, or any other vehicle was involved in the accident and since Lionel Montague, friendly with Lawrence, did not respond to A. W. Lawrence's plea for any motorcar driver at the scene of the accident to come forward, printed in the *Daily Mail* of 18 May, it is another example of the modern embellishment of the 'black car myth'.

Frank Gordon

Interview between Frank Gordon and Andrew Simpson on 25 May 1985

Frank Gordon was present at Bovington Camp's main gate entrance when Lawrence left the *Red Garage* on his Brough.

"And the last thing he done was, pulling his driving glove back over his watch, and he said, 'Well, folks, I want to be in the smoke [London] *for one o'clock if I can and I must get a move on because I want to change first.'*

With that he kicked his bike in [gear] *and roared off.*

. . . One of my drivers came into me and said, 'Hey, do you know that old Lawrence had met it?' I said 'Don't be such a B.F.' . . . 'Look,' I said, 'bloody rot, he's just been talking to me, man. What are you talking about?'

. . . I said, 'I know, I just said we were talking to him not a couple of minutes ago outside the gates [main camp entrance] *sort of business.'*

. . . I mean that ain't the old tarmac road that used to be laid there, anything dug in there'd always leave a mark there. And there was a mark in the road there sort of, . . . that shape (indicates a 'U' shape). Over on the, er . . . right hand there just a bit further was a Casualty Clearing Station, 'cause there was troops doing manoeuvres on the moors. An' they got what they call the Casualty Clearing Station that if there was any accidents say, they were brought there before they was transferred to hospital. First, one of the soldiers outside that saw the accident happen and, then, of course, they rushed across there, found he was injured, took him straight into hospital.

A.S.: So it was one of the soldiers that actually saw him?

Oh yes, one of the soldiers there. . . . All we know was they were responsible, that they'd got him into hospital before anything.

. . . that Casualty Clearing Station was just in sight of it [accident] *and they saw it happen. And they said a Corporal, it might have been a Trooper, but somebody said a Corporal, came across there, and the next thing . . . you know, picked him up on a stretcher and rushed him straight into hospital.*

A.S.: So the ambulance was right on the doorstep?

Yeh. See . . . they'd got the Casualty Clearing Station on the ground. . . . But they had the tent . . . that . . . where the memorial is [planted tree commemorating Lawrence's crash site planted in May 1983], *you know, where they planted the tree up there, well just . . . way . . . a little way this side on the flat, . . . And they had the Casualty Clearing Station on that big, flat plateau there, just . . . there's em . . . oh . . . jump there . . . tank jump* [a steep man- made ridge there today where tanks practice ascent and descent], *you know . . . just the other side of that was all flat ground, . . . So they had a pretty clear view down the road, you see . . . . a big tent, you know, one of those big stall tents . . . .*

Yes . . . a sunny day. Wasn't wet . . . 'cause otherwise we wouldn't have been stood in the road talking to him. Not like that."[8]

Conclusion: Frank Gordon was a lance corporal in the Tanks Corps in 1935 and knew Lawrence by sight.

There is no doubt that Frank Gordon talked with Lawrence before the accident. It has been accepted that after leaving the Red Garage on his Brough, Lawrence stopped at the camp gates and talked to Gordon. The authors discount the "London trip". Lawrence obviously left the gathering and headed directly for Clouds Hill.

The Casualty Clearing Station tent in the Clouds Hill summer camp on the eastern side of the road with its attendant ambulance is confirmed.

Furthermore, during May 1935, John Prentice and Duncan Montagu Cake were serving with the RAOC and undergoing a tank recovery course, seemingly at the Clouds Hill summer camp. They confirm that the summer camp was sited on the eastern side of the road near the crash site. After a walk on Sunday 12 May, *"We made our way back along a different route, arriving at Cloud's Hill our officers were at dinner in their Marquee Mess,"* confirming that the well-established campsite was in full operation.[9]

Pat Knowles

Pat Knowles wrote in 1935–47: *"Much later I became aware of the Brough's engine again. I heard it rev up as though he was changing gear, and thought 'Hello, he's stopped to chat to someone,' – something he liked to do, and thought no more about it."*[10]

During the 1960s Pat recalled, *"I heard his engine suddenly rev up and I thought he must have been stopping suddenly to speak to someone on the road."*[11]

Arthur Russell

Arthur Russell and Charles Philip Allen were indirectly involved with the crash site.

Arthur Russell interviewed in his Coventry home on 30 May 1986.

"The day before the Inquest I put the motorcycle and the cycle [Hargraves'] on this flat bed truck and took it down to the Inquest . . . .

Now the first thing I did when I went to the bike was to check the front brake. In those days it was a calliper brake and cable control. Having obviously broken two on those Broughs myself, I wanted to see if he had broken that one. Tried to pull up quickly and he had. The footrest was back a little bit, not much."[12]

Interview with Andrew Simpson on 7 December 1985. Nothing of importance added.[13]

Conversation between Arthur Russell and Paul Marriott on 20 May 1990 at Bovington Camp.

"Arthur said he was driving a coach to the Midlands on 13 May 1935. However he said he was involved with transporting Lawrence's damaged Brough to the inquest at Bovington Camp.

He recalled, when on the back of the lorry, many Press photographers had collected hoping to take a photograph of the motorbike. Arthur wanted none to be taken and said that at such a time they ought not to think of such a thing. If they insisted he would throw a sheet over it. There was no need, to Arthur's surprise, they just moved off.

He said that the Brough's right-hand brake cable had snapped. Also the left side foot rest had been moved slightly back thus slightly twisting the frame.

I asked him three times about the left foot rest but he repeated the same story."[14]

George J. Cross

In 1994 George J. Cross recalled his days in 1935 at the Bovington Military Hospital where he served as hospital clerk in the RAMC.

"My office was to the left of the main entrance of the timber hospital.

One day my work was interrupted by Private Gladden who informed me that they had just brought in Lawrence of Arabia in an ambulance, and that he was in the operating theatre. The military ambulance which brought him in was manned by Corporal Miles and Privates Singleton and Gladden. The small operating theatre was just through the passage from my office and I proceeded to it. On a stretcher, all alone and covered in a blanket, lay Lawrence. He was unconscious with what seemed to be a typical head injury. I flicked his ear but there was no reaction. No arrangements were being made at that time for the preparation of the theatre. The surgeon of the hospital was a Captain Simpson and the officer commanding the military hospital was Major Kitson." [15]

The authors found the above recollection most interesting, but contact with George J. Cross was never reciprocated and therefore the 1935 reminiscence must be left open to question.

A check on some of the names such as Captain Simpson proved elusive – so a matter of doubt remains.

Charles Philip Allen

Inquest No. 160   Dated 21 May 1935

"I am a Captain in the R.A.M.C. [Royal Army Medical Corps].

At about 11.45 a.m. on the 13th May 1935, the Deceased Mr T. E. Shaw and Hargraves were both admitted to the Hospital at Bovington.

I quickly examined Hargraves and found he was not seriously injured.

At this time Mr Shaw was being carried up to the theatre.

I then examined Mr Shaw and found him deeply unconscious.

I came to the conclusion that he was suffering from severe head injuries. I had the skull X-rayed which showed a fracture.

The Deceased remained unconscious until his death at 8 a.m. on the 19th May 1935.

With consent of the relatives I made a post mortem examination in conjunction with Mr Cairns and found a large fissured fracture 9 inches long extending from the left side of the head backwards to the middle line – across the back of the skull and forward to the right side. Also a small fracture of the left orbital plate. The brain was severely lacerated especially on the left side.

Prior to death congestion of the lungs had set in and heart failure.

In my opinion the cause of death was fracture of the skull and laceration of the brain, heart failure and congestion of the lungs.

Had Mr Shaw lived he would have been unable to speak and would have lost his memory and would have been paralysed." [16]

What then, are our conclusions as to what really happened before, at, and after the accident. With the plethora of truths, half-truths and outright lies by genuine and spurious witnesses, what is one to make of the mystery?

Often stated throughout this book, but worth repeating again, are the two golden rules for accurate research: namely always adhere to contemporary reports or statements made within, say, 1–3 days of the event in question, and focus on unimpeachable facts that remain unquestioned throughout any lengthy inquiry.

The brief scenario of events begins with Lawrence riding his Brough in top (third) gear travelling north towards Clouds Hill from Bovington Camp. He clears the first dip (a) (see p. 105) and its hill (a), enters the second dip (b) passes through it and changes down into second gear as he climbs the higher hill (b). At this stage he has encountered no traffic, no black car and his forward road vision is blind to any traffic north beyond hill (b). As soon as he motorcycles over hill (b) the sudden sight of the back of a push-bike immediately in his path causes Lawrence to instigate an emergency stop with both brakes; he skids, clips the back wheel of Hargraves' push-bike which in turn provides the lift to eject Lawrence and the Brough. The motorcycle falls on its right-hand side and skids across the road north-eastwards and Lawrence is hurled through the air landing ahead of the Brough, on his head on the road, skidding along it and finally ending up on the eastern side of the road just north of his machine.

Hargraves is also catapulted off his push-bike, and lands, then partly skids, along the road ending up on the western side and eventually becomes unconscious.

In turn the impact causes Hargraves' bike to hit Fletcher's, which dislodges him with only mild shock.

Fletcher checks out Hargraves. A civilian cyclist arrives and soldiers from the summer camp quickly appear. A passing army lorry is flagged down. Captain Anderton and Connolly arrive at the crash scene in a military ambulance, Anderton examines Lawrence, then Hargraves and Lawrence are carried on stretchers into the ambulance. Both are transported to Bovington military hospital.

An attempt has been made to estimate the weather conditions on that fateful day of Monday, 13 May 1935, especially concerning the wind strength and direction, since it plays an important role in deciding how far away the noise of Lawrence's Brough engine could be heard.

Appendices 3–4 show the meteorological pressure map and weather records for Poole, Weymouth and Shaftsbury for the day. They give a very good estimation of the weather conditions at Clouds Hill, especially during the morning in question.

At 08.00 hours local time a ridge of high pressure with its axis lying across the Irish Sea and southern England was bodily moving south-westward. This would put the wind at Clouds Hill as a light south-easterly during the early morning but gradually backing to north-easterly Force 4 by 11.30 hours. Also around midday there would have been six to seven tenths of cumulus cloud providing good sunny periods and a dry ground. Visibility was also good, at least 8 or 10 miles.[17]

In the early morning there would have been a light south-easterly wind allowing Pat Knowles to hear the drill sergeants shouting their orders on the parade ground at Bovington Camp but by 11.30 hours a fresh north-easterly wind would have cut off any loud noise from that area. Indeed it would only just be possible to hear a *loud* Brough engine, say 400 or 500 yards away from Clouds Hill, and certainly not a low tone – which is why he only heard the last rev up of the engine at the accident spot. The two boys could have heard the oncoming motorbike.

19

Clouds Hill

Clouds Hill is really the name of the high ground rising to its highest peak about 180 yards S.S.W. of Lawrence's cottage at a height of about 260 feet above mean sea level. The origin of the name is similar to *The Cloud* near Buglawton in Cheshire where it refers to a hill as far back as 1199 AD. Either the hill was shaped like a cloud or it rose to meet the clouds. Another possibility to its etymology is in the possessive 's' of Cloud's Hill - the majority of place names ending in 's' imply a personal possession; Petersfield means the field of St Peter or St Peter's field and so on. Pat Knowles believed that in medieval times a recluse, a French monk named Claude or Clowood, lived by the spring just to the north of Knowle's bungalow. Hence he thought it came to be known as the hill of Clowood or Cloud's Hill.[1] The former explanation is the most likely.

Clouds Hill is in an area of heathland with open slopes and boggy valleys in places covered with coniferous trees and summer rhododendrons growing in its yellow brown sand.

Clouds Hill land was owned by the Framptons whose family home is Moreton House. The cottage was built in 1808 and according to an old diary found in the estate office, *"Cloud's Hill Cottage built and cottage made,"* probably to house one of the foresters on the Frampton estate.[2] It was inhabited until about 1914 when it began to fall into decay. Many a tramp must have used it during the next few years. Around 1920, Staff Sergeant Arthur Knowles (Pat Knowles' father), hoping to find a permanent residence for his family, discovered the dilapidated cottage. He obtained a lease on it and its immediate surroundings for a few pounds a year from the Frampton estate agent, Mr Godwin, provided that he built an additional bungalow and reconditioned the existing cottage.[3]

In about June 1921 the Knowles family inspected Clouds Hill

which had *"no door or windows. The roof* [thatched] *had fallen in, leaving bare spars against the sky. Plaster and rubbish littered the floors. A brown lizard cocked an eye at us and scuttled up the wall and two bats hung down from the split oak battens near the chimney stack. On the walls that remained intact were sketches of women's faces, and dogs, and other crude drawings."*[4]

It is interesting to note that during the spring and summer of 1923 Lawrence had fallen in love with the countryside surrounding Bovington Army Camp (where he was stationed from 12 March), but despised its cruel ugly existence. Obviously he intended to search for a permanent residence outside the camp, preferably nearby, where he could relax and pursue his literary intentions. Alec Dixon recalled, *"he* [Lawrence] *told me that he had been searching beyond the camp boundary for rooms to which he might retire during his leisure hours."*[5] On 21 March 1923 Lawrence wrote, *"The camp is beautifully put – a wide heath, of flint & sand, with pines & oak-trees, & much rhododendron coming slowly into bloom. When the heather flowers in a few weeks there will be enough to please me;"*[6] and on 30 May, *"The perfect beauty of this place becomes tremendous, . . . The nearly intolerable meanness of man is set in a circle of quiet heath, and budding trees, with the firm level bar of the Purbeck hills behind. The two worlds shout their difference in my ears,"*[7] and finally on 27 June, *"The army is loathsome: Dorsetshire beautiful: . . . "*[8]

Elated, Lawrence invited Alec Dixon *"to appraise an excellent cottage that he had discovered hidden among the trees and rhododendrons of Clouds Hill. I laughed when I saw the place, for its roof was a mere skeleton of rafters, and the narrow stairs swayed dangerously as we climbed to inspect the floorless upper room."*[9]

The first repairs to Clouds Hill by Arthur Knowles began during the summer of 1923 when it was re-roofed. Thereafter a farm labourer, possibly Bill Hardy, lived there until he experienced a nightmare, probably caused by the returning bats, which stayed for a number of years until the oak beams were sprayed.[10]

In August or early September 1923 Lawrence arrived at Clouds Hill cottage and met the Knowles. Pat Knowles remembered, *"On the day Shaw first came, my father and I were painting the outside woodwork of the cottage. He came with two other soldiers who stood respectfully apart whilst he talked to my father about the cottage.*

He asked if it were for sale or if there was a possibility of renting it. Father told him he was going to build a wing onto it, and that he intended living in it himself; the bungalow in which we were presently living was to be for his sons.

Shaw asked father if he believed his family (four sons and one daughter) would stay around him. Eventually father said he would consider the matter and talk it over with mother, and Shaw said he would return the following week . . . . "[11]

Pat Knowles further recalled, *"The following week, one evening, he came up by himself. Father was in the garden shed cutting glass for a hot-bed frame. They talked for a while, on easier terms than before, discussing the things father was making for the cottage . . .*

My parents had decided that there was no reason why the cottage should not be rented to him temporarily, and Shaw's offer to help finance the rest of the rebuilding which father had in mind, settled the matter . . .

It was not long after that that Shaw moved into the cottage."[12]

It was agreed that Lawrence would pay ten shillings a month.[13]

On 17 September Lawrence wrote, *"I've a hut in a wood near camp wherein I spend my spare evenings. They are very few, and very spare, and I want a fire quickly when I get there, . . . The hut is very damp, and often cold."*[14] In the same letter he had asked for a special fire-lighter to ease the situation. During the remainder of 1923 Arthur Knowles and Lawrence gradually improved Clouds Hill. In October Lawrence had taken *"a ruined cottage in a wood near camp, & this I'm fitting up with the hope of having a warm solitary place to hide in sometimes on winter evenings. This district is unusually desolate (of good company) & I covet the idea of being sometimes by myself near a fire."*[15]

Originally Lawrence always wrote "Cloud's Hill" with an apostrophe which he had printed as a letterhead in spring 1924. Gradually the apostophe disappeared and "Clouds Hill" has become the accepted form.[16]

The rest of this chapter covers the history of each permanent structure of Clouds Hill.

1   Largest Room Upstairs   In late 1923 Lawrence got Arthur Knowles *"to knock down a partition in the upstairs room and put a skylight in the roof. Then furniture came: a leather-covered settee, for which it was necessary to remove a window in order to get it in, a table, two leather-upholstered chairs and a plain green carpet – faded now to the colour of moss.*

Next came a gramophone and books, which completed the furnishings of the one small upstairs room to which he came when he had the chance.

Sometimes, over weekends, he would sleep there, . . . "[17] (see Plates 54A and 54B).

On 5 November 1923, *"Have roofed it & am flooring it. . . . Am hoping for a bookcase this week, & a bed next week . . . "*[18] Also on 14 November *"fitted up a writing room in it. There I can revise my text* [Seven Pillars of Wisdom] *in about a twelve-month, allowing say 2 hrs average per day."*[19]

Also on 19 December, *"where I have a room for writing in, I have put some books in it."*[20]

E. M. Forster remembered his visits to the room in March, April and June 1924, *"We lived upstairs, and the sitting-room there looks now* [1938] *much as it did then, though the gramophone and the books have gone, and the fender with its bent ironwork has been remodelled. It was, and it is, a brownish room-wooden beams and ceiling, leather-covered settee."*[21]

Lawrence entertained his army and civilian pals in the upper room and the friendly relaxed atmosphere is recaptured by Forster, *"Here we talked, played Beethoven's symphonies, ate and drank. We drank water only or tea – no alcohol ever entered Clouds Hill, . . . And we ate – this sounds less romantic – out of tins. T. E. always laid in a stock of tinned dainties for his guests. There were no fixed hours for meals and no one sat down. If you felt hungry you opened a tin and drifted about with it . . .*

I don't know whether I'm at all conveying in these trivial remarks the atmosphere of the place – the happy casualness of it, and the feeling that no one particularly owned it. T. E. had the power of distributing the sense of possession among all the friends who came there. . . . To think of Clouds Hill as T. E.'s home is to get the wrong idea of it. It wasn't his home, it was rather his pied-à-terre, *the place where his feet touched the earth for a moment, and found rest, . . . "*[22]

Not all remained idyllic, however. Summer beetles invaded the cottage on 16 June 1924.

Lawrence describes one of his musical evenings on 30 April 1924. *"It's streaming with rain against the western window, and the trees are tossing: . . . Palmer . . . . is waiting for the Rosenkavalier waltz to end. After it he wants a bit of Mozart as played by the Lener. Palmer gets drunk on music. . . . Meanwhile I'm out over by the very wet window (but on its dry side) writing to you* [Charlotte Shaw]. *There'll be tea* [he used his own blend of China tea] *when I've finished the letter (see how short it will be!) and more and more animal contentment after that: till we wind up, when the dark comes, with a movement out of a Bach thing for two violins. We always finish with that, if the time is dark enough."*[23]

During 1923–4 a wide oak mantle-shelf was fitted over the

fireplace at a convenient height for Lawrence.

Even three years later, on 7 July 1927, Clouds Hill had *"Only two rooms, the upstairs, of the cottage, are habitable. They have three-foot walls, and nine-foot roofs, all open. A great deal of oak and chestnut on show: but my repairs to the roof had to be in deal, which are creosoted to bring it to an ancient colour. My gold Meccan dagger* [sold to Lionel Curtis in October 1923 for £125] *paid for the repair-bill, and left something for furniture."*[24]

During 1929–30 Arthur Knowles panelled the room and stained it dark brown but left it unpolished with Lawrence's instructions to leave broken glass in the cavity *"to make it awkward for the mice."*[25]

On 25 September 1933 a *"Spenser landscape was panelled into the gable, . . . "*[26] A major operation was about to be implemented on 25 September 1933, *"Upstairs is due for its second anti-wood-worm poisoning, and all stripped bare for the operation."*[27]

Books Lawrence began reading and storing a few books in the upstairs room from late 1923.[28] By early July 1924 he had accumulated 100 in number. As the collection grew he required more space so in late 1929 book shelving was erected in the room below, *"More books to go to you* [Arthur Knowles] *almost at once . . . .*

There are lots more books to follow. Let me know when the shelving gets full: . . . "[29]

Candlesticks/Holders During the winter of 1923–4 Lawrence placed two beam candle holders plus two smaller versions upstairs.[30] Alec Dixon supplied two more in the form of Jacobean candlesticks for Bernard Shaw's first visit in June 1924.

This seemed to be the main source of night light (excluding the fire) throughout Lawrence's residence. A smaller addition of a beam-candle sconce was due shortly after 6 April 1934.[31]

The introduction of two fine stainless steel candlesticks, a present from Flt. Lt.'s Norrington and Beauforte-Greenwood on 24 April 1934, finally enhanced the upper room (see p. 85).

Gramophones In late 1923 Lawrence brought a wind-up gramophone to the upper room.[32] It became a permanent fixture changing from the original *Ginn* gramophone[33] to a new Columbia *Grafonala* model in c.1928 (see Plate 54A). In 1929 he called his latest *"a super-box like a W/T set inside, with an exquisite smoothness and fullness of tone."*[34]

Florence Hardy recommended Lawrence a local carpenter called Parsons who made a stand for the gramophone.[35]

Records   A list of his record collection in the cottage after his death can be found on pages 523–9 in *T. E. Lawrence By His Friends* edited by A. W. Lawrence.

Over the years a prolific collection grew. In the period September 1923 to August 1925 his classical orchestral favourites were: Beethoven's 5th, 7th and Emperor Concerto; Delius' Hassan, Holst's The Planets. Mozart was for his delight and Beethoven for *"excursions of the spirit."*[36] He particularly liked Josef Hofmann's *The Ruins of Athens* and Kreisler's violin solos. According to the mood Bach's *Concerto in D minor* was often played and he found Haydn restful. Lawrence disliked Chopin and Grieg, and seldom played works by Bach and Wagner. He hated jazz.

His two favourite classical singers were Caruso and Gervasse Elwes; he also liked Clara Butt, Elena Gerhardz, Frieda Hemden, Chiliapine and Hackeyt, but despised Galli Curci.

On a more traditional English theme he thoroughly enjoyed 'Cherry Ripe' and 'The Lass of Richmond Hill.'[37]

Skylight   A skylight was inserted by Arthur Knowles at the request of Lawrence in late 1923.[38] On 4 May 1935 its window pane was smashed by the explosion of a nearby tree using gelignite (see p. 88).[39]

Florence Hardy's Stool   Presumably presented to Lawrence on or after the Shaw's visit in June 1924. He proposed to transfer it into the Bookroom to be used as a table in 1933.[40]

Tables   Apart from the table he originally brought to the cottage in late 1923, he took a fancy to a refectory table that Arthur Knowles had constructed. Arthur built another for Lawrence in the early years out of two wide planks from an old ship, lightly stained and oiled it. Once Arthur caught Lawrence scrubbing it with a brick and sand,[41] a task he had learnt as a soldier at Bovington.[42]

Wireless   For a weekend visit by E. M. Forster in 1924 Lawrence erected an aerial and installed a wireless set on a corner table.[43]

2   Smaller Room Upstairs   There is a smaller room upstairs adjacent to the larger one (see Plate 56); in late 1923 it was bare,[44] but during early May 1924 Lawrence installed a bed,[45] *"an ordinary camp sort of iron bed: not at all luxurious,"*[46] in which E. M. Forster slept during one of his early visits during March–June; *"When I stopped there, I used to sleep in the little room opposite . . . but then it was all anyhow."*[47] Another visitor, one of Lawrence's RAF pals, also slept there on 31 August 1924.

For years the small room remained as a bedroom with little

maintenance, although in March 1929 Bill Knowles plastered its walls.[48] In September 1933 Lawrence decided to turn it into a workroom,[49] and during November intended to install a clothes cupboard, food table (bread, cheese, butter, jam and fruit).[50] By 21 December he had *"thrown out of it the bed, . . . "*[51]

Although stripped of a bed he temporarily used a long narrow floor-cushion until he made a new bed which combined the much-needed clothes storage with a soft place to sleep. Lawrence completed a ship's bunk-bed with drawers built to his own design and body measurements (see p. 78). Included in the activity was his unusual plan to sheath its walls in aluminium foil to give warmth and dryness to the room.[52]

Lawrence installed a ship's porthole in the spring of 1935 with the help of Pat Knowles, and later 'Jock' Chambers, as an expansion of the nautical theme of the ship's bunk-bed. He obtained it from T. B. Marson, who collected it from the demolished *H.M.S. Tiger* in a Donibristle naval scrapyard[53] (see p. 83).

Food Lawrence never allowed any cooking in the cottage while he was in residence so tinned food, jams, bread, butter and cheese, with the fresh food under glass bell jars, were kept on a table in the small room.

He often ordered large bulks of rations. Between September 1923 and August 1925 there were one hundred – 1 lb jars of assorted jams, several assorted 2lb cheeses, 50 bottles of fruit salad and 50 tins of Ideal milk.[54] Alec Dixon (*Friends*, p. 375) recalled that many picnic meals of stuffed olives, salted almonds and Heinz baked beans were permanently in store. In late March 1924 E. M. Forster had a lunch of cold chicken and ham, stewed pears and cream.[55] Similarly, toast was always a standby snack.[56]

3 Bookroom The larger ground floor room was left bare and in June 1924 was full of stored firewood and lumber.[57] The walls were whitewashed in August 1924[58] and Bill Knowles converted the ground floor into a kitchen in March 1927, *"Knowles . . . is now engaged in converting Clouds Hill to a Christian way of living, with a view to letting it."*[59]

In late 1929 Lawrence decided to transfer his growing book library from the large upper room to the lower one. Shelving was erected and by February 1930 he asked Arthur Knowles to find a carpenter *"to run shelves like the present, but in oak, the full depth and height of the chimney-breast, on each side. That will hold 500 books. Years yet"*[60] (see Plates 55A and 55B).

From late October 1930 to April 1931 his mother Sarah Lawrence and brother Dr. Bob Lawrence stayed at Clouds Hill, converting the lower room with its stone-flagged floor and simple furnishings into a living room-cum-kitchen. They added a cooking range into the fireplace.[61]

By 22 November 1930 Arthur was informed, *"The book-case by the fire is point No.2: . . . "*[62]

The original west window was stone mullioned with lights but Lawrence was keen to install a central pivoting frame with a fixed frame either side. In a detailed letter to Bill Bugg, just before September 1932, he explained the particular procedures for fitting the window into the awkwardly shaped mullion frame. Frustration set in as nearly a year later on 18 July 1933 he stated, *"I wish the window-frame would come: bother the stainless steel merchants."*[63] However, soon after, on 30 July, *"We unpacked the window and frame. I think it is too long."*[64] Lawrence continued to identify the numerous faults that would have to be corrected for its precise fitting.

During late summer 1933 Bill Bugg's grandfather, a master stonemason, finished the difficult task. The result was two fixed sidepanes cemented into the stone window frame with a pivoting central panel in stainless steel to give enough light and air to the room[65] (see Plate 57).

During September 1933 the present fireplace was installed together with two shelved walls, one full of books and virtually all finished. By 25 September books filled one of the two-shelved walls (north wall).[66] They also filled one wall and one end by 5 November[67] and the room was half full by 21 December.[68]

Lawrence, much to his joy, threw out the evil-smelling cooking-range on 21 November 1933.

On 17 December local jobber William 'Bill' Bugg and carpenter Parsons had completely shelved the room and had covered the stone flags with an oak planked floor.[69]

On 26 December the stainless steel fireplace hood was expected to counter the nuisance of the smoky room.[70] To overcome this problem Lawrence intended an air-vent for drawing the fire installed after 6 April 1934.[71]

Books   From late 1929 the storing of books was confined to the bookroom. Most of his collection had been kept in friends' houses in London, mainly at V. W. Richards' home at 3 Loudoun Road, St. Johns Wood, London, NW8,[72] but by May 1933 most of the books were transferred to the cottage. K. W. Marshall, an unemployed bookseller, was staying at the cottage and helped to unpack the books and arrange them on the shelves.[73] There is some confusion to the number of books Lawrence had accumulated. It had grown to 2,000 by 9 November 1932[74] although on 15 September 1933 he stated that there were 1000 and 200–300 to be replaced.[75] After his death the library was catalogued.[76]

Chair   On 26 December 1933 Lawrence was expecting his chair to be built within one week at Southampton.[77]

Large Couch/Window Seat   In 1933 he wanted the framework of a large couch constructed to be the *"father and mother of all beds,"*[78] mainly for sleeping and reading; it was also to be a comfortable place for visitors to sit on.[79] It was built for the west window from his brother Bob's former bed, measuring six feet square, and was made to fit on 29 September 1933.[80] By 18 May 1934 it was complete.[81] A cow-hide and mattress were added to the bed.[82]

Fender   Lawrence designed the fender with a cast-iron fireback and stainless steel log box during the winter of 1933–4;[83] it was probably finished by the spring of 1934.[84]

Heating Lamps   Lawrence refers to receiving excellent service from two heating lamps obtained at Christmas 1932.[85]

Two Paintings of River Euphrates at Jerablus   In early January 1933 Lawrence thanked Ernest Altounyan for his wife's paintings of the river Euphrates, *"They delighted me. . . . These two little panels exactly fit a place in my downstairs room."*[86]

Pastel of Allenby and Oil Painting of Feisal   Edward Garnett had sent Eric Kennington's pastel drawing of Allenby to Lawrence when the cottage was completed. Lawrence still owned Augustus John's portrait of Feisal. On 10 August 1933 Lawrence wrote to Garnett, *"I shall have my dual mastership preserved in my cottage for all time . . . but the two quiet heads on the wall will let me do what I please."*[87]

RAF Rug   A small blue RAF rug, issued to married officers' quarters, was given to Lawrence at Manston by Clare Sydney Smith in the autumn of 1931.[88] It was placed in front of the bookroom fireplace, *"The rug decorates my cottage . . . They are good rugs."*[89]

Sleeping Bags   Mrs Henrietta Knowles made two simple sleeping bags into which Lawrence stitched *'Meum and Tuum'* ('mine and thine') which on 20 December 1933 were meant for Lawrence (Meum) and guests (Tuum).[90] Loose blankets, sheets, pillows and an eiderdown were also available.[91]

4 Staircase The staircase was most likely built by Arthur Knowles in 1922–3. It was certainly painted on 29 September 1924,[92] and much later it was sheathed in oak three-ply on 25 September 1933.[93] Natural cowhide leathers on hinged rods of wrought iron were hung on 6 April 1934 as substitute doors to the book and music rooms.[94]

5 Bathroom or Downstair's Small Room In the early days Jock Chambers recalls an old army boiler in the small room.[95] On 3 December 1932 Lawrence was contemplating a bath and hot water boiler – as long as his *Odyssey* money of £800 lasted[96] – to be erected in the downstair's small room. Water was pumped from the ram (see Map 10), across the road near the spring to the north of Knowles' bungalow, to Lawrence's newly installed cistern on 30 August 1933.[97]

In December 1932 Lawrence contacted his American publisher Bruce Rogers, enquiring about bathroom boilers, *"I shall label the bath Homer and the boiler B. R., upon inauguration day!"*[98] He also wrote to Charlotte Shaw (31 August) that his bath had arrived.[99] By 17 December 1933 it was fitted, having been stored in his garage since 31 August. (The boiler was manufactured by Raymond Goslett, a former fellow officer in supplies/ordnance at Aqaba.)[100]

By 21 December the boiler was erected. Also a paraffin heater called a *Selectos Water Heater* from 104 Victoria St, London, SW,[101] was erected. On Friday, 21 December 1933, he had his first hot bath.[102] In spring 1934 the boiler received its asbestos plaster cover.[103] On 6 April Lawrence wrote, *"Our last doing was to sheath the bath-room in sheet cork, laiden in slabs twelve inches by seven, and a sixteenth of an inch thick. These were glued to the walls and partition and doors and frames, bonded like bricks, in their vertical courses, . . . The cork cost about 15/-, and has done the job excellently."*[104] A bath mat was due after 6 April.[105] By 16 November the bath was housed in a demi-cupboard with its boiler covered in a full cupboard[106] (see Plates 58A and 58B).

6 Proposed Two-Room Extension Lawrence sold his other property at Pole Hill in Epping Forest for about £3,500 and decided on *"a new wing (two rooms) . . . A new wing will not harm either the smallness or the quietude of Clouds Hill, or its simplicity."*[107] One of the rooms was to house his books and he planned to build it during 1932. However he had to postpone the idea for financial reasons as the Great Depression had reduced the value of his investments, *"I have held up the improvement process which was slowly civilising my* *ruined cottage in Dorsetshire."*[108]

7   Proposed Fire-Proofing of Cottage   In April 1935 Lawrence thought of fire-proofing Clouds Hill, *"I have thought out a complex and very acute fashion of fire-proofing . . . a wooden door: the match-board lining of the under stairs cupboards: the stair risers and treads which form its roof, and the parting walls. It is going to be a work of art, involving magnesite, board, and asbestos wood – not to mention felt-nails, barbed nails and Portland (read Shipton) cement. Every day we build better and better."*[109]

8   Spring/Ram   For years all water had to be manually fetched by bucket from the spring just north of the Knowles' bungalow, *"You walk 60 yards with a bucket."*[110]

During the early 1930s Lawrence was certain that the installation of a simple ram would mechanize the flow of spring water to his cottage. He employed a hydraulic ram company to test the volume of water emitted from the spring, which measured one gallon per 70 seconds. The firm was sceptical but Lawrence went ahead.[111]

During 1933, 100 yards of long pipes were inserted across the road from the spring to his cottage. At 10.00 hours on 31 August 1933 the ram was turned on and at 13.45 hours the first water arrived at Clouds Hill tasting of red lead and galvanized iron.[112]

During the next two years the normal 700–800 gallons a day (24 hours) supply varied depending on droughts or plentiful rainfall.

9   Watertank (Reservoir)   Impressed by this initial abundance of water during the summer of 1933 Lawrence thought it an excellent idea to build a huge watertank to counter the already dangerous effects of heath fires to his cottage and Knowles' bungalow.[113]

On 5 November 1933 Pat Knowles, Way (see Plate 59) and Cooper (two of the families living to the north of the cottage) were digging the foundations for the large watertank below Mrs Knowles' garden amongst the chestnut trees. The watertank was to measure 40 × 7 × 5 feet. They intended to put a glasshouse over it to keep out the choking leaves.[114]

Difficulties were encountered in the brick cementing with the winter frosts of 1933–4[115] but in late February 1934 *Shaw's Puddle* was erected and filled from the Clouds Hill overflow. Then it was nearly 40 feet long and 7 feet wide, with enough capacity to hold 7,000 gallons.[116] Purposely built 2 feet lower than the ram for

163

gravity feed it also had the necessary fitting of a hydrant thread on the outlet pipe for instant fitting for any hose.[117]

By 21 March 1934 the wooden roofing struts were being placed and the roofing glass nearly finished. Also at each end (south and north) the framework had been extended to supply two rooms – a porch entrance to the glasshouse at the south end and a study for Lawrence at the north.[118]

By mid-April 1934 the porch entrance and flooring were laid.[119] Lawrence's Jedda doors were installed on the north entrance of his new study, having been kept in storage from 1921. He first went to Jedda in October 1916 and in *Seven Pillars of Wisdom* described them as *"heavy two-leaved slabs of teak-wood, deeply carved, often with wickets in them; and they had rich hinges and ring-knockers of hammered iron."*[120] In mid-April 1934, the study ceiling was made higher because of the tall Jedda doors,[121] which had been repaired in cedar by Florence Hardy's carpenter Parsons[122] (see Plate 60).

Lawrence also intended to use the top of the watertank as a swimming pool and during the summer of 1934 fine-cement rendering was added to the inside rim;[123] by November it had been completed[124] (see Plates 61A and 61B). Although the tank cost £120 to build it repaid itself in July 1934. The summer was very dry and many heath fires threatened local properties. On one occasion Clouds Hill was threatened but saved by using the water from the reservoir.[125] The reservoir's wooden framework was finally painted blue and its pool included white tiles. Joyce Knowles and Lawrence often swam there. Indeed it was one of Joyce's regular "jobs" to sweep the path leading to the pool.[126]

By 24 January 1935 the watertank had cracked at its northern end and had to be undercut and buttressed.[127] Digging had commenced a few days later and was expected to be repaired by April.[128] Lawrence had also nearly completed an order for an engine-and-hose-and-pump-machine[129] which may be connected with the *"oil tank"* in Lawrence's 1934 map of Clouds Hill (see Map 10).

10 Cottage Roof/Chimney Stack   In June 1921 the roof was in ruins, during 1922 it was reassembled by Arthur Knowles. New pots were attached to the stack and Lawrence referred to them in March 1929 *"as the sole disfigurement."*[130] On 22 November 1932 a local builder tried to repair the roof.[131]

11 Lintel (Architrave)   Around 1920 Joyce Dorey (later to marry Pat Knowles) discovered a large dressed stone slab in a meadow at her home at Wood Street Farm, Wool. It was stored in a barn for a number of years until Pat Knowles decided it would be useful as building material for Clouds Hill. With difficulty he transported it from Wool to Clouds Hill. He thought it had been chiselled as a building block for nearby Bindon Abbey.[132] Lawrence decided to sculpture the stone and for many days he carved out a rebate and progressed to chisel in the year "1751". The stone was eventually, probably during the summer of 1945, set in the retainng wall of the Knowles' bungalow.[133]

In 1924–5 Lawrence had a heavy stone erected over the door entrance at Clouds Hill. In the sinking he carved the words *"OU PHRONTIS"*[134] (see Plate 62). The Greek phrase came from Herodotus, VI, 129, roughly meaning 'Why worry'. It concerned a man called Hippoclides who was to marry a rich merchant's daughter. Unfortunately, intoxicated from a previous feast, he decided to perform a stupid act and stand on his head on a table dancing his legs in the air. The bride's father shouted *"Hippoclides, Hippoclides, . . . You dance your marriage off . . . 'Wyworri?'"* he answered.[135] This careless attitude was explicitly expressed by Lawrence when he said *"nothing in Clouds Hill is to be a care upon its inhabitant. While I have it there shall be nothing exquisite or unique in it. Nothing to anchor me."*[136]

Alec Dixon recalls that in July 1925, *"One afternoon I arrived at Clouds Hill to find its owner at the top of a step-ladder busily cutting an inscription on the concrete lintel of the doorway. . . . Shaw smiled down at me, and stopped work to tell the story of Hippoclides, . . . "* Lawrence explained, *"'Don't give a damn,' is a good translation, I think."*[137]

12 Front Door There was no front door when Arthur Knowles first discovered Clouds Hill in 1920. He constructed one and hinged it with the general improvements in 1922. He also attached a wrought iron knocker around 1923, which was a friend's tradesmans piece[138] (see Plate 62). House maintenance on 29 September 1924 included a good coating of paint.[139]

13 Garage *George VII*, Lawrence's Brough motorbike, urgently required a dry haven so he planned to build a garage at Clouds Hill. By 22 November 1930 the foundations were well advanced, *"Mother told me you* [W. A. Knowles] *had all the concreting done before the weather turned bad, so I suppose that will have set well. Good."*[140]

During 1933–4 the garage was sometimes used as a storage area for builders' materials and his bathroom accessories.[141]

14 Woodshed The woodshed was certainly there on 26 December 1933.[142]

15 W.C. On the map Lawrence sketched in 1934[143] there is the plan of an outside toilet just to the north of the cottage. In March 1929 Lawrence arranged for Arthur Knowles to build *"what he calls a sanitary convenience"*.[144] Joyce Knowles related to Raleigh Trevelyan, in the early 1980s, that a chemical lavatory had been put in when Sarah Lawrence had stayed at Clouds Hill (late Oct. 1930–April 1931), but by 21 December 1933[145] no such facility existed and on 26 December Lawrence refers to *"No W.C. now."*[146]

16 Trees and Shrubs Lawrence's idea of gardening was only to work at its basic upkeep, *"For me gardening is maintenance only, to be done again day after day and gone utterly the week after its creator leaves it. So I am content to leave Clouds Hill as a wilderness."*[147]

He refers to distinctive trees in the close proximity of the cottage. For example, on 3 August 1924 there was an ilex, birch, oaks, firs, rhododendrons, laurels and heather.[148] By 1927 *"a huge ilex [was] stretching arms over its [cottage] roof."*[149] During the winter of 1929–30 the 200 Scotch firs that had been planted on the nearby hill had not grown well and by spring many were lost.[150] In April Lawrence stated *"I want a row of tall red clean trunks against the skyline, like a cock's comb, on the crest of Clouds Hill, visible from Corfe and from Dorchester."*[151] By 1932 the foliage had become overgrown and a nuisance so an operation of cutting and sawing back commenced. As already mentioned (see p. 88) Lawrence, Lord Carlow and Pat Knowles went to the length of geligniting the top off an annoying tree on 4 May 1935.

He also refers to the Marsh Pimpernel flower on 17 June 1925.[152]

The abundant rhododendrons, encouraged by the Frampton estate in the nineteenth century, were added to by Lawrence by introducing the latest Tibetan and Chinese blue and pink types in November 1930.[153] Even in May 1929 he told his mother of plans to plant red and white rhododendrons, *"to mix up the colour: and a lot of magnolias, which carry beautiful great flowers."*[154] By April 1933 his *T. H. Eden Philpotts* variety, from Florence Hardy, were becoming well established.[155] Mention of waiting for a Pontina to bloom occurs in April 1933.[156]

Lawrence's mother had planted dozens of daffodils (winter/spring 1930–1) which kept growing in the grass around the cottage each spring. It was no place for flowers and Lawrence added that the rabbits liked them,[157] *"She knows I can't stand any sort of garden or plants . . . Yet she would cheerfully spoil the place for me."*[158]

For open fires he used the plentiful dead wood lying around. In 1925 dead rhododendron branches could be picked up easily for the fires, which gave a splendid glow.[159] At first all deadwood was stored in the large lower room then much later transferred for storage to the woodshed built in the early 1930s. Any loose brushwood would be sawn. On 5 March 1934 a felled chestnut tree, cleared from the water tank site, was ready for logging[160] (see Plate 27). Sometimes fire logs would be ordered from Wareham.[161]

17   The Nook   E. M. Forster recalls a pleasant circle of rising terraces that Lawrence contrived and called the *Nook* in 1924 (just east of Clouds Hill).[162]

18   Fire-Guard   There is a reference to an open track to act as a fire-guard just east of the cottage to combat heath fires.[163]

19   Telephone Poles   In 1925 Lawrence was unsuccessful with the district chief telephone engineer to remove telegraph poles that spoilt his view from Clouds Hill. However they were removed after he appealed to the Postmaster General.[164]

Renting and Purchase of Clouds Hill

The Moreton Estate (Frampton family) originally owned the Clouds Hill cottage and land and in 1920 Arthur Knowles leased it for a few pounds a year from the estate's agent Mr Godwin on the understanding that he reconditioned the cottage and built a bungalow.

On Lawrence's second visit in early September 1923 he offered to finance the rebuilding plans. On 5 November 1923 he *"found a ruined cottage near camp (a mile out) & took it for 2/6 a week."*[165]

During 1924 he persuaded Godwin to draw up a written agreement to purchase the cottage and its immediate land, excluding the Knowles' site.[166] Soon after, his brother, A. W. Lawrence, began the purchase with a deposit cheque.[167]

Godwin was slow in completing the deed of sale and Lawrence promised to pay the balance on his return from India on 2 February 1929, by selling a copy of his *Seven Pillars*.[168] On 19 March 1929 the conveyance had still not been completed.[169] Further delays annoyed Lawrence into issuing an ultimatum to Godwin to finalize the agreement within one week, but it dragged on until 12

October.[170] On 25 April 1931 the estate would not sell Lawrence the Knowles' land knowing that the lease was to terminate around 1934.[171] However, Godwin consented to prepare a lease of £15 a year for the tree part of the Knowles' land on 5 November 1933.[172] Again progress was slow and it was not until 15 April 1934 that the agent agreed to the lease.[173]

Some of the early tenants at Clouds Hill were Arnie Lawrence and his wife Barbara,[174] who stayed from July to 28 December 1925; one tenant upstairs and another below for 12/-a week in June 1927;[175] the La Mares family for 7/6 a week,[176] a fresh tenant in late May 1929; Lawrence's mother Sarah and brother Bob from late October 1930 to April 1931 and one of the original artists of *Seven Pillars*, William Roberts, his wife Sarah and son John around 1930. The Marshall and Robert families also returned in summer 1934.

Lawrence's friends visited and stayed at the cottage for their summer holidays all through his kindness and generosity.

And finally, one friend in particular, Basil Liddell Hart, recalled *"But the few with whom he made contact quickly came, then as in later years, under his spell. That much overworked word expresses the effect of his personality as no other word can."*[177]

References and Notes

Reference Abbreviations

Biographers – Hart or Graves	*T. E. Lawrence to His Biographers, Robert Graves and Liddell Hart* (Cassell, London, 1963).
Cockerell	*Friends of a Lifetime*, ed. Viola Meynell (Jonathan Cape, London, 1940).
Friends	*T. E. Lawrence by His Friends*, ed. A. W. Lawrence (Jonathan Cape, London, 1937).
Genius	*Genius of Friendship. "T. E. Lawrence"* by Henry Williamson (Faber and Faber, London, 1941).
George Brough Letters	*A Series of Letters from T. E. Lawrence to George Brough and Notes on the Identity and Use of Lawrence's Brough Superiors*, dedicated to the late Bill Beckingham, ed. Mike Leatherdale (The Brough Superior Club, December 1987).
Golden Reign	*The Golden Reign. The Story of my Friendship with "Lawrence of Arabia"* by Clare Sydney Smith (Cassell, London, 1940).
Home Letters	*The Home Letters of T. E. Lawrence and his Brothers*, ed. M. R. Lawrence (Basil Blackwell, Oxford, 1954).
Lawrence	*Lawrence of Arabia. The Authorised Biography of T. E. Lawrence* by Jeremy Wilson (Heinemann, London, 1988).
Letters – Brown	*The Letters of T. E. Lawrence*, ed. Malcolm Brown (J. M. Dent & Sons, London, 1988).
Letters – Garnett	*The Letters of T. E. Lawrence*, ed. David Garnett (Jonathan Cape, London, 1938).
Limelight	*Backing into the Limelight. A Biography of T. E. Lawrence* by Michael Yardley (Harrap, London, 1985).
National	*T. E. Lawrence* by Jeremy Wilson (National Portrait Gallery Publications, 1988).
Orientations	*Orientations* by Ronald Storrs (Ivor Nicholson & Wilson Ltd., London, 1939).
Prince	*A Prince of our Disorder. The Life of T. E. Lawrence* by John E. Mack (Wiedenfeld and Nicholson, London, 1976).

Quietness	Cloud's Hill – Dorset. "An Handful of Quietness" by Pat and Joyce Knowles and Bob Hunt (E. V. G. Hunt, Dorset, 1992).
Secret Lives	*The Secret Lives of Lawrence of Arabia* by Phillip Knightley and Colin Simpson (Nelson, London, 1969).
Solitary	*Solitary in the Ranks. Lawrence of Arabia as Airman and Private Soldier* by H. Montgomery Hyde (Constable, London, 1977).

Note: Where Lawrence emphasized the text of his letters in some way, this has been indicated by setting the emphasized words in bold italic; authors' emphasis is indicated by roman bold setting.

Chapter 1 Early Days at Bridlington, 15–21 November 1934

1   T. E. L. to Frederic Manning, 16 November 1934, *Letters – Brown*, p. 498.
2   T. E. L. to Hon. Francis Rodd, 23 November 1934, *Letters – Garnett*, p. 829.
3   Mrs J. Leng to Yvonne Argent, 18 August 1992.
4   Flt. Lt. R. G. Sims (for W/C E. B. Rice) to Hilda Barchard, 16 December 1935, copy in possession of authors.
5   R. W. Barchard (son of Mrs Hilda Barchard) to P. J. Marriott, 21 September 1992.
6   *Golden Reign*, p. 240.
7   *Prince*, pp. 434–5.
8   *Secret Lives*, p. 200.
9   Jack Alexander to P. J. Marriott, 25 November 1992.
10   James Marshall to P. J. Marriott, 7 November 1992.
11   T. E. L. to C. Day Lewis, 16 November 1934, *Letters – Garnett*, p. 826.
12   As note 1, p. 499.
13   T. E. L. to Charlotte Shaw, 16 November 1934, *Letters – Brown*, p. 498.
14   T. E. L. to Frederic Manning, 16 November 1934, *Letters – Brown*, p. 489.
15   T. E. L. to unidentified person, 16 November 1934, *Houghton Lib.*, 65M–177. bMs. Eng 1252 (267).
16   T. E. L. to Sir Ronald Storrs, 31 January 1935, *Letters – Brown*, p. 518.
17   T. E. L. to H. S. Ede, 3 January 1935, *Letters – Brown*, p. 511.
18   T. E. L. to Lorna Norrington, 23 November 1934, *Letters – Garnett*, p. 828.
19   As note 15.
20   T. E. L. to Lady Astor, 26 November 1934, *Letters – Brown*, p. 503.
21   T. E. L. to Arthur Hall, 20 November 1934, *Letters – Garnett*, p. 827.
22   *The History of the Royal Air Force Marine Craft 1918–1986* by Geoffrey D. Pilborough Mirt (Canimpex, London, 1986), p. 192.
23   *Ibid.*, p. 195.
24   *Lawrence*, p. 904.
25   R. W. Barchard to authors, 28 August 1992.
26   *Ibid.* Also T. E. L.'s notes on his last Bridlington boat headed "October 1934–February 1935" and dated 23 February 1935.
27   *Solitary*, p. 227.
28   "Lawrence in Bridlington," *The T. E. Lawrence Society Newsletter*, no. 17, November 1989, p. 16.
29   *Ibid.*
30   *Ibid.*

31   T. E. L. to Robert Graves, 4 February 1935, *Letters – Brown*, p. 521.
32   "Shifting Sands," *Daily Telegraph*, 13 April 1987.
33   As note 21.
34   T. E. L. to J. G. Wilson ,20 November 1934, *Letters – Garnett*, p. 826.
35   As note 28, p. 17. Also *"Reader, Writer and a Loner Who Fought Shy of Any Publicity,"* by Michael Chaddock, *Bridlington Free Press*, 21 February 1985.
36   Telephone conversation between Reginald Barchard and Paul Marriott, 16 March 1993.
37   Interview between Philip Donnellan and Henry Williamson in 1962, *T. E. Lawrence By His Friends*, TEL Society, Oxford, 18 September 1994, p. 14.

Chapter 2   Surroundings, 22 November–19 December 1934

1   *Friends*, pp. 550–1.
2   *Lawrence*, p. 918.
3   T. E. L. to Hon. Francis Rodd, 23 November 1934, *Letters – Brown*, p. 500.
4   *Ibid.*, p. 501.
5   T. E. L. to T. B. Marson, 23 November 1934, *Solitary*, p. 224.
6   T. E. L. to H. W. Bailey, 23 November 1934, *Letters – Garnett*, p. 828.
7   T. E. L. to Bruce Rogers, 24 November 1934, *Houghton Lib.*, 65M-177. bMs. Eng 1252 (208).
8   *Ibid.*
9   T. E. L. to Walter Williams, 24 November 1934, *Houghton Lib.*, 65M-177. bMs. Eng 1252 (252).
10   T. E. L. to Lady Astor, 26 November 1934, *Letters – Brown*, p. 502.
11   T. E. L. to Mademoiselle Schneegans, 26 November 1934, *Letters – Brown*, p. 504.
12   As note 10, p. 503.
13   T. E. L. to B. H. Liddell Hart, 28 November 1934, *Letters – Garnett*, p. 830.
14   T. E. L. to Winifred Fontana, 28 November 1934, *Letters – Brown*, p. 505.
15   *Ibid.*
16   T. E. L. to A. S. Frere-Reeves, 28 November 1934, Harry Ransom Humanities Research Center, University of Texas, Austin, USA.
17   *Friends*, p. 465.
18   *Ibid.*, p. 545.
19   *Ibid.*
20   T. E. L. to George Brough, 28 November 1934, *George Brough Letters*, no. 20.
21   As note 16.
22   *Friends*, pp. 552–3.
23   Hull Local History Library to P. J. Marriott, 13 October 1992.
24   *Friends*, p. 554.
25   *Ibid.*, p. 552.
26   *Sayings*, p. 59.
27   T. E. L. to Ezra Pound, 7 December 1934, *Letters – Brown*, p. 507.
28   T. E. L. to Henry Williamson, 9 December 1934 (but dated 11 December 1934), *Letters – Garnett*, p. 833.
29   *Ibid.*, pp. 833–4.
30   T. E. L. to Ernest Altounyan, 9 December 1934, *Letters – Garnett*, p. 831.
31   As note 28, p. 834.
32   T. E. L. to Charlotte Shaw, 11 December 1934, *Solitary*, p. 213.
33   T. E. L. to Lord Trenchard, 13 December 1934, *Solitary*, p. 232.
34   *Solitary*, p. 233.

35 *Ibid.*
36 *Friends*, pp. 557–8.
37 *Ibid*, p. 555.
38 T. E. L. to Siegfried Sassoon, 17 December 1934, *Letters – Garnett*, pp. 835–6.
39 Siegfried Sassoon to T. E. L., 19 December 1934, *Letters to T. E. Lawrence*, ed. A. W. Lawrence (Jonathan Cape, London, p. 159).
40 T. E. L. to Charlotte Shaw, mid-December 1934 (about 17th), *Letters – Brown*, p. 507.
41 *Sayings*, p. 56.
42 As note 40, p. 508.

Chapter 3   Clouds Hill for Christmas, 20–31 December 1934

1   *Golden Reign*, pp. 60–1.
2   *Ibid*, pp. 66–7.
3   *Lawrence*, p. 867.
4   *Golden Reign*, pp. 96–7.
5   *Ibid.*, p. 71.
6   T. E. L. to F. N. Doubleday, 2 September 1930, *Letters – Garnett*, p. 695.
7   T. E. L. to R. V. Buxton, 29 December 1930, *Letters – Garnett*, p. 709.
8   *Golden Reign*, p. 141.
9   T. E. L. to Charlotte Shaw, 26 June 1931, *Letters – Brown*, p. 456.
10 T. E. L. to Charlotte Shaw, 15 July 1931, *Letters – Brown*, p. 457.
11 T. E. L. to Flt. Lt. Jinman, 20 December 1934, copy made by P. J. Marriott from glass wall display in the *Blue Lobster Restaurant*, Bridlington, May 1992.
12 *Golden Reign*, p. 191.
13 *Ibid.*, p. 208.
14 *Ibid.*, p. 215.
15 As note 11.
16 *Ibid.*
17 T. E. L. to unidentified person, 3 January 1935, *Houghton Lib.*, 65M-177. bMs. Eng 1252 (268).
18 As note 11.
19 *Ibid.*
20 *Ibid.*
21 T. E. L. to C. Day Lewis, 20 December 1934, *Letters – Garnett*, p. 839.
22 T. E. L. to A. S. Frere-Reeves 20 December 1934, Harry Ransom Humanities Research Center, *University of Texas*, Austin, USA.
23 T. E. L. to Corporal Alec Dixon, 20 December 1934, *Houghton Lib.*, 65M-177. bMs. Eng 1252 (4).
24 T. E. L. to John Buchan, 20 December 1934, *Letters – Garnett*, p. 836.
25 T. E. L. to Henry Williamson, 20 December 1934, Exeter University, UK.
26 T. E. L. to A. E. 'Jock' Chambers, 26 January 1935, *Letters – Garnett*, p. 841.
27 T. E. L. to S. L. Newcombe, 20 December 1934, *Letters – Garnett*, pp. 837–8.
28 *Sayings*, pp. 27–8.
29 Lord David Cholmondeley to Yvonne Argent, 30 May 1995.
30 *Private Shaw and Public Shaw – a Dual Portrait of Lawrence of Arabia and G. B. S.* by Stanley Weintraub (George Braziller, New York, 1963), p. 260.
31 T. E. L. to Charlotte Shaw, 31 December 1934, *Letters – Brown*, p. 511.
32 T. E. L. to Arthur Russell, 3 January 1935, *Letters – Brown*, p. 512.
33 As note 31.

34 Conversation between Pat Knowles and David Garnett, *c.* 1937, *Letters –
    Garnett*, p. 844.
35 *Quietness*, p. 39.
36 Lady Pansy Lamb to John Mack, *Prince*, p. 446.
37 *Two Flamboyant Fathers* by Nicolette Devas (Collins, London, 1966), pp. 90–2.
38 As note 31, p. 510.
39 T. E. L. to G. Wren Howard, 31 December 1934, *Letters – Garnett*, p. 840.
40 As note 31, p. 510.
41 *Ibid.*
42 K. Lester to Yvonne Argent, 1 September 1992.
43 T. E. L. to Charlotte Shaw, 31 December 1934, *Letters – Brown*, p. 510.
44 *Friends*, p. 435.
45 T. E. L. to G. Wren Howard, 31 December 1934, *Letters – Garnett*, p. 840.
46 Henry Williamson to T. E. L., late December 1934, *Genius*, p. 71.
47 T. E. L. to Henry Williamson, late (probably 31st) January 1935, *Genius*,
    pp. 72–3.
48 T. E. L. to B. H. Liddell Hart, 31 December 1934, *The Memoirs of Captain
    Liddell Hart* by B. H. Liddell Hart (Cassell, London, vol. 1, 2nd edn, April
    1967), p. 352.
49 T. E. L. to Charlotte Shaw, 31 December 1934, *Letters – Brown*, p. 510.
50 T. E. L. to Alan Dawnay 16 June 1933, *Letters – Brown*, p. 474.
51 T. E. L. to Edward Garnett, 22 March 1928, *Letters – Garnett*, p. 581. Also
    T. E. L. to Sydney Cockerell, 22 March 1928, *Friends of a Lifetime – Letters to
    Sydney Cockerell*, ed. Viola Meynell (Jonathan Cape, London, 1940), p. 369.
52 As note 31, p. 510.
53 T. E. L. to Maurice Baring, end of 1934, *Prince*, p. 403.
54 As note 48.

Chapter 4   The Old Man, 1–20 January 1935

 1 T. E. L. to G. Wren Howard, beginning of 1935, *Jonathan Cape, Publisher –
    Herbert Jonathan Cape* by Michael S. Howard (Jonathan Cape, London, 1971),
    pp. 153–4.
 2 T. E. L. to Arthur Russell, 3 January 1935, *Letters – Brown*, p. 512.
 3 *Ibid.*
 4 T. E. L. to Arthur Russell, 18 January 1935, *Letters – Brown*, p. 515.
 5 As note 1, p. 154.
 6 As note 2.
 7 *Ibid.*
 8 T. E. L. to H. S. Ede, 3 January 1935, *Letters – Brown*, p. 511.
 9 *Friends*, p. 559.
10 *Ibid.*, pp. 553–5.
11 *Solitary*, pp. 231–2.
12 *Ibid.*, pp. 238–9.
13 *Sayings*, p. 52.
14 *Friends*, p. 435.
15 T. E. L. to A. S. Frere-Reeves, 7 January 1935, *Letters – Brown*, pp. 513–14.
16 *Prince*, pp. 435–6.
17 Friedericke Hilscher-Ehlert to P. J. Marriott, Autumn 1992.
18 T. E. L. to Arthur Hall, 1 February 1935, *Letters – Garnett*, pp. 848–9.
19 T. E. L. to Robert Graves, 13 January 1935, *Biographers – Graves*, pp. 178–9.
20 T. E. L. to R. A. M. Guy, 31 January 1935, *Houghton Lib.*, 65M-177. bMs.
    Eng. 1252 (117).

21 T. E. L. to Arthur Russell, 18 January 1935, *Letters – Brown*, p. 515.
22 *Golden Reign*, p. 241.
23 *Ibid.*, pp. 240–1.
24 R. W. Barchard to the authors, 23 August 1992 and to P. J. Marriott, 6 September 1992.
25 *Friends*, p. 546.
26 *Ibid.*, p. 536.
27 *Golden Reign*, p. 240.
28 As note 21.
29 T. E. L. to Clare Sydney Smith, undated but probably 18 January 1935, *Golden Reign*, p. 241.
30 *The Sayings and Doings of T. E. – Seven Stories* by R. G. Sims, Story no. 3 "The Visit," *T. E. Lawrence Studies*, ed. J. M. Wilson, vol. 1 no. 1, Spring 1976, p. 36.

Chapter 5   RAF Finale, 21 January–17 February 1935

1 T. E. L. to Hon. Edward Eliot, 24 May 1934, *Letters – Brown*, p. 489.
2 *Solitary*, p. 235.
3 T. E. L. to Bruce Rogers, 26 January 1935, *Letters – Garnett*, p. 843.
4 T. E. L. to Charlotte Shaw, 26 January 1935, *Letters – Brown*, pp. 515–16.
5 T. E. L. to Lord Carlow, 4 February 1935, *Letters – Garnett*, p. 850.
6 T. E. L. to Robert Graves, 4 February 1935, *Letters – Brown*, p. 520.
7 *Friends*, p. 306.
8 *Prince*, p. 404.
9 As note 4, p. 516.
10 T. E. L. to G. W. Dunn, 26 January 1935, *National*, pp. 222–3.
11 As note 3, p. 842.
12 As note 5.
13 T. E. L. to Lord Trenchard, 6 February 1935, *Solitary*, p. 234.
14 T. E. L. to A. E. 'Jock' Chambers, 26 January 1935, *Letters – Garnett*, p. 841.
15 As note 3, p. 842.
16 T. E. L. to Pat Knowles, 31 January 1935, *Letters – Garnett*, p. 845.
17 *Ibid.*
18 T. E. L. to Charlotte Shaw, 26 January 1935, *Letters – Brown*, p. 516.
19 Augustus John to T. E. L., 25 January 1935, *Letters to T. E. Lawrence*, ed. A. W. Lawrence (Jonathan Cape, London, 1964), p. 119.
20 As note 3, p. 842.
21 As note 3.
22 As note 3.
23 As note 14, pp. 840–1.
24 As note 14.
25 As note 18, pp. 515–16.
26 As note 18, p. 516.
27 *Bernard Shaw: Collected Letters 1926–1950*, vol. 4, ed. by Dan H. Laurance (Max Reinhardt, 1988), p. 396.
28 *Ibid.*
29 T. E. L. to Bernard Shaw, 31 January 1935, *Letters – Brown*, pp. 516–17.
30 As note 27, p. 407.
31 *Thirty Years with G. B. S.* by Blanche Patch (Victor Gollancz, London, 1951), p. 71.
32 *Solitary*, p. 236.

33 As note 29.
34 T. E. L. to James Hanley, 27 January 1935, *Houghton Lib.*, 65M-177. bMs. Eng 1252 (129).
35 T. E. L. to G. Wren Howard, 31 January 1935, *Letters – Garnett*, pp. 846–7.
36 T. E. L. to Pat Knowles, 31 January 1935, *Letters – Garnett*, p. 845.
37 *Ibid.*, p. 846.
38 T. E. L. to Tom Beaumont, 31 January 1935, *Letters – Brown*, pp. 517–8.
39 *Genius of Friendship. 'T. E. Lawrence'* by Henry Williamson (Faber and Faber, London, 1941), p. 73.
40 As note 29, p. 516.
41 As note 36.
42 T. E. L. to Sir Ronald Storrs, 31 January 1935, *Letters – Brown*, p. 518.
43 T. E. L. to R. A. M. Guy, 31 January 1935, *Lawrence*, p. 920 (Ref. 62, p. 1153).
44 *Ibid.*
45 T. E. L. to E. Spurr, 31 January 1935, *Lawrence*, p. 920.
46 *Ibid.*, pp. 1153–4, ref. note 63.
47 *"Another Lawrence – 'Aircraftsman Shaw' and Air Cushion Craft"* by H. F. King, *Flight International*, vol. 89, no. 2972, 24 February 1966, pp. 19–23.
48 T. E. L. to E. Spurr, 31 January 1935, *Lawrence*, pp. 1153–4, ref. note 63.
49 As note 36, p. 846.
50 *Friends*, pp. 573–4.
51 T. E. L. to Arthur Hall, 1 February 1935, *Letters – Garnett*, p. 849.
52 *Ibid.*
53 T. E. L. to K. W. Marshall, 1 February 1935, *Letters – Garnett*, p. 848.
54 *Broken Waters, An autobiographical Excursion* by James Hanley (Chatto and Windus, 1937), p. 246.
55 *Boy* by James Hanley (André Deutsch, unexpurgated edition, 1990).
56 T. E. L. to James Hanley, 2 July 1931. *Letters – Garnett*, p. 728.
57 T. E. L. to C. J. Greenwood, 17 July 1931, *Letters – Garnett*, p. 730.
58 T. E. L. to James Hanley, 28 December 1931, *Letters – Garnett*, p. 738.
59 *National*, p. 217.
60 As note 53.
61 T. E. L. to Lord Carlow, 4 February 1935, *Letters – Garnett*, p. 850.
62 *Ibid.*
63 Robert Graves to T. E. L., late January 1935, *Robert Graves: His Life and Work* by Martin Seymour-Smith (Holt Rinehart & Winston, New York, 1982), pp. 257–8.
64 T. E. L. to Robert Graves, 4 February 1935, *Letters – Brown*, p. 522.
65 As note 63, p. 257.
66 As note 63, p. 258.
67 Lord Trenchard to T. E. L., 7 February 1935, *Solitary*, p. 270, ch. 7, ref. 13.
68 *"Leaves in the Wind"*, 6 February 1935, *Letters – Garnett*, p. 854.
69 *Letters – Garnett*, pp. 502–3.
70 The Essential T. E. Lawrence by David Garnett (Jonathan Cape, London, 1951), pp. 298–9.
71 T. E. L. to Flt. Lt. Jinman, 9 February 1935, copied by P. J. Marriott from a glass wall display in the *Blue Lobster Restaurant*, Bridlington, on 12 May 1992.
72 T. E. L. to W. Bradbury, 13 February 1935, *Letters – Garnett*, p. 855.
73 *Ibid.*
74 T. E. L. to W. Bradbury, 15 February 1935, *Letters – Garnett*, p. 856.
75 *Friends*, p. 553.
76 *Sayings*, p. 69.

Chapter 6 Explosion, 17–25 February 1935

1   *Sunday Express*, London, 17 February 1935; *Lawrence*, p. 924.
2   T. E. L. to Tom Beaumont, 25 February 1935; *Lawrence*, pp. 925–6.
3   T. E. L. to W. Bradbury, 13 February 1935, *Letters – Garnett*, p. 855.
4   T. E. L. to unknown person, 16 November 1934, *Houghton Lib.*, 65M-177. bMs. Eng 1252 (267).
5   T. E. L. to Pat Knowles, 20 February 1935, *Letters – Garnett*, p. 857.
6   Cinema Advertisement (The Winter Gardens) in *Bridlington Free Press*, 16 February 1935.
7   *Friends*, pp. 560–1.
8   T. E. L. to W. Merton, 24 February 1935, *Houghton Lib.*, 65M-177. bMs, Eng 1252 (152).
9   T. E.L's technical details for his last boat report headed *"October 1934 – February 1935"*, dated 23 February 1935.
10 *Lawrence of Arabia and His World* by Richard Percival Graves (Thames & Hudson, London, 1976), p. 110.
11 *Friends*, p. 561.
12 *Ibid.*
13 As note 6.
14 *The Plays of John Galsworthy, "Windows"*, Act. II (Duckworth, January 1932), p. 718.
15 Interview between Air Commodore F. J. Manning and H. Montgomery Hyde, *Solitary*, p. 237.
16 *Friends*, p. 561.
17 *Ibid.*
18 As note 15.
19 T. E. L. to Lorna Norrington, 24 February 1935, *Letters – Garnett*, p. 857.
20 T. E. L. to John Buchan, 25 February 1935, *Letters – Garnett*, p. 858.
21 T. E. L. to Sir Ronald Storrs, 25 February 1935, *Orientations*, January 1943, p. 450.
22 *Solitary*, p. 241; *Friends*, p. 562.
23 *Friends*, p. 581.
24 T. E. L's RAF discharge documents, in Californian private collection, *Prince*, p. 406.
25 T. E. L. to Air Chief Marshall Sir Edward Ellington, 25 February 1935, *Letters – Garnett*, pp. 858–9.

Chapter 7 The Long Ride Home, 26 February–5 March 1935

1   T. E. L. to RAF Sgt. A. E. Robinson, 26 February 1935, *Prince*, p. 406.
2   T. E. L. to Lorna Norrington, 24 February 1935, *Letters – Garnett*, p. 857.
3   T. E. L. to Pat Knowles, 20 February 1935, *Letters – Garnett*, p. 857.
4   T. E. L. to John Buchan, 25 February 1935, *Letters – Garnett*, p. 858.
5   T. E. L. to Pat Knowles, 19 March 1935, *Letters – Garnett*, p. 862.
6   T. E. L. to Peter Davies, 28 February 1935, *Letters – Brown*, p. 525.
7   "Aircraftsman T. E. Shaw in Lincolnshire (A Last Conversation)," by Professor R. De La Bere, *Lincolnshire Magazine*, vol. 2, no. 7, September–October 1935, p. 185.
8   As note 7 plus similar article in *Journal of The Royal Air Force College*, vol.

XV, no. 2, Autumn 1935.

9   As note 7, p. 186.
10 As note 8, p. 180.
11 As note 7, p. 186.
12 As note 7, p. 190.
13 As note 8, p. 181.
14 *Golden Reign*, pp. 166 and 172.
15 As note 8, pp. 180–1.
16 As note 7, p. 188.
17 As note 8, p. 181.
18 As note 7, p. 190.
19 As note 6.
20 T. E. L. to William Rothenstein, 5 May 1935, *Letters – Garnett*, p. 870.
21 *Friends*, p. 292.
22 *Ibid.*, pp. 292–3.
23 As note 6. pp. 525–6.
24 *National*, p. 228.
25 "T. E. Lawrence and Frederic Manning" by Nicholas Birnie, *The Journal of the T. E. Lawrence Society*, vol. I, no. 2, Winter 1991–2, pp. 34–6.
26 Karen Hay to P. J. Marriott, 7 February 1992. Information mainly from Lincolnshire Street Directories and *The Holbeach of Yesteryear* by Thompson.
27 T. E. L. to Sydney Cockerell 15 November 1934, *Cockerell*, p. 371.
28 T. E. L. to Sydney Cockerell 6 March 1935, *Cockerell*, p. 372.
29 *Ibid.*
30 Interview between A. W. Lawrence and John Mack 15 July 1968, *Prince*, pp. 406 and 521.
31 *Friends*, pp. 297–8.
32 As note 28.
33 John Buchan to J. N. S. Buchan, 5 March 1935, *Buchan Papers*, 9058 2/2. Also *The Friendship of Lawrence and Buchan* by Andrew Lownie, *The Journal of the T. E. Lawrence Society*, vol. V, no. 1, Autumn 1995, pp. 64–5.
34 *John Buchan by his Wife and Friends* by Susan Buchan (Hodder and Stoughton, 1947), p. 195.
35 *Memory Hold-The-Door* by John Buchan (Hodder and Stoughton, London, September 1943), pp. 217–18.
36 "The Other Mr. Shaw – Leaves the R.A.F. and Settles in Dorset. A Lonely Cottage Retreat." *Bournemouth Daily Echo*, 2 March 1935.
37 T. E. L. to John Buchan, 1 April 1935, *Letters – Garnett*, p. 863.

Chapter 8   The Invasion, 6–26 March 1935

1   T. E. L. to L. H. Ingram, 6 March 1935, *Bodleian Res.*, MSS, b55. Although Lawrence referred to his London address as Belvedere Crescent, SE1, Philips' 1934–5 A.B.C. Pocket Atlas – Guide to London suggests a Belvedere Road, SE1, whilst 1934 directories (see note 2 below) only mention Belvedere Road, SE1.
2   Kelly's Street Directory for London SE1, 1935.
3   *Home Letters*, pp. 387 and 392.
4   T. E. L. to Ernest Thurtle, 6 March 1935, *Letters – Garnett*, p. 860.
5   T. E. L. to L. H. Ingham, 6 March 1935, *Prince*, p. 407.
6   T. E. L. to Arthur Russell, 6 March 1935, *Letters – Brown*, p. 526.
7   T. E. L. to Alec Dixon, 6 March 1935, *Letters – Brown*, p. 527.

8   T. E. L. to Florence Hardy, 6 March 1935; *T. E. Lawrence and The Max Gate Circle* by Ronald D. Knight (The Bat and Ball Press, Weymouth, 1988), p. 133.
9   T. E. L. to T. B. Marson, 6 March 1935, *Lawrence*, p. 928.
10 T. E. L. to Hon. Francis Rodd, 6 March 1935, *Letters – Brown*, p. 527.
11 As note 4.
12 As note 8.
13 As note 7.
14 As note 4.
15 As note 7.
16 As note 8, pp. 133–4.
17 As note 5 and p. 521 (ref. 8).
18 As note 8, p. 133.
19 As note 6.
20 As note 7.
21 T. E. L. to Sydney Cockerell, 6 March 1935, *Friends of a Lifetime*, ed. Viola Meynell (Jonathan Cape, London, 1940), p. 373.
22 T. E. L. to Arthur Russell, 6 March 1935, *Letters – Brown*, p. 526.
23 T. E. L. to Pat Knowles, 7 March 1935, related in letter Cliff Irwin to P. J. Marriott 25 October 1991.
24 *Lawrence*, p. 928.
25 "Letters to the Editor." *The T. E. Lawrence Society Newsletter*, no. 9, November 1987, p. 9.
26 *Friends*, pp. 303–4.
27 *Quietness*, p. 39.
28 *Ibid.*, pp. 40–1.
29 *Limelight*, p. 211.
30 *Friends*, p. 304.
31 T. E. L. to Winston Churchill, 19 March 1935, *Letters – Brown*, p. 528.
32 T. E. L. to Hon. Esmond Harmsworth, late March 1935, *Letters – Garnett*, p. 861.
33 T. E. L. to John Buchan, 1 April 1935, *Letters – Garnett*, p. 863.
34 T. E. L. to W. Merton, 1 April 1935, *Houghton Lib.*, 65M-177. bMs. Eng 1252 (153).
35 T. E. L. to Lady Astor, 10 April 1935, *Letters – Brown*, p. 531.
36 *Friends*, p. 305.
37 T. E. L. to Pat Knowles, 19 March 1935, *Letters – Garnett*, p. 862.
38 *Ibid.*
39 T. E. L. to Edward Davies, 27 March 1935, *Letters – Brown*, p. 529.
40 As note 37.
41 As note 31.
42 As note 31.
43 As note 31.
44 As note 31.
45 As note 39.
46 *Self-Portrait of an Artist. From The Diaries and Memoirs of Lady Kennet. Kathleen, Lady Scott* by Lady Kennet (John Murray, London, 1949), pp. 302–3.
47 T. E. L. to William Rothenstein, 5 May 1935, *Letters – Garnett*, p. 870.
48 *Friends*, pp. 285–6.
49 T. E. L. to C. J. Greenwood 5 April 1935, *Letters – Garnett*, p. 864.
50 *Friends*, pp. 305–7.
51 As note 34.

52   *Biographers – Hart* (Cassell, London, 2nd edn, April 1963), p. 230.

53   As note 52 but Cassell, London, 1967 edition, pp. 352–3.

54   *Shaw – Ede. T. E. Lawrence's Letters to H. S. Ede 1927–1935* (Golden Cockerell Press, 1942), pp. 59–60.

55   *Friends*, pp. 201–2.

56   As note 39.

Chapter 9   The Omen, 27 March–24 April 1935

1   T. E. L. to Esmond Harmsworth c. 20–27, March 1935, *Letters – Garnett*, pp. 860–1.

2   T. E. L. to Sir Evelyn Wrench, 1 April 1935, *Letters – Brown*, p. 530.

3   T. E. L. to John Buchan, 1 April 1935, *Letters – Garnett*, p. 863.

4   T. E. L. to W. Merton, 1 April 1935, *Houghton Lib.*, 65M-177. bMs. Eng 1252 (153).

5   John Buchan to T. E. L., 12 March 1935, *Letters to T. E. Lawrence*, ed. A. W. Lawrence (Jonathan Cape, London, 1964), pp. 21–2.

6   As note 3, p. 862.

7   As note 5, p. 22.

8   As note 3.

9   As note 2. p. 529.

10   As note 2, p. 530.

11   As note 3.

12   As note 3.

13   T. E. L. to T. B. Marson, 6 April 1935, *Lawrence*, p. 932.

14   T. E. L. to H. S. Ede, 5 April 1935, *Letters – Garnett*, p. 865.

15   *Ibid.*

16   *Ibid.*

17   *Ibid.*

18   *Horsewoman – The Extraordinary Mrs D. A Biography of Louie Dingwall, Dorset's Racehorse Trainer* by Alan R. Bennett (Dorset Pub. Co., 1979), pp. 50–4.

19   T. E. L. to George Brough, 5 April 1935, *Letters – Garnett*, p. 867.

20   *Ibid.*, pp. 867–8.

21   T. E. L. to C. J. Greenwood, 5 April 1935, *Letters – Garnett*, p. 865.

22   As note 14. p. 866.

23   T. E. L. to E. 'Posh' Palmer, 5 April 1935, *Lawrence*, p. 932.

24   As note 13, p. 932.

25   T. E. L. to T. E. Willis, April 1935, *Lawrence*, p. 932.

26   As note 21, p. 864.

27   As note 22.

28   As note 13.

29   T. E. L. to Robin White, 13 April 1935, *Letters – Brown*, p. 532.

30   T. E. L. to Lady Astor, 10 April 1935, *Letters – Brown*, p. 531.

31   T. E. L. to Robin Buxton, 13 April 1935, *Letters – Brown*, pp. 531–2.

32   T. E. L. to Ira T. 'Taffy' Jones, [13 April 1935], *Friends*, p. 349.

33   *Ibid.*

34   As note 31. p. 531.

35   T. E. L. to T. B. Marson, 5 May 1935, *Solitary*, p. 245.

36   *Ibid.*.

37   T. E. L. to Flt. Lt. H. Norrington, 20 April 1935, *Letters – Garnett*, p. 868.

38   *Ibid.*

39   *Francis Yeats-Brown 1886–1944* by John Evelyn Wrench (Eyre & Spottiswode,

1948), pp. 199–200.
40   *Quietness*, p. 42.
41   Lord Carlow to T. E. L., 4 May 1935, King's College, London.
42   Sub-note in *Letters – Garnett*, p. 868.
43· As note 37.
44   T. E. L. to Ian Deheer, 20 April 1935, *Letters – Garnett*, p. 869.
45   T. E. L. to W. E. G. Beauforte-Greenwood, 20 April 1935, *Friends*, p. 571.
46   T. E. L. to Florence Hardy, 22 April 1935, *Letters – Garnett*, pp. 869–70.
47   *T. E. Lawrence Society Newsletter*, no. 30, Spring 1994, p. 7.
48   As note 44.
49   As note 45.
50   As note 46.
51   T. E. L. to W. E. G. Beauforte-Greenwood and H. Norrington, 5 May 1935, *Letters – Brown*, p. 534.
52   T. E. L.'s wallet/purse in private English collection.

Chapter 10   Pottering, 25 April–12 May 1935

1   "'Lawrence of Arabia' – and Mountbatten," by Katie Doyce, *Plymouth Independent*, 20 January 1967.
2   *Friends*, p. 51.
3   *The Rags of Time – A Fragment of Autobiography* by William Buchan (Buchan, Ashford & Enright, Southampton, 1990), p. 174.
4   *John Buchan by His Wife and Friends* by Susan Buchan (Hodder & Stoughton, 1947), p. 195.
5   *Ibid.*
6   As note 3, pp. 174–6.
7   *T. E. Lawrence and the Max Gate Circle* by Ronald D. Knight (R. D. Knight, Weymouth, 1988), p. 135.
8   Lord Carlow to T. E. L., 4 May 1935, King's College, London.
9   *Quietness*, p. 39.
10 T. E. L. to Ernest Rhys, 5 May 1935, *Letters – Brown*, pp. 534–5.
11 T. E. L. to G. W. M. Dunn, 5 May 1935, *Letters – Brown*, p. 533.
12 T. E. L. to Sims' Family, 5 May 1935, written on back of one of T. E. L's 'cards', *Lawrence of Arabia and His World* by R. P. Graves (Thames and Hudson, London, 1976), p. 110.
13 *Ibid.*
14 *Ibid.*
15 T. E. L. to Lady Astor, 5 May 1935, *Letters – Brown*, p. 535.
16 T. E. L. to W. E. G. Beauforte-Greenwood and H. Norrington, 5 May 1935, *Letters – Brown*, p. 534.
17 As note 11.
18 T. E. L. to William Rothenstein, 5 May 1935, *Letters – Garnett*, p. 870.
19 T. E. L. to Hon. Stephen Tennant, 5 May 1935, *Prince*, p. 408.
20 T. E. L. to Bruce Rogers, 6 May 1935, *Letters – Brown*, p. 536.
21 T. E. L. to Eric Kennington, 6 May 1935, *Letters – Brown*, p. 537.
22 As note 20.
23 T. E. L. to T. B. Marson, 5 May 1935, *Solitary*, p. 245.
24 T. E. L. to Eric Kennington, 6 May 1935, *Letters – Garnett*, p. 870.
25 *Ibid*, pp. 870–1.
26 T. E. L to Bruce Rogers, 6 May 1935, *Letters – Brown*, p. 536. Also addressed envelope T. E. L. to Bruce Rogers, franked 7 May 1935, *Houghton Lib.*, 65M-177. bMs. Eng 1252 (210).

27　T. E. L. to E. M. Forster, 7 May 1935, *Letters – Garnett*, p. 871.
28　T. E. L. to K. W. Marshall, 7 May 1935, *Letters – Garnett*, pp. 871–2.
29　T. E. L. to K. W. Marshall, 7 May 1935, *Letters – Garnett*, p. 872.
30　*Ibid.*
31　*Nancy Astor – A Life* by Anthony Masters (Book Club Associates, London, 1982), p. 151.
32　T. E. L. to Lady Astor, 8 May 1935, *Letters – Brown*, p. 537.
33　Lady Astor to T. E. L., 7 May 1935, *Lawrence*, p. 934.
34　*Ibid.*
35　T. E. L. to E. 'Posh' Palmer, 10 May 1935, *Letters – Brown*, p. 540.
36　*Friends*, p. 544.
37　As note 35, pp. 539–40.
38　T. E. L. to G. W. M. Dunn, 10 May 1935, *Letters – Brown*, p. 538.
39　*Friends*, p. 350.
40　T. E. L. to R. H. Kiernan, *c.* 10 May 1935, *Lawrence of Arabia* by R. H. Kiernan (George C. Harrap, dustjacket of 13th imprint, November 1951).
41　T. E. L. to Ralph Isham, 10 May 1935, *Letters – Brown*, p. 539.
42　*Ibid.*
43　*National*, p. 229.
44　T. E. L. to K. T. Parker, 12 May 1935, *Letters – Brown*, pp. 540–1.
45　*Still Digging* by Sir Mortimer Wheeler (Michael Joseph, 1955), p. 103.
46　*Quietness*, p. 42.

Chapter 11　Brough Superior, GW 2275 – George VII

1　*The Mint* by T. E. Lawrence (Penguin, 1978), pp. 226–8.
2　T. E. L. to George Brough, 7 February 1932, *Lawrence*, p. 891.
3　*Lawrence*, p. 891.
4　T. E. Lawrence's log book for GW 2275, copy in possession of authors.
5　As note 3.
6　T. E. L. to George Brough, 5 March 1932, *Letters – Garnett*, pp. 738–9.
7　*Ibid.*
8　T. E. L. to George Brough, 20 April 1932, *A Series of Letters from T. E. Lawrence to George Brough* by Mike Leatherdale, *Brough Superior Club*, December 1987, letter no. 7.
9　*Ibid.*
10　T. E. L. to Arthur Hall, 22 October 1932, *Letters – Garnett*, p. 750.
11　As note 8, T. E. L. to George Brough, 26 January 1933, no. 8.
12　*Ibid.*
13　T. E. L. to Sir Philip Sassoon, 21 March 1933, *Letters – Garnett*, p. 763.
14　*Biographers – Hart*, p. 71.
15　As note 8, T. E. L. to George Brough, 13 June 1933, no. 10; also T. E. L. to George Brough, 16 July 1934, no. 16.
16　*The Memoirs of Captain Liddell Hart* (Cassell, London, vol. 1, 2nd edn, April 1967), p. 349.
17　As note 8, T. E. L. to George Brough, 12 September 1933, no. 11.
18　T. E. L. to Lady Astor, 31 December 1933, *Letters – Garnett*, p. 788.
19　As note 8, T. E. L. to George Brough, 10 April 1934, no. 12.
20　T. E. L. to George Brough, 3 May 1934, *Letters – Brown*, p. 485.
21　As note 8, T. E. L. to George Brough, 3 May 1934, letter no. 13.
22　As note 8, T. E. L. to George Brough, 18 May 1934, no. 14.
23　As note 8.
24　As note 8, T. E. L. to George Brough, 16 July 1934, no. 16.

25   T. E. L. to Lord Carlow, 14 September 1934, *Letters – Garnett*, p. 818.
26   As note 8, T. E. L. to George Brough, 28 November 1934, No.20.
27   T. E. L. to Arthur Russell, 18 January 1935, *Letters – Brown*, p. 515.
28   George Brough to T. E. L., 11 March 1935, *The Journal of the T. E. Lawrence Society*, vol. I, no. 2, Winter 1991–2, p. 90.
29   *Quietness*, p. 38.
30   T. E. L. to George Brough, 5 April 1935, *Letters – Brown*, p. 531.
31   *Shaws Corner* by Stephen Winstein (Hutchinson, London, 1952), p. 82.
32   As note 21, pp. 15–16.

Chapter 12   On the 13th Day of May

1   *Quietness*, pp. 42–4.
2   *Limelight*, p. 213.
3   *The Crash That Killed T. E. Lawrence* by Andrew Simpson, privately printed, late 1980s.
4   Telegram, T. E. L. to Henry Williamson, 13 May 1935, *National*, p. 229.
5   As note 3.
6   *Daily Dispatch*, 15 May 1935.
7   *Ibid.*
8   *The Life and Times of Joyce Knowles* by Bob Hunt (E.V. Hunt, Dorset, 1994), pp. 52–3.
9   As note 6.
10   "Lawrence's Death Crash at 50 to 60 M.P.H. Mystery of a Black Car. Boy Asked to Mount Cycle in Court," *Daily Telegraph*, 22 May 1935.
11   Corporal E. H. Catchpole's sworn signed Inquest statement, 21 May 1935, copy in possession of authors.
12   *Quietness*, p. 44.
13   Note in public scrapbook dated 11 June 1989 in St Martin's Church, Wareham, Dorset, unsigned.
14   *Biographers – Hart*, pp. 230–1.

Chapter 13   The Long Wait, 14–19 May 1935

1   "'Lawrence of Arabia' : Grave Condition – Concussion: Fracture of Skull Feared – Smash Scene Barred to Public," *Oxford Mail*, 14 May 1935.
2   *Ibid.*
3   *T. E. Lawrence* by Desmond Stewart (Hamish Hamilton, London, 1977), p. 334, ref. 46.
4   *Daily Dispatch*, 15 May 1935.
5   As note 1.
6   *Limelight*, p. 214.
7   *Leicester Mercury*, 14 May 1935.
8   *Daily Sketch*, 15 May 1935, p. 2.
9   "Lawrence Dead. Fatal End to Cycle Crash," *The Times*, 20 May 1935.
10   "Lawrence Still Unconscious – 'Fighting Chance' Say Doctors," *Oxford Mail*, 15 May 1935.
11   *Ibid.*
12   *Ibid.*
13   *Ibid.*
14   *Solitary*, p. 250.
15   As note 6, p. 210.
16   "Stop Press," *Oxford Mail*, 17 May 1935.

17 "Lawrence Still Unconscious. Congestion of Right Lung Now – Story of Accident," *Oxford Mail*, 18 May 1935.
18 *Ibid.*
19 "Lawrence: A Despairing Night," *Daily Dispatch*, 19 May 1935.
20 *Ibid.*
21 "Tragic End of Lawrence of Arabia", *Daily Dispatch*, 20 May 1935.
22 As note 19.
23 As note 17.
24 *A Macabre Mystery Solved!* by Ronald Knight (1990), copy with authors.
25 "Lawrence, The Last Hours. A Tragedy Had He Lived – His Mind Damaged. Simple Village Funeral for Uncrowned King of the Desert. His Own Wish," *Daily Sketch*, late London edn, 20 May 1935, p. 3.
26 "T. E. Lawrence: A Brother Gives His Testimony" by A. W. Lawrence, *The Times*, 22 November 1969, p. 7.
27 "Dorset Village Grave for Lawrence. Famous Men and Former Comrades at Funeral. Inquest Fails to Solve Mystery of Crash on Heath," *Dorset Chronicle and Somerset Gazette*, 23 May 1935.
28 *Daily Sketch*, 20 May 1935, p. 3.
29 As note 25.
30 As note 28.
31 *In Broken Images, Selected Letters of Robert Graves 1914–1946*, ed. Paul O'Prey (Hutchinson, 1982), pp. 247 and 249.

Chapter 14   Inquest and Funeral, 21 May 1935

1   "T. E. Lawrence: A Brother Gives His Testimony" by A. W. Lawrence, *The Times*, 22 November 1969, p. 7.
2   *Biographers – Hart*, p. 232.
3   "Lawrence's Death Crash at 50 to 60 M.P.H. Mystery of a Black Car. Boy Asked to Mount Cycle in Court," *Daily Telegraph*, 22 May 1935.
4   "Dorset Village Grave for Lawrence. Famous Men and Former Comrades At Funeral. Inquest Fails to Solve Mystery of Crash on Heath," *Dorset Chronicle and Somerset Gazette*, 23 May 1935.
5   *Leicester Mercury*, 21 May 1935, p. 21.
6   *Ibid.*
7   "Lawrence's Will. Brother Appointed Literary Executor," *Daily Telegraph*, 22 May 1935.
8   *Solitary*, p. 253.
9   *Secret Lives*, p. 275.
10 *Orientations*, pp. 453–4.
11 "Quiet Funeral for Lawrence of Arabia. His Will, which is at Oxford, Will Not Be Read after the Service," *Oxford Mail*, 20 May 1935.
12 *Ibid.*
13 As note 2, p. 232.
14 As note 4.
15 As note 3.
16 *Ibid.*
17 As note 4.
18 *Great Lives. T. E. Lawrence* by Peter Brent (Weidenfeld & Nicholson, London, 1975), p. 223.
19 *T. E. Lawrence* by Desmond Stewart (Hamish Hamilton, London, 1977), p. 306.
20 *Golden Reign*, pp. 240 and 243.

21 As note 1.
22 As note 1.
23 Tom Beaumont to "Leo" 6 February 1973, in archives of The Tank Museum, Bovington, Dorset.
24 Telephone conversation between Stella Loader (daughter of P.C. 26 Sidney Frank Loader) and Paul Marriott, 12 September 1991.
25 As note 4.
26 Telephone conversation between Nick Birnie and P. J. Marriott, 14 April 1991. Also as note 4.
27 As note 3.
28 As note 4.
29 As note 3.
30 Information from a scrapbook compiled by Roland Hammersley, Bovington, 1991.
31 *Orientations*, p. 454.
32 A. W. Lawrence to George S. Hymes, 5 June 1935, *"You will have probably seen from the papers (not that I told them, the news got out somehow) that the piece of rush or grass, from Akaba, X Flight, was placed with my brother's body inside the coffin,"* Houghton Lib., f. bMs. Eng 1252 (285).
33 *Siegfried Sassoon: Poets Pilgrimage*, assembled by D. Felicitas Corrigan (Victor Gollancz, London, 1973), p. 238.
34 "Lawrence's Funeral," *Bournemouth Evening Echo*, 8 April 1972.
35 "Memories of Lawrence," by Jack Easton and Arthur Russell, *Sunday Express Magazine*, 4 December 1988, p. 25.

Chapter 15   Crash Witnesses – Corporal E. F. Catchpole

1 "'Lawrence of Arabia'. Grave Condition – Concussion: Fracture of Skull Feared. – Smash Scenes. Barred to Public." *Oxford Mail*, 14 May 1935.
2 *Limelight*, p. 214.
3 "Lawrence's Death Crash at 50 to 60 M.P.H. Mystery of a Black Car. Boy Asked to Mount Cycle in Court," *Daily Telegraph*, 22 May 1935.
4 Official Deposition signed by Ernest Catchpole, 21 May 1935, copy with authors.
5 *Lawrence of Arabia in Dorset* by Rodney Legg (Dorset Publishing Co., 1988), p. 104.
6 Commonwealth War Graves Commission to P. J. Marriott, 18 February 1991.

Chapter 16   Crash Witness – Frank Fletcher

1 *T. E. Lawrence* by Desmond Stewart (Hamish Hamilton, London, 1977), pp. 302 and 334 ref. 46.
2 "Lawrence of Arabia. Mother, Aged 73, Told of Death. World Tributes," unknown newspaper, 18 May 1935.
3 "Lawrence Still Unconscious Congestion of Lungs Now – Story of Accident," *Oxford Mail*, 18 May 1935.
4 Inquisition no. 160. Signed Inquest report by Frank Fletcher, 21 May 1935, copy in possession of authors.
5 " Lawrence's Death Crash at 50 to 60 M.P.H. Mystery of a Black Car. Boy Asked to Mount Cycle in Court," *Daily Telegraph*, 22 May 1935.
6 *Lawrence of Arabia. The Facts Without the Fiction* by Harry Broughton (Harry

Broughton, Wareham, 2nd edn, August 1972), p. 7.
7   *Bournemouth Evening Echo*, early 1985.
8   Interview between Frank Fletcher and authors, 13 August 1991.
9   Frank Fletcher to P. J. Marriott, 2 October 1991.
10   Frank Fletcher to P. J. Marriott, 8 November 1991.
11   *Ibid.*

Chapter 17   Crash Witness – Albert Hargraves

1   Interview between Roland Hammersley and the authors, Bovington, August 1990.
2   "Lawrence's Death Crash at 50 to 60 M.P.H. Mystery of a Black Car. Boy Asked to Mount Cycle in Court," *Daily Telegraph*, 22 May 1935.
3   Inquiry Statement signed by Albert Hargraves, 21 May 1935.
4   "My Accident That Shocked The World," by Stewart Rigby, unknown newspaper, 1982.
5   "Crash That Cost the World a Hero and Scarred a Man for Life," by Noel Wain, *Bournemouth Evening Echo*, 13 May 1966, p. 26.
6   *Ibid.*
7   Frank Fletcher to P. J. Marriott, 8 November 1991.
8   As note 5.
9   As note 4.

Chapter 18   Indirect Witnesses

1   *The Life and Times of Joyce Knowles* by Bob Hunt (E. V. Hunt, Dorset, 1994), pp. 52–4.
2   Interview between Roland Hammersley and Joan Hughes, February 1986, copy of Hammersley's conclusions in possession of authors.
3   *Limelight*, p. 217.
4   *Ibid.*
5   "There Was a Car!", *Bournemouth Evening Echo*, 5 September 1985.
6   "Fresh Thoughts on Lawrence," *Bournemouth Evening Echo*, 31 December 1985.
7   Interview between Margaret Montague and Andrew Simpson at her home in Wimborne, *The Crash That Killed T. E. Lawrence* by Andrew Simpson, privately printed, late 1980s.
8   From transcript of interview between Frank Gordon and Andrew Simpson at Bovington, 25 May 1985, pp. 1–14.
9   Letter by John Prentice, *Dorset County Magazine*, 2nd Issue, 1968.
10   *Quietness*, p. 44.
11   *Secret Lives*, p. 274.
12   Interview between Arthur Russell and authors Malcolm Brown and Julia Cave at his Coventry home, 30 May 1986.
13   Interview between Arthur Russell and Andrew Simpson, 7 December 1985, *The Crash That Killed T. E. Lawrence* by Andrew Simpson, privately printed, late 1980s.
14   Conversation between Arthur Russell and P. J. Marriott, 20 May 1990.
15   *The T. E. Lawrence Society Newsletter*, 32, Autumn 1994, p. 6.
16   Inquisition no. 160. Inquiry statement signed by Charles Philip Allen, 21 May 1935, copy in possession of authors.
17   Data extracted from the actual weather records stored at the Meteorological Office Archives, Eastern Road, Bracknell, Berkshire, England, by authors in

Summer 1992.

Chapter 19   Clouds Hill

1   *Quietness*, p. 51.
2   *Ibid.*, p. 20.
3   *Ibid.*, p. 24.
4   *Ibid.*
5   *Tinned Soldier – A Personal Record, 1919–1926* by Alec Dixon (Jonathan Cape, London, 1941), pp. 307–8.
6   T. E. L. to A. E. 'Jock' Chambers, 21 March 1923, *Letters – Brown*, p. 230.
7   T. E. L. to Lionel Curtis, 30 May 1923, *Letters – Brown*, p. 239.
8   T. E. L. to Eric Kennington, 27 June 1923, *Letters – Brown*, p. 240.
9   As note 5, p. 308.
10   As note 1, p. 26.
11   *Ibid.*
12   As note 1, p. 27.
13   T. E. Lawrence at Clouds Hill by Jeremy Wilson, *Journal of the T. E. Lawrence Society*, vol. III, no. 1, Summer 1993, p. 46.
14   T. E. L. to F. N. Doubleday, 17 September 1923, as 13.
15   T. E. L. to R. V. Buxton, 4 October 1923, *Letters – Garnett*, p. 435.
16   As note 13, p. 47.
17   As note 1, p. 27.
18   T. E. L. to A. E. 'Jock' Chambers, 5 November 1923, *Letters – Brown*, pp. 249–50.
19   T. E. L. to D. G. Hogarth, 14 November 1923, *Letters – Garnett*, p. 440.
20   T. E. L. to mother, 19 December 1923, *Home Letters*, pp. 356–7.
21   "Clouds Hill," by E. M. Forster, *The Listener*, 1 September 1938, p. 426.
22   *Ibid.*
23   *National*, p. 225.
24   T. E. L. to D. G. Hogarth, 7 July 1927, *Letters – Garnett*, p. 528.
25   As note 1, p. 30.
26   T. E. L. to mother, 25 September 1933, *Home Letters*, p. 380.
27   *Ibid.*, p. 379.
28   T. E. L. to mother, 19 December 1923, *Home Letters*, p. 357.
29   T. E. L. to Arthur Knowles, 10 February 1930, *Letters – Garnett*, pp. 679–80.
30   As note 25.
31   T. E. L. to mother, 6 April 1934, *Home Letters*, p. 389.
32   As note 27.
33   T. E. L. to G. W. M. Dunn, 15 December 1932, *Letters – Garnett*, p. 757.
34   *National*, p. 226.
35   As note 13, pp. 53–4.
36   *Friends*, pp. 377–8.
37   *Ibid.*
38   *Quietness*, p. 27.
39   *Ibid.*, p. 39.
40   As note 26.
41   As note 38, p. 24.
42   As note 5, p. 296.
43   As note 36, p. 377.
44   T. E. L. to mother, 19 December 1923, *Home Letters*, p. 356.
45   T. E. L. to mother, 9 May 1924, *Home Letters*, p. 357.

46 T. E. L. to A. E. 'Jock' Chambers, 24 August 1924, as note 13, p. 48.
47 As note 21, p. 427.
48 T. E. L. to Lionel Curtis, 28 March 1929, as note 13, p. 51.
49 T. E. L. to mother, 5 November 1933, *Home Letters*, p. 383.
50 *Ibid.*
51 *National*, p. 224.
52 T. E. L. to mother, 6 April 1934, *Home Letters*, p. 389.
53 *Solitary*, p. 245.
54 *Friends*, p. 364.
55 E. M. Forster to Alice Clara Forster, 23 March 1924, *Selected Letters of E. M. Forster*, vol. 2, ed. M. Lago and P. N. Furbank (Collins, London, 1985), p. 50.
56 T. E. L. to private 'posh' Palmer, 15 March 1927, as note 13, p. 50.
57 As note 21.
58 As note 46.
59 As note 56.
60 T. E. L. to W. A. Knowles, 10 February 1930, *Letters – Garnett*, p. 680.
61 *Quietness*, p. 30.
62 T. E. L. to W. A. Knowles, 22 November 1930, *Letters – Garnett*, p. 706.
63 *The Life and Times of Joyce Knowles* by Bob Hunt (E. V. Hunt, Dorset, 1994), p. 59.
64 *Quietness*, pp. 35–6.
65 T. E. L. to mother, 25 September 1933, *Home Letters*, pp. 379–80.
66 *National*, p. 224.
67 As note 49.
68 T. E. L. to W. E. Jeffrey, 21 December 1933, *Letters – Garnett*, p. 784.
69 As note 1, p. 32.
70 T. E. L. to A. W. Lawrence, 26 December 1933, *Letters – Garnett*, p. 786.
71 T. E. L. to mother, 6 April 1934, *Home Letters*, p. 389.
72 T. E. L. to A. E. 'Jock' Chambers, 27 April 1929, *Letters – Garnett*, p. 655.
73 As note 13, p. 55.
74 T. E. L. to G. W. M. Dunn, 9 November 1932, *Letters – Garnett*, pp. 752–3.
75 T. E. L. to Edward Garnett, 15 September 1933, *Letters – Garnett*, p. 777.
76 *Friends*, pp. 476–510.
77 As note 70, p. 787.
78 *Quietness*, p. 32.
79 *National*, p. 224.
80 As note 66.
81 T. E. L. to K. W. Marshall, 18 May 1934, *Letters – Garnett*, p. 803.
82 T. E. L. to K. W. Marshall, 10 July 1933, as note 13, p. 55.
83 T. E. L. to mother, 25 September 1933, *Home Letters*, p. 380.
84 T. E. L. to mother, 6 April 1934, *Home Letters*, pp. 388–9.
85 T. E. L. to Lady Astor, 31 December 1933, *Letters – Garnett*, p. 788.
86 T. E. L. to Ernest Altounyan, 5 January 1933, as note 13, p. 54.
87 T. E. L. to Edward Garnett, 10 August 1933, *Letters – Garnett*, p. 774.
88 *Golden Reign*, pp. 167–8.
89 As note 88, p. 225.
90 As note 78.
91 T. E. L. to A. W. Lawrence, 26 December 1933, *Letters – Garnett*, p. 786.
92 T. E. L. to E. M. Forster, 29 September 1924, *Letters – Garnett*, p. 467.
93 As note 66.
94 As note 71.

95 Presentation "T. E. Lawrence by His Friends," by Malcolm Brown in Oxford, 17–18 September 1994, *T. E. Lawrence Society*, p. 11.

96 T. E. Lawrence at Clouds Hill by Jeremy Wilson, *The Journal of the T. E. Lawrence Society*, vol. III, no. 1, Summer 1993, p. 51.

97 T. E. L. to R. G. Goslett, 31 August 1933, *Letters – Garnett*, p. 775.

98 T. E. L. to Bruce Rogers, 19 December 1932, *More Letters From T. E. Shaw to Bruce Rogers* (privately printed, 1936).

99 T. E. L. to Charlotte Shaw, 31 August 1933, *Letters – Brown*, p. 476.

100 T. E. L. to mother, 17 December 1933, *Home Letters*, p. 384.

101 Information obtained at Clouds Hill by authors, Summer 1992.

102 T. E. L. to Charlotte Shaw, 31 December 1933, as note 13, p. 58.

103 As note 71.

104 *Ibid.*

105 *Ibid.*

106 T. E. L. to Hon. Francis Rodd, 23 November 1934, *Letters – Garnett*, p. 830.

107 T. E. L. to Charlotte Shaw, 19 November 1929, as note 13, p. 51.

108 T. E. L. to F. N. Doubleday, 5 September 1931, as note 13, p. 53.

109 T. E. L. to S. F. Newcombe, 10 April 1935, as note 13, p. 63.

110 T. E. L. to Lionel Curtis, 28 March 1929, as note 13, p. 51.

111 As note 78.

112 T. E. L. to Charlotte Shaw, 31 August 1933, *Letters – Brown*, p. 476.

113 As note 49.

114 *Ibid.*

115 T. E. L. to mother, 2 February 1934, *Home Letters*, p. 386.

116 *Ibid.*

117 *Ibid.*

118 T. E. L. to mother, 21 March 1934, *Home Letters*, p. 387.

119 T. E. L. to mother, 6 April 1934, *Home Letters*, p. 389.

120 *The Seven Pillars of Wisdom* by T. E. Lawrence (Jonathan Cape, London, 1935), chapter 9, p. 72.

121 As note 119.

122 T. E. L. to mother, 21 March 1934, *Home Letters*, p. 387.

123 As note 119.

124 T. E. L. to Frederic Manning, 16 November 1934, *Letters – Brown*, p. 499.

125 As note 13, p. 61.

126 As note 63, pp. 68–9.

127 T. E. L. to A. E. 'Jock' Chambers, 26 January 1935, *Letters – Garnett*, p. 841.

128 T. E. L. to Pat Knowles, 31 January 1935, *Letters – Garnett*, p. 846.

129 *Ibid.*

130 T. E. L. to mother, 19 March 1929, *Home Letters*, p. 376.

131 T. E. L. to G. W. M. Dunn, 22 November 1932, *Letters – Garnett*, p. 753.

132 As note 1, p. 41.

133 As note 63, p. 112.

134 *Quietness*, p. 28.

135 T. E. L. to Mrs Eric Kennington, 18 October 1932, *Letters – Garnett*, p. 746.

136 *Ibid.*

137 *Tinned Soldier, A Personal Record, 1919–1926* by Alec Dixon (The Right Book Club, London, 1941), pp. 308–9.

138 *Quietness*, pp. 24 and 30.

139 As note 92.

140 T. E. L. to W. A. Knowles, 22 November 1930, *Letters – Garnett*, p. 706.

141 T. E. L. to A. W. Lawrence, 26 December 1933, *Letters – Garnett*, pp. 786–7.
142 *Ibid.*
143 T. E. L. to mother, 17 April 1934, *Home Letters*, p. 391.
144 T. E. L. to Lionel Curtis, 28 March 1929, as note 13, p. 51.
145 *Writers at Home*, National Trust Studies (Trefoil Books, London), 1985, p. 154.
146 T. E. L. to Alec Dixon, 21 December 1933, *Letters – Brown*, p. 480.
147 As note 142, p. 787.
148 T. E. L. to unidentified person, 16 November 1934, *Houghton Lib.*, 65M-177. b.Ms. Eng 1252 (217).
149 T. E. L. to A. E. 'Jock' Chambers, 3 August 1924, *Letters – Garnett*, p. 436.
150 T. E. L. to D. G. Hogarth, 7 July 1927, *Letters – Garnett*, p. 528.
151 T. E. L. to Dick Knowles, 19 April 1928, as note 13, pp. 50–1.
152 T. E. L. to E. M. Forster, 17 June 1925, *Letters – Brown*, p. 282.
153 T. E. L. to W. A. Knowles, 22 November 1930, *Letters – Garnett*, p. 706.
154 T. E. L. to mother, 1 May 1929, *Home Letters*, p. 377.
155 T. E. L. to Florence Hardy, 25 April 1933, *Letters – Garnett*, p. 767.
156 *Ibid.*, pp. 767–8.
157 *Ibid.*, p. 768.
158 T. E. L. to Mrs Knowles, 23 November 1932, as note 13, p. 53.
159 As note 21, p. 427.
160 T. E. L. to A. E. 'Jock' Chambers, 5 March 1934, *Letters – Garnett*, p. 791.
161 T. E. L. to Pat Knowles, 31 January 1935, *Letters – Garnett*, p. 846.
162 As note 21, p. 427.
163 T. E. L. to mother, 6 April 1934, *Home Letters*, p. 390.
164 *Prince*, p. 513, ref. 46. Also T. E. L. to Lady Astor, 26 November 1934, *Letters – Brown*, p. 503.
165 T. E. L. to A. E. 'Jock' Chambers, 5 November 1923, *Letters – Brown*, p. 249.
166 *Quietness*, p. 28.
167 T. E. L. to mother, 28 December 1925, *Home Letters*, p. 360.
168 T. E. L. to mother, 4 November 1927, *Home Letters*, pp. 369–70.
169 As note 130.
170 *Lawrence*, p. 850.
171 T. E. L. to mother, 25 April 1931, *Home Letters*, p. 379.
172 As note 49.
173 T. E. L. to mother, 17 April 1934, *Home Letters*, p. 390.
174 T. E. L. to mother, 28 December 1925, *Home Letters*, p. 360.
175 T. E. L. to D. G. Hogarth, 7 July 1927, *Letters – Garnett*, p. 528.
176 As note 13, p. 50.
177 *"T. E. Lawrence" in Arabia and After* by Liddell Hart (Jonathan Cape, London, May 1935), p. 18.

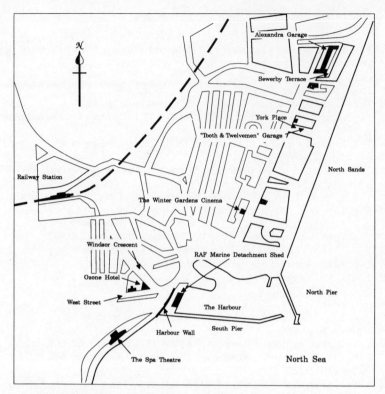

MAP 1   Bridlington, East Yorkshire, 1934–5.

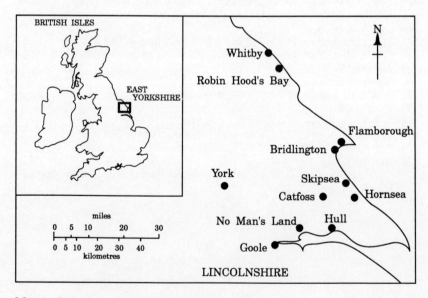

MAP 2   Text place names in East Yorkshire, 1934–5.

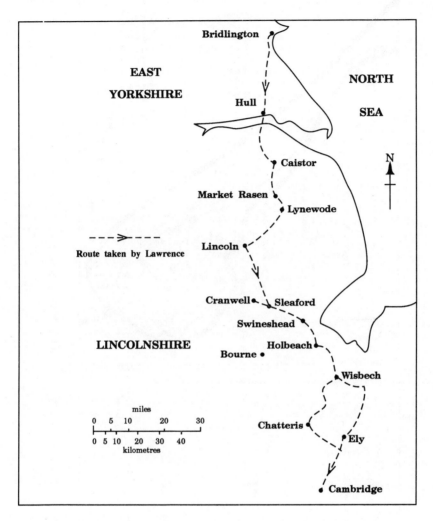

MAP 3 Lawrence's push-bike trip: Bridlington to Cambridge, 26 February to 1 March 1935.

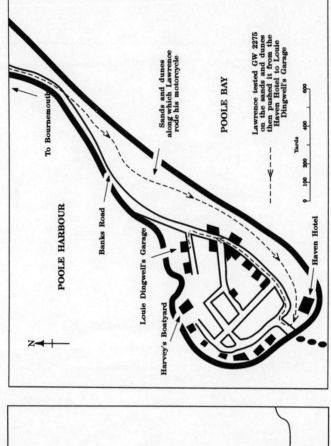

MAP 5 Sandbanks, Bournemouth, 1935.

Sands and dunes along which Lawrence rode his motorcycle

POOLE HARBOUR

POOLE BAY

To Bournemouth

Banks Road

Louie Dingwell's Garage

Harvey's Boatyard

Haven Hotel

Lawrence tested GW 2275 on the sands and dunes then pushed it from the Haven Hotel to Louie Dingwell's Garage

Yards

0   100   200   300   400   500

N

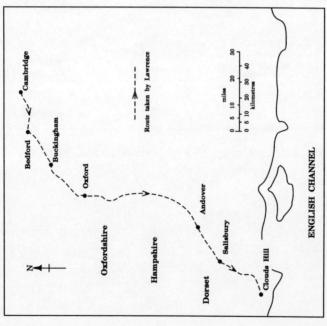

MAP 4 Lawrence's push-bike trip: Cambridge to Clouds Hill, 2–4 March 1935.

Cambridge

Bedford

Buckingham

Oxford

Oxfordshire

Hampshire

Andover

Salisbury

Dorset

Clouds Hill

ENGLISH CHANNEL

Route taken by Lawrence

miles
0   5   10   20   30

kilometres
0 5 10   20   30   40

N

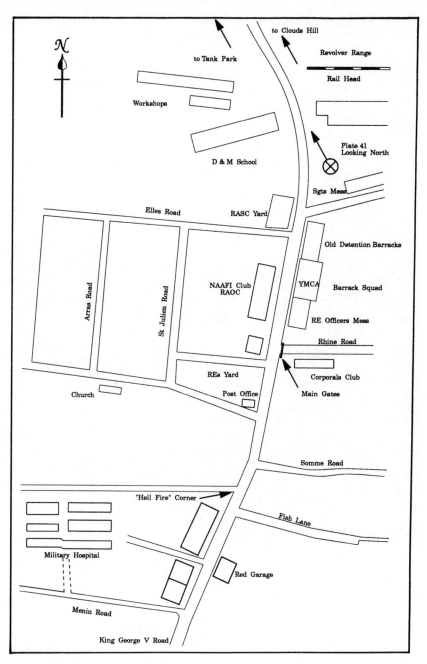

MAP 6 Bovington Camp, 1935.

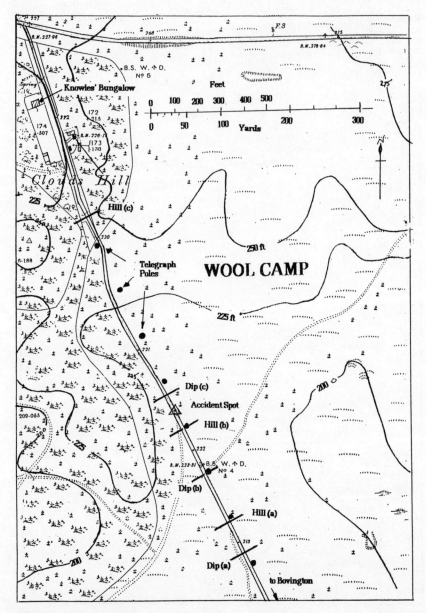

MAP 7 Crash site and surroundings, 1935.

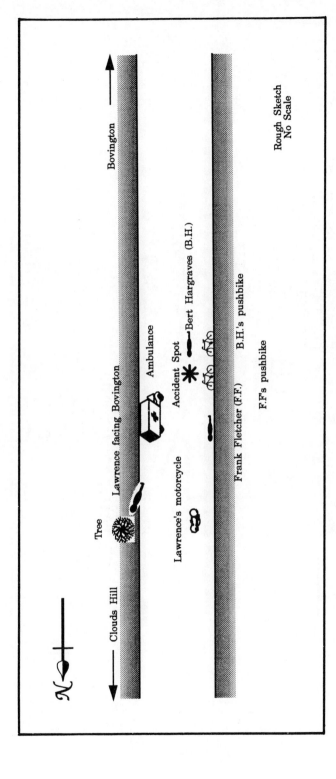

Map 8   Frank Fletcher's sketch map of the crash on 13 May 1935.

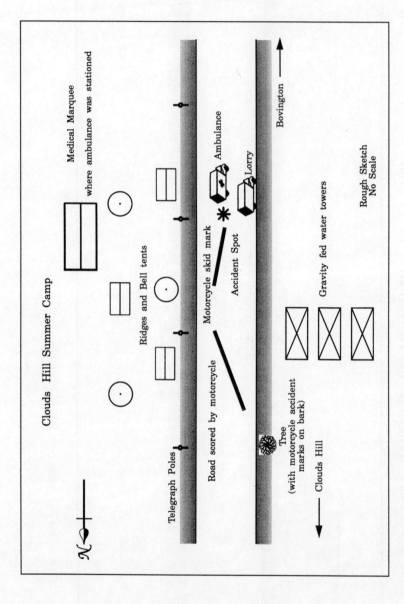

MAP 9 Joan Hughes' sketch of the crash on 13 May 1935.

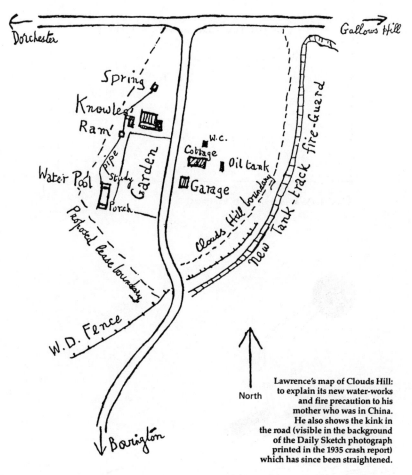

Dorchester

Gallows Hill

Spring

Knowles
Ram'

pipe

Water Pool

Study

Porch

Garden

W.C.

Cottage

Oil tank

Garage

Clouds Hill boundary?

New Tank-track fire-Guard

Proposed lease boundary

W.D. Fence

Barington

North

Lawrence's map of Clouds Hill: to explain its new water-works and fire precaution to his mother who was in China. He also shows the kink in the road (visible in the background of the Daily Sketch photograph printed in the 1935 crash report) which has since been straightened.

MAP 10   Lawrence's sketch of Clouds Hill, 17 April 1934.

To tell you that in future I shall
write very few letters.
                                        T. E. S.

DIAGRAM 1 Lawrence's printed card.

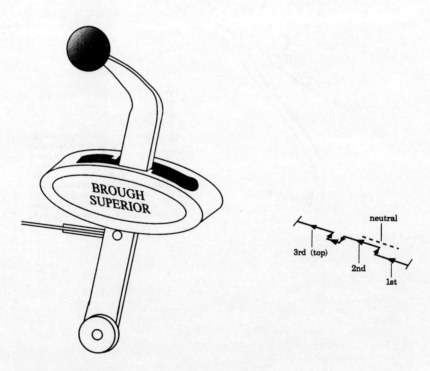

DIAGRAM 2 Manual gear change and gate on Lawrence's Brough Superior
GW 2275.

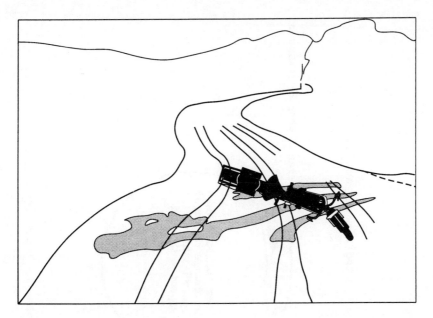

DIAGRAM 3A Demonstrated skid.

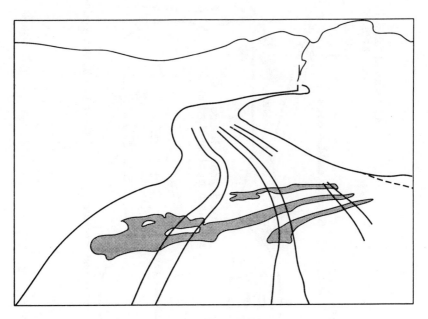

DIAGRAM 3B Details of skid marks in Plate 37A.

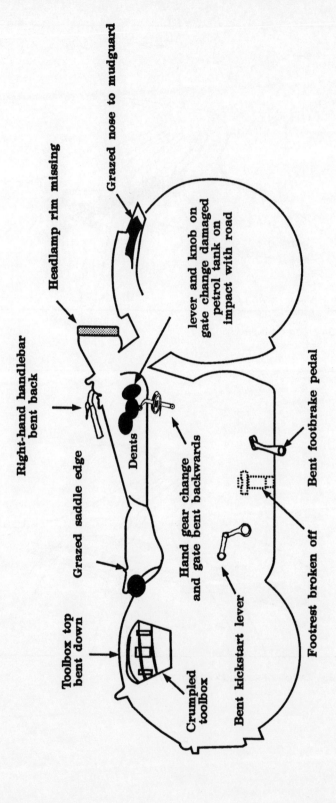

Headlamp rim missing

Grazed nose to mudguard

lever and knob on
gate change damaged
petrol tank on
impact with road

Right-hand handlebar
bent back

Grazed saddle edge

Dents

Bent footbrake pedal

Hand gear change
and gate bent backwards

Toolbox top
bent down

Footrest broken off

Crumpled
toolbox

Bent kickstart lever

DIAGRAM 4   Crash damage to Lawrence's Brough Superior GW 2275 taken from a late May 1935 photograph.

Date.	Wind.		State of Sea.	Weather.	Port.		Hour.		Duty Employed on.	No. of Passengers.	Time under Weigh. (To be totalled weekly.)
	Direction.	Force.			From	To	Departure.	Arrival.			
									Brought Ford.		

APPENDIX 1   Lawrence's last Bridlington boat report, 26 February 1935.

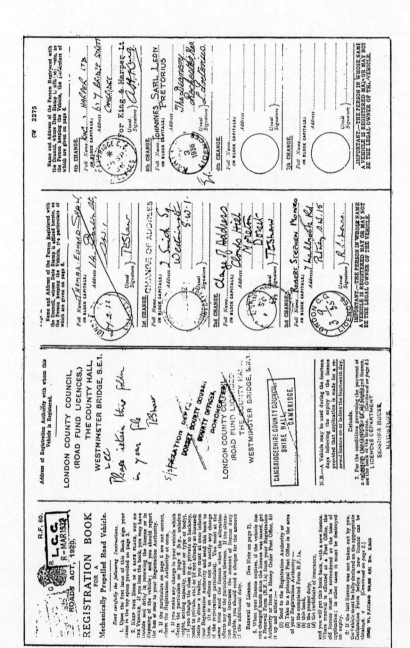

APPENDIX 2 Lawrence's log book for his Brough Superior GW 2275.

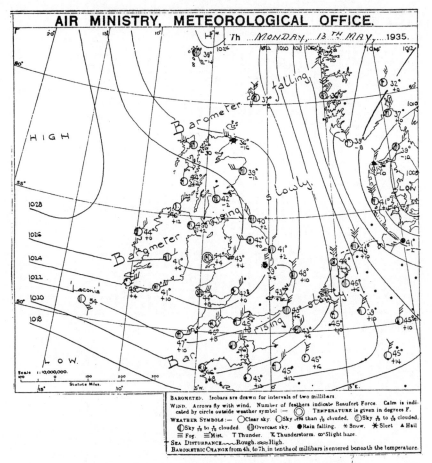

APPENDIX 3   Weather map for 17:00 hours, 13 May 1935.

Weather Records at 1000 hours on 13 May 1935

Station	Cloud wind Vis. Pressure	Temp wet-Bulb R.H. Max.	State of Ground	Weather			
Poole	6/10 N.E. Cu force J* 1023.4mb 5	48.4F 41.8F 52% 55F (9.1C) (5.4C) (13C)	0	bc	bc	bc	c
Shaftsbury	7/10 S.E. force — — 2	49.8F 39.8 31% 50F (9.9C) (4.3C) (10C)	—	bc		bc	
Weymouth	7/10 E. force — 1023.5mb	49.6F 41.6F 44% 53F (9.8C) (5.3F) (12C)	—	c	c	bc	

* Coded visibility, J = 6.25 – 12 statute miles.

(Cloud coverage is recorded in tenths; wind speed in the Beaufort Scale; pressure in millibars; temperature in degrees Fahrenheit; R.H. = relative humidity – the dryness of the air in percentages and weather letters bc mean partly cloudy and c cloudy.)

APPENDIX 4   Weather records for Dorset, 13 May 1935.

1 9 3 4

	JANUARY	FEBRUARY	MARCH	APRIL	MAY	JUNE	
S	7 14 21 28	4 11 18 25	4 11 18 25	1 8 15 22 29	6 13 20 27	3 10 17 24	S
M	1 8 15 22 29	5 12 19 26	5 12 19 26	2 9 16 23 30	7 14 21 28	4 11 18 25	M
Tu	2 9 16 23 30	6 13 20 27	6 13 20 27	3 10 17 24	1 8 15 22 29	5 12 19 26	Tu
W	3 10 17 24 31	7 14 21 28	7 14 21 28	4 11 18 25	2 9 16 23 30	6 13 20 27	W
Th	4 11 18 25	1 8 15 22	1 8 15 22 29	5 12 19 26	3 10 17 24 31	7 14 21 28	Th
F	5 12 19 26	2 9 16 23	2 9 16 23 30	6 13 20 27	4 11 18 25	1 8 15 22 29	F
S	6 13 20 27	3 10 17 24	3 10 17 24 31	7 14 21 28	5 12 19 26	2 9 16 23 30	S

	JULY	AUGUST	SEPTEMBER	OCTOBER	NOVEMBER	DECEMBER	
S	1 8 15 22 29	5 12 19 26	2 9 16 23 30	7 14 21 28	4 11 18 25	2 9 16 23 30	S
M	2 9 16 23 30	6 13 20 27	3 10 17 24	1 8 15 22 29	5 12 19 26	3 10 17 24 31	M
Tu	3 10 17 24 31	7 14 21 28	4 11 18 25	2 9 16 23 30	6 13 20 27	4 11 18 25	Tu
W	4 11 18 25	1 8 15 22 29	5 12 19 26	3 10 17 24 31	7 14 21 28	5 12 19 26	W
Th	5 12 19 26	2 9 16 23 30	6 13 20 27	4 11 18 25	1 8 15 22 29	6 13 20 27	Th
F	6 13 20 27	3 10 17 24 31	7 14 21 28	5 12 19 26	2 9 16 23 30	7 14 21 28	F
S	7 14 21 28	4 11 18 25	1 8 15 22 29	6 13 20 27	3 10 17 24	1 8 15 22 29	S

1 9 3 5

	JANUARY	FEBRUARY	MARCH	APRIL	MAY	JUNE	
S	6 13 20 27	3 10 17 24	3 10 17 24 31	7 14 21 28	5 12 19 26	2 9 16 23 30	S
M	7 14 21 28	4 11 18 25	4 11 18 25	1 8 15 22 29	6 13 20 27	3 10 17 24	M
Tu	1 8 15 22 29	5 12 19 26	5 12 19 26	2 9 16 23 30	7 14 21 28	4 11 18 25	Tu
W	2 9 16 23 30	6 13 20 27	6 13 20 27	3 10 17 24	1 8 15 22 29	5 12 19 26	W
Th	3 10 17 24 31	7 14 21 28	7 14 21 28	4 11 18 25	2 9 16 23 30	6 13 20 27	Th
F	4 11 18 25	1 8 15 22	1 8 15 22 29	5 12 19 26	3 10 17 24 31	7 14 21 28	F
S	5 12 19 26	2 9 16 23	2 9 16 23 30	6 13 20 27	4 11 18 25	1 8 15 22 29	S

	JULY	AUGUST	SEPTEMBER	OCTOBER	NOVEMBER	DECEMBER	
S	7 14 21 28	4 11 18 25	1 8 15 22 29	6 13 20 27	3 10 17 24	1 8 15 22 29	S
M	1 8 15 22 29	5 12 19 26	2 9 16 23 30	7 14 21 28	4 11 18 25	2 9 16 23 30	M
Tu	2 9 16 23 30	6 13 20 27	3 10 17 24	1 8 15 22 29	5 12 19 26	3 10 17 24 31	Tu
W	3 10 17 24 31	7 14 21 28	4 11 18 25	2 9 16 23 30	6 13 20 27	4 11 18 25	W
Th	4 11 18 25	1 8 15 22 29	5 12 19 26	3 10 17 24 31	7 14 21 28	5 12 19 26	Th
F	5 12 19 26	2 9 16 23 30	6 13 20 27	4 11 18 25	1 8 15 22 29	6 13 20 27	F
S	6 13 20 27	3 10 17 24 31	7 14 21 28	5 12 19 26	2 9 16 23 30	7 14 21 28	S

APPENDIX 5 1934–5 calendar.

(Old) shillings and pence		*(Decimal) new pence*
1/4d	(farthing)	–
1/2d	(halfpenny)	–
1d	(penny)	0.5p
3d	(threepence)	1.25p
6d	(sixpence)	2.5p
1/-	(shilling)	5p
2/-	(two shillings or florin)	10p
2/6	(two and sixpence or half a crown)	12.5p
10/-	(ten shilling note)	50p
£1 (20/-)	(pound note)	100p
21/-	(guinea)	105p
£5 (100/-)	(five pounds)	500p

APPENDIX 6 Conversion of old pounds, shillings and pence (£.s.d.) into new decimal currency.

Index

Index

Index

211